SOCIAL CHANGE IN WESTERN EUROPE

**PRIVATIZATION IN W**

C000156847

# SOCIAL CHANGE IN WESTERN EUROPE

The *Social Change in Western Europe* series developed from the need to provide a summary of current thinking from leading academic thinkers on major and economic issues concerning the evolving policies of Western Europe in the post-Maastricht era. To create an effective European Union governments and politicians throughout the region must work to provide satisfactory social, economic and political conditions for the populations of Europe, and each volume affords an opportunity to look at specific issues and their impact on individual countries.

The series is directed by an academic committee composed of Arnaldo Bagnasco (Turin University), Henry Mendras (CNRS, Paris) and Vincent Wright (Nuffield, Oxford), assisted by Patrick Le Galès (CNRS, Rennes), Anand Menon (University of Oxford) with the support of Michel Roger and Olivier Cazenave (Futuroscope in Poitiers).

SOCIAL CHANGE IN WESTERN EUROPE

# PRIVATIZATION IN WESTERN EUROPE
## PRESSURES, PROBLEMS AND PARADOXES

edited by
VINCENT WRIGHT

**PINTER**
PUBLISHERS

DISTRIBUTED IN THE USA AND CANADA BY ST MARTIN'S PRESS INC

**Pinter Publishers**
25 Floral Street, Covent Garden, London, WC2E 9DS, United Kingdom

First published in Great Britain 1994

© Actes Sud 1994

Distributed exclusively in the USA and Canada by St Martin's Press, Inc., Room 400, 175 Fifth Avenue, New York, NY10010, USA

**British Library Cataloguing in Publication Data**

A CIP catalogue record for this book is available from The British Library

ISBN 1 85567 246 4 (hbk)
    1 85567 213 8 (pbk)

**Library of Congress Cataloging-in-Publication Data**

Industrial privatization in Western Europe : pressures, problems, and
  paradoxes / edited by Vincent Wright.
     p.   cm. – (Social change in Western Europe)
  Includes bibliographical references and index.
  ISBN 1-85567-246-4. – ISBN 1-85567-213-8 (pbk.)
  1. Privatization–Europe–Case studies.   I. Wright, Vincent.
II. Series.
HD4138.153 1994
338.94–dc20
                                                      94–7280
                                                        CIP

Typeset by Florencetype Limited, Kewstoke, Avon
Printed and bound in Great Britain by SRP Ltd, Exeter

# CONTENTS

# LIST OF CONTRIBUTORS

**Rudy Andeweg** is Professor of Political Science at the University of Leiden.

**Sabino Cassese** is Professor of Public Law and Director of the Institute of Public Law, Rome.

**Delia Meth-Cohn** is the Politics and Economics editor of the Economist Group magazine, *Business Central Europe*.

**David Corkhill** is a Principal Lecturer and Coordinator for Iberian and Latin American Studies at the University of Portsmouth.

**Hervé Dumez and Alain Jeunmaître** are Heads of Research at CNRS in Paris.

**Josef Esser** is Professor Political Science at the University of Frankfurt.

**Oscar Fanjul** has been Chairman of the Instituto Nacional de Hidrocarburos (INH) since 1985 and Chairman of REPSOL since its creation in 1987.

**Jan-Erik Lane** is Professor in Politics at the University of Oslo and pro tempore professor at the Norwegian School of Management.

**Luis Mañas** is currently General Manager of the Chairman's Office at REPSOL, SA.

**Wolfgang Müller** is Professor in Political Science at the University of Viennna.

# CHAPTER 1

## INDUSTRIAL PRIVATIZATION IN WESTERN EUROPE: PRESSURES, PROBLEMS AND PARADOXES

### Vincent Wright

There is nothing new about privatization: there are examples to be found in the 1960s and 1970s in Ireland (with the sale of assets of Dairy Disposal Company in 1972), in the United Kingdom (where in 1977 a Labour government sold shares in British Petroleum), in West Germany (where there was a privatization programme carried out by the CDU government in the 1960s, and where, in the 1970s, a minority share of Lufthansa was sold) and in Italy (whose major state holding, IRI, rid itself of several companies in the 1950s and 1960s). France had a long history of 'back-door' privatization of industry through the sale of the subsidiaries of public sector holdings, a policy denounced by the Socialists in opposition in the 1970s and practised by the same Socialists when in power after 1981. It should be noted that this policy, delicately termed '*respiration*', was accompanied by a no less extensive programme of back-door nationalization, with the acquisition by the public sector of the subsidiaries of private groups.

What is unique about the 1980s and early 1990s is that the sporadic and limited phenomenon of the 1960s has become widespread and frequent, almost routine.[1] It has been calculated that between 1985 and 1993 governments in 100 countries raised some $328 billion by selling state-owned firms to private investors. In 1992 alone the proceeds amounted to some $70 billion. All European countries, without exception, and whatever their political complexion, are privatizing and at an accelerating pace. Sales proposed in Western Europe alone could raise $150 billion by 1998 (*Economist*, 21 August 1993).

This book seeks to describe and explain the pressures for, the extent and nature of, and the reasons for the privatization programmes of several West European countries: the United Kingdom, France, Germany, Italy, Spain, Austria, Sweden, the Netherlands, and Portugal.

It also briefly assesses the political and economic impact of the various programmes, and points to some of the problems and paradoxes which have emerged in their implementation. The central themes of the book, which are summarized in this Introduction, may be stated quite simply: privatization strategies are being pursued throughout Western Europe under the impact of convergent pressures (I). However, an analysis of the reshaping of the wider public sector – of which privatization is an element – reveals that other more important and country-specific pressures are at work, leading to somewhat different reform programmes (II). Furthermore, even the type of privatization strategy differs from country to country (III). The result is great diversity in the extent and nature of the privatization programmes, even with respect to industrial privatization – the focus of this book (IV). The reasons for this diversity must not be sought only in the different pressures being exerted. Governments, in responding to convergent pressures, do so with different degrees of enthusiasm and for different motives (V). Obviously, too, the scale and type of privatization are dictated by the scale and the nature of the sector to be privatized (VI); by the tissue of political and institutional constraints (VII); and by the capacity of domestic financial markets to absorb privatization programmes (VIII). Consequently, the impact of privatization varies widely (IX). Yet, even where it has been carried out extensively and with commitment its impact may have been exaggerated, since it has sometimes been negated by other policies or it has generated unintended – and often unwelcome – consequences which have diluted the impact (X).

# I  Privatization: convergent pressures

Since the early 1980s the intellectual, economic and financial environment has not proved a favourable one for public enterprises. Hirschman has argued that Western Europe oscillates between periods of preoccupation with expanding the public sector and those concerned with broadening the frontiers of the private sector and strengthening the market. Such a cycle is allegedly generated, in large measure, by disappointment with the side effects – unintended or underestimated – of the previous phase of the 'involvement cycle' (Hirschman, 1982). While Hirschman's dialectic raises more questions than it answers, it nevertheless points to the first factor in the general environment since the early 1980s – what may be termed the intellectual disenchantment with *dirigisme* and Keynesianism in many circles. Scepticism about the efficacy of state intervention has become manifest in many countries, and notably in right-wing circles in the United Kingdom, Portugal and Sweden. Yet even Socialist France clearly expressed its doubts, as it quickly discovered the constraints of the international economy, and 'rediscovered the firm' – the principal instrument of wealth creation.

Reactions against high taxation, coupled with worrying levels of inflation and high public indebtedness, have also forced several governments to question the bases of many of their economic policies, and to call into question the 'distributional coalitions' which sustained them. In that sense, neo-liberalism may be seen in some European countries as a backlash against the prevailing neo-corporatism – that comfortable, collusive and costly institutionalized relationship between the state, the employers and trade unions.

The second element in the environment has been the changing nature of some industries. Part of the argument for nationalization had always resided in the need to control natural monopolies in strategic areas – telecommunications, railways, gas and electricity – or in high-risk industries requiring heavy investment and promising low returns. Yet massive technological advances are weakening the extent of natural monopoly in several industries (notably in telecommunications) as well as introducing new products into the sector, driving down costs, altering production processes and lowering barriers to entry into existing markets, thus transforming single-product monoliths into complex multi-product enterprises. If the traditionally reluctant management of Telekom, Germany's state telecommunications monopoly, has become increasingly pro-privatization it is because it is aware that BT, US Sprint and many others can now transmit data across borders for German companies, and even carry voice messages around international private networks of companies, their suppliers and customers: by diverting messages first to the UK (where international calls are lower than in Germany) BT claims to be able to cut charges by up to 30 per cent. Another argument, the 'commanding heights' argument, which had been used to justify the nationalization of industries such as rail transport, coal and steel, looks singularly unconvincing as these industries have lurched into deeper financial crisis, becoming costly political embarrassments rather than engines of growth. Thus, by the end of 1992, IRI, Italy's biggest industrial holding company, had run up debts of 73 trillion lire (nearly $60 billion) and losses for 1993 were estimated at 5 trillion lire (*Economist*, 2 October 1993) and French public companies were demanding FF20 billion ($3.5 billion) of state funding to cover their capital requirements. Moreover, technological changes have transformed erstwhile 'strategic industries' into industrial dinosaurs. Indeed, for many observers the very concept of strategic industry is highly suspect, or they argue that new strategic industries based on services and knowledge are much less susceptible to state control because they are more fragmented, function in mercilessly competitive markets and are subject to rapid innovation.

The third element in the general environment allegedly unfavourable to public enterprises has been the increasing internationalization of both product markets and financial markets. Many industries have become much more complex and necessitate international co-operation because of problems of scale and compatibility. Economies of scale in some industries are now on a European or world level: take-overs, mergers, the purchase of equity and joint venture, are increasingly common at the international and European level. These processes of internationalization are blurring the national identities of many major enterprises in some sectors (notably automobile), rendering them somewhat problematic as 'national champions'. Nevertheless, governments throughout Western Europe are tolerating or even facilitating such processes. However, ultimately, they are demanding reciprocity, and governments in countries such as the USA and the UK are increasingly intolerant towards the predatory activities of major foreign public enterprises which acquire private stock without running the risk of being acquired themselves. Moreover, it has been alleged by many, including the bosses of nationalized firms, that industrial decisions rooted in national politico-bureaucratic compromises are hindrances in an internationalized and liberalized environment which demands increasing flexibility and speed in decision-making (Feigenbaum, 1982).

The challenges of an increasingly integrated European market – the fourth major element in the changing general environment for public firms – which sees the removal, at least in principle, of all trade barriers within the European Union has been a frequently cited reason for changes in company law, in the reduction of customs formalities, in competition policy and in the general move towards liberalization. Although the existence of public enterprises is tolerated by the Treaty of Rome, there are aspects of the open market – monetary convergence, competition policy, public procurement policy – which logically prevent dirigiste governments from fully exploiting their public enterprises as instruments of industrial, regional policy or of purely political patronage. Furthermore, the control exercised by Brussels over public sector firms has frequently irritated their managers, furnishing them with another reason for willing privatization. Nationalized enterprises therefore, appear ill-equipped to meet the requirements of a change of international and European environment.

Another major change in the environment – the fifth – and it is linked with the previous four, is the massive capital needs of major enterprises, whether public or private. Governments, squeezed everywhere in Europe, have encouraged or forced their public sector firms to become profitable (thus inducing them to act like private firms) or to seek recapitalization through the international financial markets. The French Socialist governments of 1988 to 1993 were obliged to loosen their declared policy of *'ni-ni'* (neither nationalization nor privatization) by allowing private, and often foreign, shareholders to enter into the capital of public sector firms. In so doing they invented a wealth of ingenious financial instruments in an attempt to prevent foreign ownership from weakening control.

A final important element in the general environment has been the emergence and diffusion of a pro-privatization model based on the experience of the UK. The apparent success of the privatization model – one of Britain's few successful exporting industries – was diffused with remarkable success across Europe (both Western and Eastern), feeding the ideological aspirations of the neo-liberals, whetting the appetite of revenue-hungry governments of all political colours, and pressuring the sceptics and critics into apologetic and defensive postures. The British model also influenced the mechanics of other European privatization programmes: selling by tranches; spreading the payments period; reserving a share of the privatized stock for employees or the public at below-market prices.

There are, therefore, several broadly convergent pressures at work in Western Europe, which combined have led to a serious questioning of the existing public industrial sector. However, it should be emphasized that each of these pressures has been felt with different degrees of intensity and at different times (for instance, the budgetary pressure was most acutely and most quickly felt in the UK). It should be noted, too, that while privatization has been placed on the political agenda everywhere it has not always been the most important policy priority. Indeed, even within the general restructuring of the public sector which has taken place in Western Europe, pressures for privatization, though real, have often been displaced by more pressing needs – a point to which we now turn.


## II Privatization: the wider policy context

Privatization must be seen as part of a much wider policy response (if not always conscious strategy) in the restructuring of the relationship between state, market and society which has characterized the politics of West European states since the early 1980s (OECD, 1992). This restructuring is multidimensional, and its forms may be summarized as follows:

- budgetary squeeze (or even contraction in some sectors) which has had a direct impact on the scale of resources and of state personnel;
- deregulation, a many-layered phenomenon comprising, for example, the dismantling of controls (notably in the currency markets and over prices), the reduction of administrative formalities (often in planning), and the simplification of administrative procedures;
- liberalization, or the breaking up of monopolistic or dominant market positions to encourage and facilitate greater contestability or entry into the market (notably in financial markets and in the transport and telecommunications sectors);
- financial market modernization and the creation of new financial instruments to ensure growth, greater transparency and increased efficiency;
- the creation or strengthening of more effective competition policy;
- marketization – a fashionable term which means the introduction of competitive forces into the purchase of public goods and the provision of public services;
- customarization – the pressure to see citizens as clients whose needs (and not those of the suppliers) should be viewed as critical;
- the introduction of new management techniques and organizational structures, often borrowed from the private sector;
- decentralization – the enforced or voluntary devolution of administrative and political authority and implementation to elected local governments. The UK is a glaring exception to the general rule, since it has experienced a process of rapid and brutal centralization. In some cases, a cynical desire by central government to reduce their financial commitments by transferring service responsibilities to the local level is legitimized in the name of strengthening local democracy;
- deconcentration, which is the devolution of authority down to non-elected state officials at the local or regional level;
- diffusion – a policy of transferring to semi-automous agencies, appointed by the government, or to voluntary or charitable organizations, tasks previously managed by central state administrations.

Privatization is therefore part of a wider package of reducing the size and reshaping the role of the central state, of allocating resources and wealth differently, and of providing collective goods in a different fashion. In some cases, this package is ideologically inspired (the

Conservative governments in the UK since 1979, the Centre Right government elected in 1982 in the Netherlands, the PDS government in Portugal, the New Democracy government in Greece, the Centre Right government in Sweden), in others it represents merely a reluctant managerial adjustment to changed economic and financial circumstances.

In some countries privatization is intimately linked with one or more of these strands of the general reform programme – notably deregulation and liberalization. In others the reform programme may have quite distinctive features as the result of specific pressures: the administrative adjustment to asymmetrical regionalization in Spain; the tightening up of rules in the Italian public sector to combat corruption and absenteeism; the creation of new public sector institutions to adapt to radical federalization processes in Belgium.

As a result, the total public sector reform package displays wide variations across Europe. Thus, Britain has proved to be a zealous privatizer and liberalizer and a no less zealous centralizer. France is both a fairly enthusiastic privatizer and a limited decentralizer whilst Belgium has been a timid privatizer but radical decentralizer.

## III  Privatization – types

Privatization, interpreted broadly, is that wide range of policies designed to reduce the scope, limit the functions and generally weaken the influence of the public sector. It too constitutes a package with distinct yet overlapping contents, motivations and analytical ramifications. It is therefore essential to disentangle these various elements (Glade, 1986). Again, a brief summary may be useful. Privatization, broadly conceived, involves:

- the abolition or severe curtailment of public services, on the assumption that private provision will fill the gap (the proliferation of private security firms is a much-quoted example);
- the squeezing of the financial resources of publicly-funded bodies, in the hope of inducing them to seek compensatory private funding (the drive for increased sponsoring of the arts provides a good illustration);
- the increase in the financial contribution of consumers for public goods such as medicine – a policy partly inspired by the desire to reduce the role of the state as purchaser;
- the direct transfer to the private sector (often voluntary and charitable) of total policy responsibilities which were previously public:

the growth of the so-called 'third sector' has been one of the most striking changes in service delivery since the early 1980s;

• the contracting out of public service implementation to private agents; there is some connection with the previous policy although it is quite distinct, since the former involves a complete withdrawal of the state from service delivery whilst the policy of contracting out involves state withdrawal only at the level of implementation. Contracting out is practised at both national and local level and covers services such as cleaning, office security, accounting, personnel training programmes, catering. It is one of the most widely practised forms of privatization in Western Europe;

• the sale of land and publicly-owned housing stock, as in Sweden and even more so in the UK where more than one million homes have been sold to people who were renting them.

## Industrial privatization

Finally, there is industrial privatization which is the essential focus of this book. It must not be confused with other forms of privatization, since it raises different questions, involves different actors and policy networks, is often motivated by different ambitions, and generates different constraints.

Industrial privatization – perhaps the most dramatic and visible dimension of privatization – has taken many forms, some direct, others indirect:

• the encouragement of the private sector to share in public investment projects – a policy long practised in countries such as France, Spain and Belgium through the *sociétés d'économie mixte* – but which has become increasingly fashionable in the UK (which launched the Private Finance Initiative in 1992 and which listed 70 projects in October 1993 and which at that date was seeking private financial backing for projects such as the East London river crossing and the £3 billion high-speed tunnel link to London) and in Germany (for instance, for the planned expansion of Berlin's airport capacity). Highly complex issues of risk and rate of return are raised by this form of privatization because major infrastructural projects involve big political and regulatory risks.

• the promotion of joint public-private (sometimes foreign) production ventures; thus, the steel producing subsidiary of IRI, the Italian state holding, is involved in a joint venture with Lucchini, the private steel group, while the Swedish state steel group SSAB produces electrical steels as part of a joint venture with British Steel, the steel group privatized by the Thatcher government;

- the introduction of private sector managers, criteria of efficiency and procedures into the public industrial and banking sectors in countries such as Spain and the UK, in the hope of instilling more market orientation into their ethos and objectives;

- the deregulation and liberalization of certain sectors (particularly posts, telecommunications and transport) to facilitate private sector competition with the public sector. Thus, in Sweden, the newly elected centre-right government broke up the monopolies in telecommunications, the railways and electricity distribution. But it is in Portugal that this policy has been carried furthest, with the dismantling of monopolies in petrol, telecommunications, cereals, alcohol and sugar;

- the sale of subsidiaries belonging to nationalized industries and banks – a policy favoured by many public sector bosses;

- the creation of subsidiaries within the public group, but providing them with separate market-oriented managements and pay structures (Deutsche Telekom hived off its mobile telephone business in this way to make it more competitive in a liberalized market).

- the recapitalization of public companies by allowing the participation of private investors, thus reducing the quota held by the state;

- the sale of a minority of the stock in companies totally owned or largely controlled by the state – this is the principal form of privatization in most European countries;

- the sale of the majority of shares in a nationalized company, leaving the state with a minority, often destined for future sale, or a blocking minority to ensure control;

- the outright sale of public firms to private investors – a policy pursued by more radical and ideologically-inspired governments.

There is, therefore, great diversity in the types of privatization available to governments, and this diversity is reflected in the extent to which European governments have availed themselves of the various types. Unquestionably, the UK has adopted the widest approach to privatization: it has privatized most of the major public sectors (see below) and its current plans embrace immigration controls at ports and airports, parts of the prison service, the fire service inspectorate, the computerization of police records. The government has even sought legal advice on whether the Inland Revenue would be within its legal rights to hand over tax codes and assessments of 34 million individuals to a private company. In all these cases – as in many others – the government has seemingly been oblivious to the delicate political and regulatory issues raised (Graham and Prosser, 1991). The British government has also gone much further than any other government in Europe in forcing local councils to contract out part of their services.

## IV  Privatization: the degree and the diversity

Without doubt, the UK has been and remains Europe's most resolute industrial privatizer: it accounted for nearly a third of the total assets privatized in the world between 1984 and 1991. As Richardson points out in Chapter 3, the British programme has involved 46 large companies and dozens of smaller ones, and has included international competitive firms (Amersham), and strategic companies (British Aerospace, British Airways). The sectors affected include energy, steel, transport, shipbuilding, ports, airports. Even the great public utilities of water, gas, electricity and telecommunications have been sold to the private sector. By 1993 the programme had raised some £40 billion. As a result of the programme, nearly a million jobs have been transferred to the private sector, and nationalized industries which accounted for 9 per cent of GDP in 1979 saw that figure reduced to barely 3 per cent by 1993. Only the railways and coal mines (both due for privatization) and the postal services and London Transport remain in the public sector.

The first French privatization programme from 1986 to 1988, as Dumez and Jeunemaitre point out in Chapter 4, was in some respects even more radical than that of the British. In the space of a legislature it was proposed to privatize 66 *grandes entreprises* (1454 if subsidiaries are included): 42 in the banking sector, 13 in insurance, 9 in the industrial sector, and 2 in communications. Some 750,000 employees were involved in the programme which corresponded to a 30 per cent increase in the capitalization of the Paris Bourse in 5 years. The October 1987 financial market crash effectively brought the programme to a halt, and the re-election of François Mitterrand to the Presidency of the Republic in 1988 led to its official abandonment. Nevertheless, about a third of the programme was completed in less than two years. Moreover, the policy of *ni-ni* (no more privatization, no more nationalization) promised in President Mitterrand's electoral programme was soon transformed into a policy of *oui-oui*. Nationalization (for example, the Air France take-over in January 1990 of UTA) and, more especially, privatization were tolerated and even encouraged. Starting with Prime Minister Rocard, the *ni-ni* intentions were weakened and they were further undermined by Prime Ministers Cresson and Beregovoy. Nationalized companies were allowed to sell subsidiaries and to raise an increasing proportion of their capital needs on the stock market. By the spring of 1993 when the Right returned to power, public asset sales had involved major banks and enterprises such as Rhône-Poulenc, Elf Aquitaine, Crédit Local de France and Total, and had raised nearly FF50 billion – a remarkable balance sheet for the *ni-ni* policy. But the amount is insignificant when compared with the promised proceeds of the ambitious privatization proposals of the new Right-wing government elected in 1993. The new privatization legislation envisages the transfer to the private sector of 21 major banking and industrial enterprises. The new list of *privatisables* includes national champions such as Renault, the national flag carrier Air France, and strategic industries such as the oil group ELF. The state's 51 per cent stake in ELF could fetch $9 billion, making it one of the world's biggest privatization deals. Within six months of the passage of the Act, significant tranches of Crédit Local de France, the Banque Nationale de Paris and of Rhône-Poulenc had been sold to the public.

Plans for privatization have also been announced by the Right wing in Germany where the Kohl government has disposed of the central state's stakes in Veba (energy), Volkswagen, Viag (metals and chemicals), and Salzgitter (steel and engineering), raising DM10 billion; where the government has reduced its holding in Lufthansa from 80 per cent to barely 50 per cent; and where the Treuhandanstalt, a new body specifically charged with the responsibility of privatizing the state sector of East Germany, had by the end of 1993 sold all but 1392 firms, of the 13,200 initially acquired. The proceeds amounted to DM 180 billion (*Financial Times*, 29 October 1993). The German government has even pushed along negotiations with the Social Democratic opposition with a view to privatizing Telekom, the country's sleepy telecommunications monopoly.

Governments are also privatizing state assets in Belgium, in the Netherlands (where over 100,000 employees have moved from the public to the private sector), in Norway, and in Sweden which, as Lane points out in Chapter 9, hopes to privatize, in a $10 billion programme, 35 state-owned companies, including SSAB (steel), LKAB (ore-mining), Vettenfalls (electric power), and the giant holding Procordia (food, tobacco and pharmaceuticals).

Portugal, studied by David Corkill in Chapter 11, has been implementing at an accelerating pace since 1989 its 1986 plan to transfer to the private sector 60 major public companies and 450 companies indirectly controlled by the State. The 60 major firms are active in key sectors such as steel, petro-chemicals, paper, cement, banking and insurance, air transport and post and telecommunications. The fifteen biggest privatizations represent no less than one third of Portugal's GDP. Between April 1989 and April 1992 18 major state companies, worth ESc 600 billion, were sold and by the end of the programme only a few utilities will be left in state hands.

Not only zealous right-wing governments have indulged in privatization. The Amato and Ciampi governments of Italy, after years of procrastination by their predecessors, and a reluctant programme of partial privatizations, were determined to press ahead with more ambitious privatization proposals (worth a calculated $10 billion). To facilitate this programme the state holdings IRI, ENEL, INA and ENI have been converted into joint-stock companies, with the Treasury as the sole shareholder. Amongst the important companies affected by the programme are Agip (the oil and gas exploration business), SNAM (gas pipelines) and Nuovo Pignone (turbines and engineering), all subsidiaries of ENI, Banca Commerciale Italiana and Credito Italiano, of the banking sector owned by IRI. The highly successful 15-trillion-lire ($1.2 billion) flotation of a fifth of the capital of Istituto Bancario San Paolo di Torino, Italy's biggest bank, was one of the largest flotations in the history of the Milan bourse and was hailed as a milestone in the reform of the country's antiquated banking system and an encouragement for other privatization ambitions.

The intention to sell majority stakes or entire companies – and by public flotation – bears witness to the increasingly radical nature of the Italian programme. So, too, does the ambition to sell 30 per cent of the financial services group Istituto Mobiliare Italiano and to privatize completely INA (a major insurance group), ENEL (the state electricity generating authority) and even Stet (the public telecommunications monopoly). While the implementation of the programme remained modest by the end of 1993, for reasons provided by Cassese Chapter 6, the ambitions are clear and the opportunities much more obvious.

As Oscar Fanjnl and Luis Manas point out in Chapter 7, the Spanish public sector has also been raising considerable sums of money through privatization even though the programme has been relatively timid. Between 1984 and 1986 it dissolved or sold off more than 30 companies and since then it has been selling off minority stakes in the three state holdings. Some of these sales, notably Repsol (1989), Argentaria (the banking group), Telefonica (1988) and Endesa (1988)) have been immensely lucrative, raising nearly $8 billion dollars.

While privatization is on the policy agenda everywhere in Europe and the pace of implementation appears to be accelerating, each country retains its own mix. The great diversity of privatization programmes may be seen not only in the scale and types of privatization but also in the procedures adopted for each type and the use of the proceeds (when there are any). Procedures for privatization of companies have ranged from public flotations on the stock exchange (notably in the UK and France from 1986 to 1988); sales to another company (generally favoured in Italy and Spain); management and even employee buy-outs (for sales of smaller companies); issuing bonds convertible into shares of state-owned companies due for privatization (a policy practised in Italy); auctioning to the highest bidder (the case, for example, of Cemitir, the cement subsidiary of IRI); and even to exchange (for instance, in 1987 Thomson sold CGR in exchange for the electronic activities of General Electric (RAC)). The proceeds have been used in some cases for recapitalizing the firm or the holding company (Austria, Italy, Spain), providing capital for the public sector in general, paying off the public debt, reducing the budget deficit, or for a combination of these objectives. Occasionally, the proceeds are earmarked for a specific purpose: the money raised by the sale of Salzgitter, the German public sector steel company, was used to finance a foundation involved in environmental protection; part of the proceeds of the French Socialist programme of partial privatizations was used to fund policies to boost employment.

We note, therefore, diversity in the extent, nature and procedures and use of the proceeds of the various privatization programmes. This diversity springs from the differing needs, ambitions, opportunities and constraints of governments. Before looking at these factors it is worth looking at the motives which have shaped the policy ambitions of governments.

## V  Privatization: the motives

It is not always easy to analyse the motives of the privatizers. In the first place, motives vary widely across and within European countries, which is scarcely surprising since different interests defend privatization for different and often diametrically opposed reasons. Second, motives may even change over time as in the UK. Indeed, the reasons for many of the privatizations in Britain followed rather than preceded the programme: they were invented after the events to justify them. Finally, it is not always easy to unravel unspoken motives from declared reasons. Broadly speaking, however, one can distinguish between the ideologically and politically inspired privatization ambitions of the neo-liberal conservative governments of Britain, France (1986–8), Portugal and Norway, and the more pragmatic and limited ambitions of governments elsewhere.

The first series of motives may be described as broadly ideological. For the radical right, especially in Britain and France, privatization is part of a general strategy to shift the boundary between public and private in favour of the latter, and is nourished by a deep-seated anti-state sentiment. In France, a first wave of privatization was linked with the struggle against not only the technocratic elites entrenched in the state sector but also against the long tradition of *dirigisme* or *Colbertisme*. The title by the Minister of Finance Edouard Balladur of his defence of his programme is inelegant yet highly revealing: *Je crois en l'homme plus qu'en l'Etat*. In the UK privatization has been seen as an integral part of the onslaught on the social-democratic, semi-collectivist consensus of the post-war era. In both countries privatization has been the focus of a campaign to push back the frontiers of the state – which for the neo-liberal Right is the stultifying and inhibiting state that erodes personal responsibility and undermines individual initiative. Self-help and self-reliance are the cardinal virtues of the neo-liberals, and they are seen as being undermined by collective provision. This anti-state philosophy has found favour in some right-wing circles in other European countries (notably in Greece and Portugal), but little echo in the debates in Christian Democratic circles in Italy, West Germany, Belgium and the Netherlands. It has also been singularly absent from right-wing thinking in Spain. It is instructive that parts of the French right and of the British Conservative Party do not share the anti-state enthusiasm of their leaders. Interestingly, the tone of the public and parliamentary debates on the French privatization programme of 1993 compared with that of 1986–8 was very low key: '*le débat idéologique est clos*' declared Edmond Alphandéry, the Economics Minister, to a group of bored senators who were discussing the privatization bill in June 1993. A second ideological underpinning of privatization is the belief that public industries and services limit the choice of consumers because of their monopolistic positions. It is further argued that public ownership deprives individuals of economic freedom by forcing them to take 'implied shareholdings' in public sector enterprises that they might not chose to hold if given the choice. The third ideological strand in the privatization argument, widely used in France and the UK, lies in the desire to create a 'property-owning democracy'. From this motivation stems the drive to sell shares in the denationalized industries to as wide a public as possible and especially to the employees of those industries, and, in practice 'popular capitalism' has been nurtured by a battery of incentives to buy and to hold those shares.

The second general argument for privatization may be described as economic, and again there are several interconnected strands within the argument. In Britain and France the economic aims are ambitious: in the UK claims have been made that privatization has helped to produce 'a sweeping and irreversible shift in the structure of the economy' while in France it is part of the policy to 'change the rules of the game of our economy'. The rules, it is argued, may be altered in several ways. In the first place privatization has been perceived as a means of furthering liberalization. As noted above, many of the state monopolies are not natural monopolies (even in gas and electricity there may be a natural monopoly in transmission through the national grid, but not in production), and are becoming less so because of technological change; once broken up there would be greater scope for competition. It has been argued that for politically and socially inspired loss-making services it is more efficient to target specific subsidies to needy consumers, or to private suppliers of those services. In Italy there are many, including Romano Prodi, head of IRI since May 1993, who now view wholesale privatization as a means of revitalizing Italian capitalism by expanding the stock exchange, creating a share-holding public and by introducing into the private sector major competitors to the small number of powerful family-based groups.

A second economic argument has been that public sector production and services are intrinsically less efficient than those in the private sector. They are allegedly less efficient because they are not vulnerable to the bracing winds of market forces, and are cushioned by the statutory obligation by the state to pick up the bill for any losses made. They face no threat of bankruptcy or take-over and they have no private shareholders to satisfy. Furthermore, deprived of the possibility of direct personal financial gain, public sector managers will wastefully pursue their own non-pecuniary goals. Moreover, when they are motivated by the need for greater efficiency and profits they may be frustrated by governments pursuing their own macro-economic and income redistribution objectives. At bottom, there is a deep-seated suspicion in neo-liberal circles of politico-bureaucratic compromises which usurp the role of the market as the mechanism for allocating resources. Uninhibited, market-oriented, profit-seeking entrepreneurs are preferred to budget-maximising bureaucrats and vote-maximizing politicians. Yet, it should be emphasized that this is primarily a Franco-British motivation: the managers of the major state holdings in Spain and Italy who have privatized parts of their empires have entertained no great belief in the intrinsic merits of market mechanisms. Nor has there been any atavistic attachment to the market evident in European Christian Democratic circles, where the principles of the social market economy still find sturdy defenders.

A third economic reason for privatization is that it facilitates the adoption of tough labour policies by distancing governments from unpalatable political choices. Private management, it is alleged, is more likely to tackle the unions which protect inefficient work practices and employment levels. The evidence from the European steel and coal industries, some of which carried out massive slimming-down operations under public ownership, has not dented the enthusiasm for this argument. The need to spread 'the enterprise culture' by familiarizing the public, through ownership, with the mechanisms of the market provides the fourth economic argument of the privatizers. The final economic argument has been that employed by the pragmatists who head the vast and rambling state holding companies in Italy and Spain. For them privatization is generally viewed as a means of rationalizing asset portfolios and reorganising investment strategies. By hiving off loss-making or marginal operations they can improve their balance sheets, induce greater sensitivity to product specialization, and even facilitate the process of mergers thought necessary to bring about the economies of scale required by international competition and an increasingly integrated European market. The sale of the Spanish State company SEAT to Volkswagen, and of the Italian state-owned Alfa Romeo to Fiat were justified in these terms. Interestingly, some of these managers have now become converted to more radical privatization plans.

Linked to the economic motivation for privatization has been the managerial one. Privatization is seen as a means of breaking up the vast public sector empires – each characterized by internal feuds among warring barons – and held together by statute and public subsidy. Privatization should facilitate the sale of 'incoherent' parts, and the rationalization of managerial structures. Even more important for the privatizers is the fact that it enables ministers to extricate themselves from time-consuming and debilitating relationships with the public sector. Ministers, it is contended, either 'go native' and espouse the cause of the industries they are supposed to control, or they interfere too much in the daily operations of those industries. Everywhere in Europe there have been constant confrontations between ministers and public sector managers over wage levels, investment plans, borrowing requirements, restructuring projects and the right to raise capital outside Ministry of Finance control. The relationship has become 'a muddle', full of 'ambivalence, indecision and vacillation'. It is therefore argued that privatization might ensure both autormomy and incentives.

The fourth set of reasons for privatization has been party political and clearly popular with the party faithful. More significantly, it has been alleged that the sale of privatized stock to a wide public in some European countries is part of a strategy to create right-wing voters and to undermine the unions and deprive the left of one of its traditional bastions of support.

Finally, a variety of financial reasons have been given to justify private programmes. The first financial reason often cited is that privatization provides quicker and more direct access for the firms involved to international capital markets (although it is unclear why nationalized firms should be totally deprived of such a right). A second financial reason for privatization, heard in Britain but more especially in France, Italy, Sweden and Norway, is that it fosters the growth of the domestic stock exchange: it can widen capital markets by bringing in many new investors and 'deepen' them by introducing mature companies with strong market positions. Thus, the French Bourse has always been thought to be too small by successive French governments, which have since the 1950s tried to enhance its place in the world's capital markets; privatization is yet another device for strengthening Paris, threatened by the 'big brother' across the Channel.

A third financial reason sometimes invoked by proponents of privatization is that the sale of public assets reduces commercial risk for a government by diminishing the state's exposure to the vagaries of recession and the volatile currency exchange and business climate. It would also, it is alleged, also put an end to the immensely costly rescue operations of public enterprises. However, it should be pointed out that such rescue operations have not been restricted to the public sector: indeed, nationalizations have often been precisely the result of the state bailing out private firms in dire financial difficulty.

Finally – and here perhaps we touch upon the most important single reason for privatization: selling state assets raises money for public sector managers (Spain, Italy, Norway and Portugal) and for hard-pressed governments which are struggling to reduce large budget deficits (this reason has been invoked several times by the Italian government), and huge public debts and enables them to cut personal and corporate taxes and to finance public expenditure. It should be noted, however, that asset sales improve short-term cash flow in a once-and-for-all manner: in general they do not enhance a government's long-term net worth, and may even cause it to deteriorate if profitable assets are sold off too cheaply (which is too frequently the case).

It follows from this brief exploration of the reasons and motives of the privatizers that, whereas in the UK (at least since 1983) and France (from 1986 to 1988) the programmes have been ideologically inspired and rooted in a wider strategy, elsewhere they are responses to more pragmatic requirements. It follows too that privatization was likely to be more ambitious in scope and nature in these two countries than in the rest of Europe.

However, programmes are shaped not only by ambitions but also by opportunities and constraints to which we must now turn.

## Privatization: public sector opportunities

Since the pattern of privatization in any country depends on what there is to privatize, the size and nature of the various public sectors in Europe must be considered. There are difficulties in establishing meaningful comparative data on the size of state-owned industrial sectors, since the definition of public enterprise varies so greatly. It is not surprising that problems of definition and calculation exist. In some countries the public industrial sector is constantly being expanded or contracted as holding companies sell off or acquire subsidiaries – often quietly or even unlawfully. In some enterprises the state enjoys control but with only a minority stake, while in others it has a majority stake but chooses not to exercise control. In some countries state control is indirect, being exercised through financial holding companies such as the Société Nationale d'Investissement in Belgium or through state-owned banks such as the Caisse des Dépôts in France. Hybridization (a subject to which we shall return) singularly complicates any assessment of the scope of public sector industrial activity. In short, public industrial sectors are often bewildering mazes. Of course, it is possible to establish a crude guide: by whatever criteria, Sweden, Denmark and Holland have small public industrial and banking sectors while Austria, Spain, Italy and France have extensive ones. But a totally accurate comparison is not possible.

The size of the state sector clearly determines the potential for privatization – a point made with some force by Rudy Andeweg in Chapter 10 on the Netherlands: it is difficult to indulge in extensive privatization if there is little to privatize. But size is not the only factor. For instance, in West Germany in 1982 the Federal government held at least a 25 per cent stake in 958 companies, controlling 102 of them directly and 856 indirectly. The sudden expansion of the German public sector after reunification involved the unwelcome acquisition of over 13,000 firms, most of which were hopelessly inefficient. While privatization in the Eastern part of the country has been rapid, even brutal, privatization proposals for Western Germany have remained modest, as Josef Esser explains. Similarly, Austria and Italy have very extensive public industrial sectors but initially only modest privatization ambitions.

Part of the explanation for the relative modesty of some programmes lies in the structure of the public sector. In some countries it is organized through vast industrial holding companies such as the ÖIAG in Austria, the Instituto Nacional de Industria (INI), Instituto Nacional de Hidrocarbidros (INH) and Patrimonio del Estado in Spain, and the Statsföretag Convention (renamed Procordia in 1984) in Sweden. The best example is probably that of Italy, with its three major *enti*: EFIM, ENI and, of course, IRI, which together had accumulated several hundred companies. IRI, a vast ramshackle empire, controls amongst many other things, 100 per cent of the production of cast iron, two thirds of special steels, and a fifth of ice-cream and of peeled tomato production. In many cases direct stakes are complemented by extensive indirect stakes through state-controlled financial institutions. Thus, the Dutch state has direct stakes in some 40 companies but holds stock in many others through institutions such as the National Investment Bank and the Industrial Guarantee Fund, while the Belgian government, through the Société Nationale d'Investissement, owns shares in many strategic companies. In all these cases the state has to filter its policies through the management of the holdings: its leverage is less direct and effective than in the UK. It is significant that radical privatization in Italy has required a restructuring of the relationship between the *enti* and the government.

The scope of the activities of the public sector is no less important than its structure. In terms of the political and economic justification of privatization it makes a difference whether a firm represents a big public service monopoly (which is often constitutionally protected), a small domestic competitive enterprise or a major internationally competitive group.

The nature of the relationship between central government and public enterprise is also significant. The fact that parts of the West German public industrial sector are in the hands of the Länder, or that Swedish localities run some public utilities, present difficulties to the central government that are absent in countries such as Britain and France where most nationalized industries are truly national. Yet even in centralized systems state-public industry relations vary across European countries and within each according to sector and to time, and depend on factors such as the perceived strategic value of an industry, the extent of *dirigisme* willed by the government, the degree of technical competence required to run an industry, the legal relationship, and its profitability.

The very weak financial position of many European public enterprises since the early 1980s is another relevant factor. In Portugal the state industrial sector accumulated losses between 1974 and 1986 that were the equivalent of a third of annual GDP, while in Spain the public sector was losing over $1 billion a year in the mid-1980s. The financial losses of the Italian *enti* were staggering in their proportions: in 1984, for instance, IRI was losing 4.5 million lire for every one of its 500,000 employees, and by 1992 had consolidated debts of 60,000 billion lire (£28 billion). In July 1992 the new government felt obliged to issue a decree announcing the liquidation of EFIM, a state holding company with a crippling 8.5 trillion lire ($7.5 billion) debt. The government declared itself willing to guarantee the repayment of principal by issuing up to 4 trillion lire of Treasury bonds, but that it intended to freeze interest payments for up to two years. During that time the administrators of the group would try to repay as much as possible by privatizing some of its assets (including Agusta, the helicopter manufacturer). The Austrian state-holding ÖIAG (traditionally a key instrument of government stabilization policy) ran into severe difficulties in the 1980s, with Voest-Alpine, its steel group, piling up vast losses. In France while the overall performance of the state sector greatly improved after 1982 there remained throughout the decade politically damaging black spots. As many public enterprises collapsed financially (sometimes as the result of politically-inspired decisions) politicians were increasingly looked to for resources. This rendered the enterprises unpopular with politicians, whose own interventions, by curtailing managerial autonomy, had been unpopular with managers. Thus a slow spiral of unpopularity was created and sustained.

In West Germany, most of the public sector has been relatively successful, and little need has been felt to change the structures of the public-private relationship. But West Germany has been the exception. Elsewhere the image of public sector industries has been far from flattering. They have been perceived as bastions of archaic, self-interested and obstructive trade unionists anxious to defend over-staffing and costly work practices, as over-centralized and bureaucratized empires run by demotivated managers who were imbued with '*la logique technocratique*' rather than '*la logique industrielle*', as havens of waste and inefficiency cushioned against consumer pressure and market forces, and propped up by excessive subsidy – at a time when state resources were being squeezed by recession and fiscal resistance. This image has not only damaged the public sector in the eyes of the public and provided ammunition for the privatizers, but has also delegitimized it among groups of managers and employees, thus rendering it politically vulnerable.

Finally, the role of the public sector has been a key element in shaping the various privatization programmes. That role was often forged by the historical circumstances that led to the original creation and extension of the public sector. Where technology was naturally monopolistic – that is, where single firm production was the most efficient – there was a strong case for tight state control or even ownership of such a monopoly. In some countries – Italy, Germany (under both Weimar and the Third Reich) and Spain – nationalization had strong nationalistic roots: IRI dates from Mussolini in 1933 and INI from Franco in 1941. In others, notably Britain and France, nationalization was seen as an imperative linked with combating the dominant industrial oligarchies, with gaining control over 'the commanding heights of the economy', with refashioning state-industry relations, and with introducing new patterns of management-worker relations. The French Socialist nationalization programme of 1982 involved a dramatic expansion of the public sector and was inspired by many (not always compatible) motives. Perhaps the most politicized extension of the public industrial sector took place in Portugal after the 1974 Revolution, when a relatively small public sector of the Salazar years (characterized, however, by extensive state regulation of private-sector investment, wages and prices) became one of the biggest in Western Europe, and was given constitutional protection as 'an irreversible victory of the working class'.

In the post-war period in countries such as Italy, France and Spain, public sector firms played a major role as 'agents of growth' both at national and regional level, in industrial construction or reconstruction: for elements of the European left, IRI was once a model to be emulated. However, in the 1970s and early 1980s, when parts of the private sector were in financial crisis, the state sector came to be seen as a haven for bankrupt firms by politicians of all political parties. In Spain, Portugal and Greece, the public sector also became entangled in issues of democratic transition and consolidation as an instrument for buying social and political acquiescence (Bermeo). Reticent public sector managers were obliged, under political pressure, to bail out insolvent private sector enterprises – often small and generally peripheral to the major interest of the state holdings. Thus, IRI in Italy developed into a Hapsburgian empire, vast, rambling and incoherent, while INI in Spain was transformed into 'a golden dustbin filled to the brim with the unprofitable refuse of the private sector'. By the time of the death of Franco the state had a stake in 747 industrial companies and a controlling interest in 379 others. Enforced diversification was accompanied by a more voluntary form: the managers of ÖIAG in Austria, IRI in Italy, INI in Spain and the French state industrial groups all made important acquisitions to expand their empires.

Nationalism and regime consolidation were not the only motives behind nationalization: in Italy it became integrally linked with a widespread system of political patronage. In Italy the public sector grew under Christian Democracy (DC), which saw in it an instrument of economic interventionism that gave it independence from private industrialists who constituted the core of the traditional liberal oligarchy. The DC extended the public sector as part of its *sottogoverno* or 'iceberg' – the submerged power structure which underpinned its political hegemony. As that hegemony came increasingly to be questioned, public sector posts became bargaining counters between and within the governing coalition parties, each with a keen eye on their patronage potential. For the critics, therefore, an extensive public sector was a means of consolidating power of the political parties. Close links between political parties and the public sector also existed in Spain, Portugal, Greece and Austria.

Finally, the public sector in some countries was expanded and consolidated as part of a much wider political settlement: public enterprises were clearly used as buffers, designed to lessen sectoral or regional tensions in culturally and socially divided countries, the case most notably in Belgium. Consequently, as instruments of economic and social regulation they became less vulnerable to emasculation by politicians fearful of the political impact of such policies.

The creation, extension and protection of the public sector was the result, therefore, of pressures emanating from governments, political parties, regional and local interests, trade unions, certain client groups, and, on occasion, private sector industrial and financial interests ready to exploit state enterprises to socialize losses. Consequently, the public sector became saddled with wide-ranging and not always compatible political, economic, social and financial objectives. Furthermore, where conflicting and mutually inconsistent goals seemed to exist, politicians found it undesirable, even dangerous, to clarify the ambiguity. Only in Britain under the Conservatives, and increasingly in France, were some attempts made to clarify the ambiguity, as governments embraced a purely economically functional conception of state industry, in which it was to be judged solely by its efficiency and financial performance. That being so, the step to private ownership is not as great as when public enterprise is traditionally associated with non-economic functions. In other words, British and French right-wing governments divested public sector industry of its political and social role, and were able to act more radically and more effectively in adopting privatization measures. Other governments, locked into a more socio-political conception of the public sector, were unwilling or unable to proceed in so radical a fashion: only privatization of a limited sort was therefore available to them, and in the event it was carried out largely by public sector managers. However, increasingly, under pressure of financial imperatives, some governments have been converted to the British view.

The origins, size, scope, role, organizational structure, financial condition, and pattern of state-sector relations have clearly helped to determine the extent and nature of privatization programmes. But there are other political and economic constraints of a more explicit nature, and it is to these that the next section is addressed.

## VII  Privatization: political, legal and institutional constraints

Several major political factors may be identified as shaping the various European privatization programmes. The first is linked to the previous discussion: protection will be afforded to the public sector, or parts thereof, according to the perception of its political or strategic importance. It has already been argued that in several European countries the public sector is deeply embedded in a general political settlement. Tampering with its ownership has wider ramifications that may be politically dangerous or destabilizing. In France, for example, the aerospace and aircraft industry initially escaped the attention of the privatizers because of its significance for national defence, and the oil industry (represented by ELF) because it was intimately involved in French policy in Africa. Initially, there was no question, unlike in Britain, of transferring such industries to private ownership.

But perceptions are not immutable and this attitude changed with the second privatization programme of 1993. There is, perhaps, a more fundamental point that needs to be raised in explaining the ease or otherwise of implementing radical privatization programmes: a country's conception of the state. The British have always felt uncomfortable with the very concept, and have never really elaborated a juridically-rooted definition of the state: the government, the crown, the administration have been seen largely in functional terms, and, paradoxically, it is only under the self-proclaimed anti-statist government of the 1980s that the nature and proper role of the state have been explored. Unlike in

Britain, debates about privatization in many continental European countries raise the issue of the inalienable sphere of state activity (tax collection, prisons, certain monopolies, defence), thus imposing limits (often internalized and unspoken) on some of the more radical schemes. In some cases, certain state activities are protected constitutionally. Thus, state-owned public monopolies are afforded constitutional protection in France, and attempts to denationalize them would certainly run into difficulties. The Constitutional Council and the Council of State were responsible for tightening some provisions of the July 1986 *ordonnance*, notably those dealing with the rights of shareholders, with fixing the price of the initial issue, and with foreign acquisitions. Moreover, the 1986 Enabling Act on privatization specified the companies to be privatized, fixed a date limit for completion of the programme and laid down the rules on matters such as the use of receipts, the amount of capital to be sold to employees, and the preferential rights of individual small investors. No such legal provisions constrain a British government, which is free to privatize as it wishes, when it wishes.

The West German Basic law also provides constitutional protection for the public monopolies. Privatization of the railways and the postal services (including telecommunications) requires a two-thirds majority in the Bundestag and the Bundesrat to pass the necessary constitutional amendment: hence the drawn-out negotiations between the Kohl government and the Social Democrats (who advocate only partial privatization) to privatize Deutsch Telekom. Similar situations pertain in Spain and Portugal. In Portugal it took more than five years of protracted negotiations between the PSD and the Socialists to revise the Constitution to enable the privatization of certain industries, even though certain public utilities were excluded from the revision. Legal obstacles to privatization may also abound: these range from the need to settle the time-consuming legal dispute between Freddy Laker and British Airways, to the requirement to change the structure of the holding companies of the public enterprises into joint-stock companies (as in Italy and France), and the highly charged problem of altering the civil service status of workers in some sectors (notably telecommunications) in several European countries.

The third major political factor shaping the various privatization programmes has been the commitment and will as well as the structure and durability of executive power. The governments of Thatcher and Chirac, each with a majority in parliament, were zealous privatizers and did not have to contend with the constraints of coalition-building and maintenance. Of course, Prime Minister Chirac in 1986 had to suffer the delaying tactics of President Mitterrand who exercised his constitutional prerogatives in vetoing the initial *ordonnance*, but the delay was short and the legislation was finally passed with only minor modifications. During the second period of *cohabition* which began after the 1993 elections, Mitterrand expressed his serious reservations about certain privatizations, but made no attempt to block them. Perhaps of equal importance is the ability to reduce the number of actors involved in the privatization programme at the executive level, and to ensure that those actors are enthusiastic pro-privatizers: this has occurred in the UK, France, Greece under the New Democracy government, and in Italy under the Ciampi government (which deliberately tightened Treasury control over the programme), although an unseemly public dispute over the method of privatization between Romano Prodi (head of IRI) and Paolo Savano (Industry Ministry) in October 1993 revealed the tensions within the small group involved in the privatization programme. The durability of a privatizing government is, of course, essential. The privatization programmes of right-wing governments in France and Greece were dramatically curtailed with their defeat at the polls in 1988 and 1993 respectively, although Prime Minister Papandreou may be obliged to imitate the French Socialists by implementing a programme of partial privatization.

The constraints of party coalition – the fourth major political factor – have been felt most acutely in West Germany and until recently in Italy. In the Federal Republic only the Free Democrats (FDP) have been enthusiastically in favour of widespread privatization, and in 1984–5 coalition politics reduced the list of candidates for privatization from thirteen to five. In Italy the fragile balance within government coalitions traditionally accorded disproportionate leverage and veto power to the obstructive, and this was clearly illustrated in the fate of several early privatization proposals.

The state of internal party politics has been the fifth factor in facilitating or hindering a drive to privatize. The ascendancy of Mrs Thatcher and her supporters within the Conservative Party, especially after 1983, greatly eased the implementation of the programme, in spite of grumblings in certain Conservative Party circles about the government 'selling off the family silver'. Yet even Mrs Thatcher was obliged by Conservative back-benchers to drop plans to sell off the Austin-Rover volume car business to Ford: they clearly abandoned their market principles and remembered their nationalism. Accordingly, they greeted with enthusiasm the news in 1988 that British Aerospace was acquiring the Rover group (with the help of illegal under-the-counter sweeteners provided by a market-loving Industry Minister). In France the dominance of the Prime

Minister and his close ally, Edouard Balladur, Minister of Finance, enabled them to push forward the programme at a very rapid rate, in spite of carping criticisms by some members of the right-wing coalition. Similarly, the personal authority of Felipe Gonzales did much to convince reluctant elements in the Spanish Socialist Party of the need to sell off certain parts of the major state holding.

The structure of territorial power may be seen as a sixth political factor in shaping a privatization programme. While this is most apparent in the contracting-out type of privatization (since local authorities are major service deliverers), it has also influenced industrial denationalization in Austria (where provincial reticence is apparent), in Italy (where the hostile activity of the local authorities in Naples contributed to the failure of the SME sale, for example) and, more especially, in West Germany. In the Federal Republic, as noted above, the Länder hold stakes in the banking and industrial sectors, and they have proved reluctant to part with them: for instance, Lower Saxony refuses to sell its 20 per cent stake in Volkswagen since the firm is seen as too important for the local economy.

Any consideration of public policy-making must take into consideration the nature of policy networks. Privatization is no exception (Richardson et al, 1992). The Thatcher government after 1979 slowly restructured a number of policy networks to diminish the power of interests such as the unions and local government, and this capacity to restructure was important in removing obstacles to privatization. Not only were the unions excluded but even management were on occasions left out of decisions to privatize. The announcement of the sale of BT, the telecommunications giant, apparently came as a complete surprise to management, but after they had displayed some enthusiasm for privatization they were brought back into the decision-making process. In France the unions wield considerable influence in the public service monopolies (though much less than in the past) but have very little power in the public sector competitive industrial groups. In a strategic industry such as aerospace there is a tightly-knit policy community comprising a small group of politicians, defence officials (from the powerful Direction Générale de l'Armament) and technocrats from the enterprises, all of whom were traditionally committed to retaining the industry firmly in the public sector. But in general the structure of public sector policy has not been a brake on the declared privatization ambitions in France. Indeed, the October 1993 strikes that grounded Air France, which were called to protest against the necessary programme of restructuring the loss-making company before privatization, revealed the mobilizing potential of the shop floor rather than the effectiveness of the unions.

In most European countries policy networks tend to be more decen-
tralized and diffuse, and policy styles more consensual. Radical policies
run the risk of being emasculated in such circumstances. It is clear that
a centralized political system focused essentially on the prime minister
and a friendly finance minister with a capacity to shape and reshape the
appropriate policy is better placed to promote radical policies than one
with a fluid and diffused political system, or one in which industrial
policy networks are stable and characterized by close and collusive
relationships rooted in consensus building. When both conditions exist
– as in several European countries – policy space is clearly reduced, and
radical policies such as extensive privatization are precluded.

The final political factor that has had an impact on the privatization
drive lies in the nature and organization of the constituencies for and
against privatization. Since the early 1980s there has been a weakening
of the coalition that is committed to the extension or maintenance of
public sector industry. The major political parties that favour the public
sector have either been seriously weakened (the case of the British
Labour Party and certain Scandanavian Social Democratic parties and a
number of European Communist parties), or increasingly sceptical about
the merits of nationalization (the Austrian, Spanish and French Socialist
parties). On the other hand, Social Democratic parties in West Germany,
Sweden and the Netherlands have never been ardent supporters of an
extensive public industrial sector.

The trade union movement has also been on the defensive during this
period, being weakened by government legislation, unemployment, the
changing structures of the labour market, the introduction of new style
shop-floor relations, internal divisions and falling membership. Despite
being entrenched in the public sectors of Western Europe, the unions
have been unable to protect their strongholds. In Austria, the ÖGB exercised some moderating influence on privatization plans through its links
with the SPÖ; in Italy, where the unions are generally better informed
and more widely consulted, they helped to block the sales of Maccarese
and SME. But, as elsewhere in Europe, unions in Italy now seem
powerless to prevent more radical privatizing programmes.

If trade union leaders remain generally in favour of nationalized
industries, the same cannot always be said of their members. Many have
become disabused with the public sector (which in many countries has
been ruthless in reducing the workforce), or, in some cases (Britain,
France, and Germany) seduced into privatization by the offer of shares
at preferential rates. Perhaps the most serious dilution of support for the
public sector is to be found among its managers. Indeed, by the mid-
1980s they were among the principal proponents of the privatization

movement. In Britain, the chairmen of public monopolies fought to retain their monopoly positions, but within the private sector: for keen privatizers, such as Lord King of British Airways, competition was not to stand in the way of privatization. The management of British Telecom, after a period of strained relations with the government, came to be influential supporters of privatization. In France even some nationalized industry chairmen appointed by the Socialists have been in favour of private sector minority stakes, and a small group has become converted to outright privatization. After the electoral victory of the right in March 1986, public sector managers pressed the Treasury to sell off their companies as quickly as possible.

In Italy and Spain the most explicit support for partial privatization has come from the managers of the state holding companies. As in Britain and France, they wish to organize their enterprises without undue political interference, without constant recourse to unsympathetic finance ministries, and without being enmeshed in the web of politico-bureaucratic compromises which characterized public sector decision-making. All public sector managers resent the second-guessing of civil servants and the constant political interference in purely operational matters. Most also resent the use of public sector firms as crude instruments of governmental macro-economic policy or regional policy. They dislike being pressured into 'irrational' investments and diversification strategies, and politically-inspired rescue operations of bankrupt private companies. All too frequently they were squeezed into financial crisis – for which they were then blamed.

For public sector managers in Britain and France privatization, which was placed on the political agenda by governments, was a means of acquiring commercial autonomy. Their colleagues in Italy, Portugal and Spain, where privatization was not politically promoted initially and where outright denationalization was politically infeasible, saw in privatization a means of acquiring great autonomy *vis-à-vis* the politicians by introducing a buffer zone of private investors. Partial privatization was also favoured because it enabled them to restructure their ramshackle holdings, rid themselves of loss-making peripheral activities, and improve their financial position (thus lessening their dependence on the Treasury) by ploughing back into the holdings the proceeds of the privatization operations. It must be recalled that in Austria, Italy, Spain and Portugal public sector holdings and firms which engaged in partial privatization were often able to use the funds raised to recapitalize their enterprises – once again a clear inducement to action.

The pro-privatization constituency was therefore strengthened by the addition of public-sector managers. But the constituency would have been powerful and vocal even without them. Central banks, finance ministries, private industry and particularly banking interests have welcomed the privatization programmes, although with varying degrees of enthusiasm both across European countries and within each one of them. While the Confederation of British Industry (CBI) has been generally enthusiastic, the French *patronat* in the shape of the CNPF has given a more cautious response (it is worried about unbalancing the Bourse and about foreign acquisitions), and the largest Dutch employers' organization (VNO) is lukewarm. The Austrian Business League, which is generally in favour, contains elements that are also far from enthusiastic. The keenest support for privatization has come from those most likely to profit from it: the financial lobby comprising institutional investors, stock exchanges, merchant bankers who have organized flotations, and underwriters who often make considerable gains. Again, however, the weight of these groups varies considerably across Europe: thus the banking lobby is powerful in Britain, France and Spain but weak in Greece and Portugal. Finally, there has existed a group of neo-liberal intellectuals who have been active in promoting the case of privatization: in Britain, the Institute of Economic Affairs and the Centre for Policy Studies; in France, the Club '89 and the Clubs Perspectives et Réalités; in West Germany, a group of influential neo-liberal economists. Writings advocating privatization or attacking nationalization have proliferated, preparing the intellectual groundwork and furnishing the rationalizations for pro-privatization politicians.

An analysis of the political background to privatization reveals the importance of the interplay of constitutional and institutional arrangements with policy aspirations. It suggests that such arrangements may have an inhibiting effect on some governments, but that resolute governments in propitious political and institutional circumstances have the capacity to effect very far-reaching change – certainly more far-reaching than traditional models of policy-making based on incrementalism and policy networks (which may be restructured or marginalized) might suggest. It is perhaps revealing that public opinion, as expressed in opinion polls, has played little part in shaping the privatization debate. Indeed, in the UK the privatization of the public utilities was supported by only a very small minority of the population.

## VIII   Privatization: the financial parameters

The nature of industrial capital and the structure and state of financial markets have influenced the courses that privatization have taken in

European countries. At one level privatization may be regarded as a way of changing the mechanism whereby a company is financed. Public ownership transfers individuals' savings to industrial companies by such means as taxation, government borrowing, or through publicly-owned banks. When privatization occurs, other channels of funding must be found. The basic alternatives are take-over by private industrial or holding companies, intermediation by private banks, management buy-outs, or direct investment via the stock exchange by private individuals or institutions such as pension funds or insurance companies.

The small size and weak structure of many European financial markets have ruled out the 'popular capitalism' which has inspired privatizations of the British and French variety. The capitalization of the London Stock Exchange has enabled it to absorb all the privatizations without difficulty (indeed, as noted above, the City has been one of the most ardent promoters of the privatization programme). But in countries such as Portugal, Denmark, Finland, Norway and Austria, fears about the small size of the financial market initially precluded massive and rapid sales because it was felt that they might crowd out investment in other equity or lead to foreigners (particularly unwelcome neighbours) buying substantial stakes. In Italy various reforms (including the expansion of mutual funds) may help the Milan stock exchange to expand, but currently it is totally unable to manage a major flotation. Even the size of the Paris Bourse continues to give rise to disquiet in French political, financial and industrial circles that it is incapable of digesting a rapid and radical privatization programme: this may explain the government's decision to sell the bigger enterprises (notably ELF, France's biggest company, with a capitalization of over $18 billion) in tranches. Fears are also expressed that private companies looking for new capital would be crowded out. It is contended that the Bourse is too small and inefficient, that already a large volume of trade in French securities is being carried out by American or British brokers in London, and that several major French banks – including BNP and Paribas – have based their international capital operations in London. Yet fears of saturation and crowding out have so far proved to be unfounded. This has partly been as a result of the growth of the French equity market, which has increased sharply since 1982, partly a consequence of government measures designed to facilitate and increase transactions (easing of exchange controls, new computerized trading techniques, tax incentives) and also because privatization at below market values has not unnaturally attracted the French public into the purchase of equity.

Elsewhere, fears about the incapacity of domestic stock markets to cope with a major privatization have largely been misplaced (even the tiny Danish Stock Exchange comfortably dealt with the sale of half of the state's stake in Kryolitselskabet Öresund, the biggest equity sale in the country's history). Nevertheless, it is clear that very few stock exchanges could cope with a sale as big as British Gas or British Telecom. Moreover, there is another factor that must be considered: the absence of efficient institutional investors and the investment culture of many European countries which has also prevented popular capitalism-type privatizations. Thus, the Spanish and Austrians have a strong tradition of bank saving, while the Italians buy government bonds rather than equity. There is a similar lack of culture of individual equity buying in Germany: this became clear in the early attempts to privatize Volkswagen. This poses no political problem if a wide range of other institutions purchase privatized equity. But this is not always the case. One of the fears expressed in Italy of massive privatization is that it might consolidate the hold of the very small number of 'barons' who already dominate the private sector.

The final financial market consideration in the privatization debate is the state of the financial markets and of the firms to be privatized. The privatization programmes of the early and mid-1980s were greatly facilitated by the world-wide increase in share transactions. The Stock Market crash of October 1987 led to the disastrous affair of the £7.2 billion British Petroleum issue, and had a damaging impact on the French and Spanish privatization programmes. The financial plight of many nationalized industries has also prevented their privatization. Investors are unlikely to buy unprofitable (for example, railways) or highly risky (nuclear power stations, for example) ventures. The experience of the Treuhand in East Germany has been highly instructive in this respect.

## IX  Privatization: the impact

Assessing the impact of the privatization programmes requires making distinctions between the Franco-British radical models and the more piecemeal and limited measures of other countries; between the financial, economic and political consequences; and between the short- and possible long-term effects, some of which already hint at being of an unanticipated and unwelcome sort. It also requires isolating the variable of privatization from other accompanying pressures and policies such as deregulation. Part of the assessment must therefore be somewhat speculative. Clearly in the UK there has been some redrawing of the public-private boundary. Elsewhere, even in France, after the 1986–8 period, which saw the completion of a third of the promised privatization programme, the results have so far been modest. It must be emphasized that even if the Chirac privatization programme had been fully implemented, public utilities and major 'strategic' firms would have remained in state hands.

It is no less difficult to evaluate the impact of privatization on the performance of the companies involved. There is the problem of isolating the ownership variable from a host of other factors that bear on performance. In principle, privatization can improve industrial efficiency in several ways. One of its effects may be to remove financial constraints on the firms in question. Thus, IRI in Italy has been raising capital for some of its subsidiaries by selling shares in others, thereby circumventing cash controls set by the government. In France only two uses were allowed by the 1986 Act of the proceeds of privatization: repayment of the public debt (or disindebtment), thus reducing the state's demands on the bond market, and capital increases for enterprises that remained in the public sector. In fact the government used 72 per cent of proceeds for disindebtment and the remaining 28 per cent for recapitalizing state companies.

Second, private ownership may sharpen incentives for internal efficiency by stimulating the profit motive. This is most likely to be achieved in competitive market conditions. But in the UK some industries were transferred to the private sector with the dominant market positions unaltered. The flotations of British Telecom (much of whose business, for example, local network operation is naturally monopolistic at the current state of technology), of British Gas and of the British Airports Authority were carried out (in 1984, 1986, and 1987 respectively), with their integrated near-monopoly structures intact. This led to considerable criticism. When the electricity and water distribution industries were privatized attempts, not entirely successful, were made to introduce greater competition into the sectors. Third, privatization can improve industrial efficiency by preventing government from exploiting the firms as instruments to pursue other goals – macro-economic, employment distributional or regional. It is clear that privatization in some cases has led to massive redundancy programmes. The Treuhand has been heavily criticized by many in the Eastern Länder for doing little to protect jobs and prevent closures; by the end of 1993 an estimated 3000 firms had been closed as a result of the privatization programme, with the direct loss of over 300,000 jobs. Similarly, British Telecom has a well-earned reputation for a radical slimming down of its labour force. However, it must be recalled that many state industries in the 1980s and early 1990s earned a well-justified reputation for ruthless cutting of manpower.

In truth, there are great problems in comparing the performance of public and private enterprises because the criteria for assessing performance are varied, and because their activities do not always overlap sufficiently to permit meaningful comparison. Furthermore, private sector management has a basic duty to maximize profits for shareholders, which is not the case with public sector firms which are frequently bound by other objectives: low profitability is not necessarily inconsistent with efficient management. Difficulties of comparing have not, of course, prevented comparisons – but the evidence is confused and far from conclusive. It is generally argued that performance, in terms of production, sales and profits, has improved in the UK since privatization. It has even been argued that the privatized companies are imbued with a commercial culture, and that this culture has, by way of ripple effect, spread to the remaining public sector. A recent report by the World Bank (a believer in privatization) has clearly suggested that privatization does improve efficiency, but the weight of evidence does not appear to support any general propositions about the superiority of private over public ownership or vice versa. The scale and nature of competition in the relevant market emerges as a key factor, with private ownership appearing relatively more efficient in competitive conditions. Efficiency also appears to be enhanced when the owners are closely involved in management (which is not always the case in major international holdings). The record of many nationalized industries in several European countries suggests that public sector firms are capable of transforming their performance. Indeed, rather embarrassingly, public sector productivity grew faster than that in the private sector in the UK under the Thatcher government. By being accorded greater autonomy and encouraged to make unpopular decisions on lay-offs, by tightening up financial management and by requiring higher product and service standards, many public sector firms have become distinctly more profitable and are thus, perhaps paradoxically, preparing the path for their own privatization.

The general impact of privatization on corporate structures in Western Europe varies from country to country. In most the impact has been negligible because the programmes so far implemented have been so limited. In Italy, however, the effect so far has been to strengthen certain already powerful private sector groups (such as Agnelli, De Benedetti), which alone have the financial capacity to acquire privatized stock. In the banking sector privatization has also been a spur to the rationalization of a fragmented and inefficient system. In France the early claims for privatization were certainly ambitious: according to Edouard Balladur, French Finance Minister, *'le capitalisme français d'après les privatisations ne ressemblera pas à celui d'avant*, but the statement was exaggerated and misleading: exaggerated because traditional French capitalism will certainly be readily recognizable after the privatization programme, and misleading because privatization will not herald in a more market-oriented economy but rather a restructured private capitalism. In the 1986–8 programme the Finance Ministry was clearly trying to establish an interlocking network of French-controlled holdings in the privatized groups through the core controlling interests – the *noyaux durs* – which are carefully selected by itself. By March 1988 the Rue de Rivoli had chosen 73 mainly French groups to control 16 billion francs of capital in the privatized firms. As a result of complex cross-shareholding, a small number of groups, some still linked to state banks, were emerging as the props of French industry. In the post-1993 programme, aware of the pressures of internationalization, the French government has decided to widen the scope of the core shareholding to include foreigners. In the case of the Banque Nationale de Paris, 16 friendly institutional investors will own 30 per cent of the Banque's shares, and these include its German partner, the Dresdner Bank, Britain's BAT, Hoffmann-La Roche of Switzerland, General Electric of the USA, and two Kuwaiti government bodies. With the privatization of 43 per cent of the capital of Rhône-Poulenc in November 1993, the Italian Group Fiat and Crédit Suisse joined other stable shareholders to hold a combined 24 per cent of the total. In Italy the privatization of Credito Italiano was structured around Mediobanca, the highly influential Milanese merchant bank. The result of privatization in France, as in Italy, is likely to be a greater concentration of private economic power and not necessarily a more competitive economy.

Take-over bids by newly privatized companies in the UK (e.g. British Telecom/Mital, British Airways/British Caledonian and then DanAir, BP/Britoil, and British Aerospace/Rover) suggest that similar forces may be at work there as well. On the whole, privatization may be seen as a mechanism for facilitating rationalization processes already at work in the national, European and international economies. Mergers, with take-overs of and increased equity holdings in domestic and foreign firms form an integral part of the modern industrial scene, and are clearly linked with the process of privatization. It is difficult to imagine, for instance, the necessary process of the rationalization of European airlines without a significant degree of privatization: Air France's purchase of a 37.6 per cent stake in Sabena after its partial privatization is but one more step in the rationalization process; the Spanish government sold its stake in the Spanish subsidiary of SKF to the Swedish parent company in 1985, transferred its control of the debt-laden SEAT car firm to West Germany's Volkswagen, and of the troubled lorry-and bus-maker ENASA to America's General Motors. It also allowed Telefonica to sell its 49 per cent stake in Intelsa, its switching equipment joint venture with Ericsson, to the Swedish partner. IRI justified its sale of Alfa-Romeo to Fiat in terms of achieving economy of scale at European level, and has entered a number of joint public-private ventures to achieve competitive scale in the telecommunications and electronics sectors. Strategic foreign firms such as Fiat and Crédit Suisse have now been introduced into the hard-core stable share ownership of French privatized firms, and in the UK, by the end of 1987, foreigners already held 45 per cent of Jaguar, 20 per cent of Rolls Royce and 15 per cent of British Aerospace.

In some cases in Britain, France and Portugal, foreign ownership is higher than that permitted by the law. Nationalization of key industries or the introduction of foreign capital into their ownership may raise delicate questions of national sovereignty in countries such as France with a strongly nationalist industrial culture, or Italy and Greece where very few laws restrict foreign direct investment, or in Portugal and Sweden where such laws have been severely weakened.

The political ramifications of privatization have yet to be fully explored. Curiously, even the political implications of the transfer of wealth that has been enormous in Britain and considerable in France, through equity holding, have attracted little attention in political science literature. Ownership has two dimensions: the entitlement to a share of the profits of an enterprise in the form of dividends, and some say in determining its policies. The latter aspect raises thorny questions, because the links between ownership, control and the distribution of power are often very tenuous, especially if shareholding is widely dispersed, as in French and British privatized companies. Corporate control is likely to remain firmly in the hands of management in the UK since the major institutional investors, banks, insurance companies, pensions funds and unit trusts, show little interest in control. In any case, as in France, the creation of millions of new shareholders is unlikely to have an impact on the distribution of corporate power.

Between 1986 and 1988 the number of shareholders tripled in France: the sale of Paribas in January 1987 attracted no fewer than 3.8 million people. The early results of the 1993 programme are no less promising: the first three sales were vastly oversubscribed, with the Banque Nationale de Paris stock being distributed amongst 2.8 million shareholders. The United Kingdom privatization programmes have resulted in a bigger increase to about 13 million shareholders by the end of 1992. Both the British and French governments have proudly proclaimed the establishment of a new and large share-owning class, and each has claimed that there are now as many shareholders as trade-union members. Each has also deliberately sought to widen share-ownership by selling privatized stock at very attractive prices. This new class of shareholders is supposedly more independent and more free, and displays greater responsibility because it is sensitized to the requirements of the firm and to the exigencies of the market: with a direct personal stake greater interest would be stimulated in the performance of industry. While there is no doubt about the popularity of many of the major flotations in Britain and France (most were massively over-subscribed), a close look at the figures it not so reassuring. Many new small investors simply had an eye for a bargain, and made quick and easy profits by selling their newly acquired shares – to the institutional investors. Survey evidence shows that the majority of shareholders in Britain have holdings in just one or two privatized companies. Even the massive privatization drives of Britain have done nothing to reverse the trend towards a progressive reduction in the proportion of equity held by individuals. Thus, although 22 per cent of the British held shares in 1992 compared with only 7 per cent in 1981, only 20 per cent of the country's shares were in the hands of individuals (compared with nearly 40 per cent on the New York stock exchange). Institutional investors now own almost half of the stock privatized since 1979 (*Financial Times*, 10 August 1993; *Economist*, 6 November 1993). In short, individual share ownership has been spread more widely by privatization, but very thinly.

Not unnaturally, quick profit-making and taking has led to criticisms in both Britain and France of privatization creating a nation of share stags and '*une économie de casino*' more reminiscent of the bingo hall than the bourse, and that far from creating a realistic understanding of the market, the sale of stock at below market value was projecting a totally false vision of how the market operates. More important, it is clear that the creation of a vast group of new shareholders does little to alter the control of industry. Atomized, ill-informed and largely uninterested, individual shareholders have very few effective powers. Popular capitalism is clearly not going to disturb corporate managers, and a consideration of property rights in Britain and France as the result of privatization should perhaps lead to a debate about the concentration of economic power rather than its much acclaimed diffusion. It should also be underlined that the *General Household Survey* of 1990 indicated that even after the British 'popular capitalism' programmes of the 1980s only 6 per cent of unskilled manual workers (compared with 43 per cent of professionals) and 7 per cent of council tenants (53 per cent of home owners) were shareholders. The claim made by Norman Lamont that

Britain has 'within its grasp the possibility of a dream come true, a nationwide capital-owning democracy' in which every person is an owner (quoted in *The Independent*, 3 January 1992) must be treated with some scepticism.

Conservative parties may gain votes where shareholding has massively expanded as the result of privatization. There is some poll evidence from the British elections to suggest that this may have happened. This is scarcely surprising: the underpricing of privatization issues is appreciated more by those who gain than depreciated by the general public that loses. Secondly, the election of a party that sought – or might seek – to reverse privatization or introduce tougher regulatory policies would jeopardize the value of shares held by millions. Yet in bearish markets holders of devalued equity may not be so well-disposed towards the privatizers and tighter regulation is being introduced. In other words, in most European countries with modest privatization programmes the political impact is naturally limited, and there are too many imponderables to hazard any predictions about the impact of radical privatization on the longer-term distribution of political power.

A further political dimension of privatization warrants further analysis: the extent to which it has contributed to a restructuring of traditional policy communities and networks. Once again, however, disentangling cause from effect may prove a futile exercise.

One final question needs to be addressed: does privatization mark a fundamental break with state intervention? Again, the modest scope and extent of privatization in most European countries has been such that change is unlikely, while in France and Britain privatization has represented an adjustment in the intensity and pattern, and not the scope of the state-industry relationship. In France, it must be recalled, there is no intention to privatize the great public sector utilities (EDF, GDF, SNCF, France Télécom) even though the question was raised in the *Projet de l'Union pour la France* – the 1993 electoral platform of the Right. In spite of an expansion of allocation through markets rather than through politico-administrative compromise there has been no systematic withdrawal of the state. Moreover, in Britain the effect of privatizing monopoly utilities has resulted in more detailed and more explicit interventionism through the publicly appointed regulatory authorities that have come to enjoy wide discretion to shape the terms and conditions on prices and the services provided. Indeed, the relationship between these new regulating agencies and the privatized utilities has often bordered upon open warfare, with the latter accusing the former of 'changing the rules of the game'. Perhaps the most spectacular expression of the tension between the regulators and the regulated was the referral of British Gas to the Monopolies and Mergers Commission, which in August 1993 recommended that the company be broken up and its domestic monopoly be abolished.

Everywhere in Western Europe the state continues to intervene massively in the economy by regulating the terms and influencing the environment of both public and private industry operations. In spite of the very real constraints of the international economy and of the European Community, European states retain a vast range of industrial control mechanisms, some of which are of an undifferentiated nature affecting the industrial environment in general, others of a more specific, micro-economic nature. The state continues to be provider, regulator, entrepreneur, purchaser (its procurement policies remain vital for several privatized companies), umpire and travelling salesman in industrial affairs, imposing a corset on some actors, providing a safety net for others and opening up opportunities for others.

State involvement in the affairs of privatized companies – before, during and after their sale – may be seen very clearly in Britain and France where their governments closely controlled the date, conditions, price and initial structure of shareholding of the firms to be privatized. In East Germany, the Treuhand has often privatized a company only after negotiating very detailed conditions relating to investment and employment with the purchasers. The attitude of the government towards British Airways is a good illustration of persistent intervention. It protected the airline before privatization against British Caledonian, the private airline and its main competitor, in heated negotiations over route allocations (thus being partly responsible, according to some observers, for the eventual demise of British Caledonian). It ensured successful privatization of British Airways by the favourable conditions pertaining to the sale, and it continued to protect the company after privatization. When the partly state-owned SAS made its bid during November–December 1987 to buy a controlling stake in British Caledonian in an attempt to form the first major cross-border airline in Europe, it was blocked by the Thatcher government, which allowed a counter-bid by British Airways to succeed, thus consolidating BA's hold on the market. The Conservative government also allowed BA to swallow another private sector competitor in 1992. It was clearly more concerned with protecting a national champion (even if privatized) than furthering competition. The history of BA since privatization reveals fully the clash between the demands of the market, the requirements of management, and the exigencies of sovereignty.

Perhaps one of the most significant political features of the impact of the privatization programmes in Europe has been the increase in industrial hybridization – a traditional feature of the industrial landscape of France, Belgium and Italy, which has been accentuated even in these countries. This public-private hybridization takes many forms, but particularly at the level of equity. We now witness public enterprises taking stakes in national and foreign privately-controlled firms, public firms buying minority stakes in other national public and foreign public enterprises as well as private firms buying stakes in state-controlled national and foreign public companies. The diversification strategies of major British and French firms provide numerous examples of this increasingly intricate process of national and international hybridization. Hybridization also takes the form of joint ventures.

More interestingly, several governments have retained important stakes or a blocking minority of shares (the case of Sabena, the Belgian flag carrier) or a 'golden share' in some privatized firms. This 'golden share' enables worried governments, in order to protect the national interest, to block unwelcome take-over bids. This veto may prove to be more theoretical than real. Nevertheless, the continuing state presence raises a series of complex and unanswered questions about the relationship with the industries involved. Arrangements vary from hybrid to hybrid, resulting in nebulous and unpredictable situations: it is difficult to know in what circumstances governments might activate their rights. The result is that public-private industrial relationships as the result of hybridization in some areas may well have been obfuscated rather than redefined. Thus, an element of uncertainty remains, partially undermining one of the major reasons for privatization.

The interpenetration of public and private industry has long been the subject of academic enquiry: Lindblom, Galbraith, Shonfield and Andrew Berle were among many who pointed to the inextricable mixing of the two – a mixing rooted in mutual dependence (in sectors such as aeronautics, atomic energy, electronics and telecommunications), and overlapping functions (both make regulations, employ people, produce goods and services, are major investors, generate national income, and deliver social welfare). Major public and private firms are both subject to varying degrees of political authority, both function in the same environment shaped by the state, and suffer the same ambiguities of purpose and problems of multiple oversight. In many countries, such as France, intimate and collusive relationships exist in certain sectors between ministry officials, public technocrats and managers in the public and private sectors. There are, of course, differences between public and private firms, but these should not be exaggerated. It may be possible to adjust state-industry relations but it is intrinsically

impossible to eradicate them: we may be witnessing less the process of
state retreat than of state reshaping.


## X   Privatization: problems and paradoxes

The privatization programmes of Western Europe have been shaped by
common pressures and by conditions specific to each country, and
almost everywhere have to be set in the wider context of the restructuring of state-market-society relations. As such they cannot be divorced
from the wider environment of internationalization, Communitarization
and liberalization: the fact that a Dutch-based company should now be
managing the Immigration Centre near Heathrow airport or that French
companies are sweeping the streets of some British cities should come
as no more of a surprise than that the Spanish government have floated
privatized stock on the London stock exchange or that the French
government have included major foreign companies amongst the
stable core share-holders of its privatized enterprises. The pressures for
privatization are real, and they are growing. Yet it would be simplistic
to see the various privatization programmes as merely the reaction of
governments to the demands of strategically placed pressure groups
responding to technological change. We have seen that there are
significant differences across Europe and that these differences in the
privatization programmes may be explained by several interrelated
factors:

- the perceived intensity of the pressures pushing towards privatization;
- the motives, ambitions and political will and durability of the privatizers, who have harboured various mixtures of ideological, economic, political and financial objectives;
- the different starting points from which privatization is proceeding,
  as defined by the origins, nature and scope of public sector enterprises in European countries;
- the political and institutional opportunity structures in which the
  privatizers operate, including the stability and structure of executive
  power, the nature of their respective party political systems, the
  degree of centralization of political and industrial power, the structure of policy networks, and the prevailing styles of policy-making;
- the technical ease with which privatization of the industry may be
  pursued;
- the financial systems through which the transfer of ownership to
  private investors is carried out.

To appreciate the extent, the timing, the pace and the type of privatization strategies deployed, consideration must be paid to all the above factors. It is not simply a technology-driven phenomenon forcing governments to react in common fashion. Rather, it is a political process responding to a variety of pressures (Henig *et al.*, 1988).

If privatization has become a 'policy fashion' it is because it appears to offer solutions to at least some of the economic problems facing European governments. The 'demonstration effect' of the UK programme has also clearly influenced its European neighbours. Yet, as has been shown, the constitutional, institutional and political circumstances (including especially the political will) are highly propitious in the UK, and are unlikely to be reproduced in their entirety elsewhere. Moreover, as the UK experience shows, even radical privatization has had a limited impact on the role of the state in the economy and the overall wealth of that economy. It has raised vast sums of money for the government, redistributed wealth, and has improved the performance of some firms. But the British economy is in many respects in a worse mess than it was before its radical privatization programme. We need not go as far as one observer on the *Financial Times* who argued that 'the abiding impression of the whole programme is that it was unexceptional in principle and irrelevant to practice' (*Financial Times*, 16 June 1993). However, we must accept that privatization is no panacea, and no substitute for a more balanced macro-economic strategy. Furthermore, it must be recognized that all forms of privatization have raised delicate problems of timing, method, permissible foreign ownership, and price. More importantly, partial privatization often gives rise to acute problems of transparency and accountability while the privatization of a state monopoly may leave the government with the complex issue of the necessary competitive or regulatory regime as well as the definition of the social obligations of the company.

The privatization programmes have produced not only problems but also paradoxes. We have the spectacle of some socialist governments indulging in privatization as well as right-centre governments displaying scepticism about its desirability. We witness a Conservative government in Britain fully mobilizing state power to push through its privatizations in the name of reducing that power. The same government proclaims the virtues of the market yet it frequently privatized according to political rather than strictly market criteria. We note some governments refusing the logic of the European open market by protecting their industries behind the barrier of state ownership yet indulging in sustained pro-European rhetoric. We recognize that privatizers denounce the inefficiency of public firms but have privatized mainly those making comfortable profits. Indeed, in some countries (see, for example, Sweden, Chapter 9) governments have had to strengthen the private sector (notably the financial markets) in order to ensure the success of their privatization programmes. We perceive the frenetic activity of French state-owned banks preaching the virtues of privatization in Eastern and Central Europe. We hear Italian and Spanish state-sector industrial bosses arguing that privatization would leave the public sector stronger not weaker. We see that eradicating one form of state regulation (nationalization) may lead to re-regulation – and of a more detailed and interventionist sort. We note the purchase of privatized or private stock by foreign (often French) state-owned companies, which when criticized for introducing 'backdoor nationalisation' innocently protest that they acting as private entrepreneurs. Of course, many of these paradoxes are more apparent than real, and most spring from a combination of the complex and constant interplay of public and private interests and the ambiguous and often conflicting motives and aims of European governments.

Despite its problem-ridden and paradoxical nature privatization will remain on the European policy agenda, if only for financial reasons. It is a pot of gold for governments short of money and unwilling to raise taxes. Privatization may be yet another example of governments doing the right thing for the wrong reasons, masking need by virtue, and cloaking necessity with a rationalizing ideological discourse.

## Note

1.  The literature on privatization is very extensive For comparative analyses of the phenomenon see: W.P. Glade (ed.) *State Shrinking: A Comparative Inquiry into Privatisation*, Austin, Texas, Institute of Latin American Studies, 1986; D.J. Gayle and J.N. Goodrich (eds), *Privatization and Deregulation in Global Perspective*, London, Pinter Publishers, 1990; W.T. Gormley, *Privatization and its alternatives*, Madison, University of Wisconsin Press, 1991; K. Kernaghan (ed.), 'Symposium on the Progress, Benefits and Costs of Privatization', *International Review of Administrative Sciences*, 56(1), 1990; P.W. Macavey *et al*, *Privatization and State-Owned Enterprises*, London, Kluwer Academic Publications, 1989; J.J. Richardson (ed.), *Privatization and Deregulation in Canada and Britain*, Aldershot, Dartmouth Publishing Company, 1990; R. Ramamuri and R. Vernon (eds), *Privatization and Control of State-Owned Enterprises*, Washington, World Bank, 1991; E.N. Suleiman and J. Waterbury (eds), *The Political Economy of Public Sector Reform and Privatization*, Oxford, Westview Press, 1990; J. Vickers and V. Wright (eds), *The Politics of Privatization*, London, Frank Cass, 1989; Ferdinando Targetti, *Privatization in Europe: West and East Experiences*, Aldershot, Dartmouth Publishing House, 1992.

# References

Bermeo, Nancy (1990), 'The politics of public enterprise in Portugal, Spain and Greece', in E.N. Suleiman and J. Waterbury, *The Political Economy of Public Sector Reform and Privatization*, Oxford, Westview Press, 137–62.

Feigenbaum, Harvey (1982), 'Public enterprise in comparative perspective', *Comparative Politics*, October: 101–22.

Glade, William P. (1986), 'Services and forms of privatisation' in Glade, *State-Shrinking: a Comparative Inquiry into Privatisation*, Austin, Texas, Institute of Latin American Studies: 10–14.

Graham, Cesmo and Prosser, Tony (1991), *Privatizing Public Enterprises: Constitutions, the State and Regulation in Comparative Perspective*, Oxford, Clarendon Press.

Henig, Jeffrey R., Hamnett, Chris and Feigenbaum, Harvey (1988), 'The politics of privatization: a comparative perspective', *Governance*, **1** (4), October: 442–68.

Hirschman, A. (1982), *Shifting Involvements: Private Interest and Public Policy*, Oxford, Basil Blackwell.

OECD (1992), *Regulatory Reform, Privatisation and Competition Policy*, Paris, OECD.

Richardson, Jeremy J., Maloney, William A., and Rüdig, Wolfgang (1992), 'The dynamics of policy change: lobbying and water privatization', *Public Administration*, **70**, Summer: 157–75

# CHAPTER 2

## ECONOMIC ASPECTS OF PRIVATIZATION IN BRITAIN

### Ray Rees

### Introduction: some history

From the late 1960's the general policy of 'rolling back the frontiers of the state', of which privatization is of course a part, was a central element of Conservative party policy. In the early days of the Heath government of 1970–4 an initial attempt at mounting a 'denationalization programme' was made, with very modest results, and the pressure rapidly faded as the famous 'U-turn' in the economic policy of that government took place. Both this failure to carry through the policy, and the series of confrontations with trades unions that ultimately resulted in the defeat of the government, must have given Conservative party strategists considerable food for thought during the period, up to 1979, in which they were out of power. What they would no doubt judge as the outstanding success of the privatization programme[1] over the past decade suggests that the lessons from the experience of the Heath government were learned. A sector which in 1979 accounted for over 10 per cent of UK gross domestic product, 8 per cent of employment, and 17 per cent of the capital stock has been reduced to less than a fifth of that size. An extensive portfolio consisting of holdings in manufacturing industry and ownership of the major energy, transport and communications utilities has been contracted to a rump consisting of British Rail, a much reduced coal industry, and postal services. Following the re-election of a Conservative government for a fourth term of office, many of these remaining activities will also be privatized.

It seems clear that a privatization programme of this extent was beyond the expectations, though presumably not the hopes, of Mrs Thatcher's government when it took office in 1979. For example, it was initially denied that the recently privatized water industry would in fact be privatized. The success of early parts of the programme, and political gains from it which may not have been fully anticipated at the outset, clearly led to its extension and intensification. In fact the programme can be divided into two overlapping phases. The first, earlier phase was that of the sale of a number of smaller, predominantly manufacturing enterprises. Some of these, such as Rolls Royce, Jaguar, and a number of shipbuilders, had been taken into public ownership because of their bankruptcy as privately owned firms. Others, such as Amersham International and Cable and Wireless, had evolved out of government activities, (for example the development and manufacture of radioactive materials), but which clearly could be viable as commercial concerns. Still others, such as British Steel, British Airways (BA), Associated British Ports and British Petroleum (BP), were in the public sector because of the belief of earlier Labour governments that they should be state owned.

The central characteristic of all these enterprises from the economic point of view is that they raised no real issue of market failure[2], at least not to an extent that could not be dealt with by the standard instruments of economic policy. They were all actually or potentially subject to some degree of competition, whether from domestic or foreign firms, and none raised acute environmental issues comparable with, say, nuclear energy or water supply.

The second phase of the programme was inaugurated by the sale of (the first tranche of) British Telecom (BT) in 1984. This began the process of selling off the major public utilities which, in at least some of their major activities, possessed considerable monopoly power. To follow were sales of the gas, electricity and water industries and the south-east airports. As well as on the whole being much larger than the enterprises in the first phase (with, of course, some exceptions: the British Airports Authority is much smaller than British Steel, for example), so that the process of selling them off was in itself more challenging, privatization of these utilities raises deeper issues concerning market failure and regulation, which will be discussed later in this chapter.

## Motives for privatization

The objective of substantially reducing the extent of state economic activity, in pursuit of which privatization is one instrument, has its roots both in political philosophy and economic theory. Comparative advantage dictates that I confine myself to the latter. The economic argument for private ownership rests on the idea that the pursuit of profit by the owner(s) of a firm leads first to closer attention to the wishes of consumers, second to a higher rate of technological progress and innovation, and third to greater efficiency and lower costs of production. The last follows because a corollary of making as much profit as possible is the desire to make the costs of producing any given output as low as possible. This is then seen as a benefit to the entire economy, since minimizing cost of producing one output frees resources for producing more of other outputs. Adherents to this view, among whom are three economists who were most influential in providing the intellectual underpinnings for the privatization programme, Sir Alan Walters, Michael Beesley and Stephen Littlechild, criticize in contrast the lack of incentives provided by public ownership to identify and satisfy consumer demands, to innovate and to produce efficiently.

Note that according to this view it is the nature of ownership that matters, and not whether the structure of the market at a given time is monopolistic or competitive. The view of the so-called Austrian School, in particular of Joseph Schumpeter (1883–1950), is that competition should be viewed as a dynamic process in which new products and production techniques, which must be searched for and developed by profit-hungry entrepreneurs, drive out the old. The concern of neo-classical economists with the evils of monopoly power is regarded as misplaced: such power is short-lived given the gales of creative destruction sweeping through the economy, and in any case may be advantageous to innovation. The possibility of achieving monopoly power by introducing a new product or process provides an incentive to innovate (c.f. the case for patents); existing monopoly profit provides a pool of funds to finance innovation. Given their view of the lack of incentives for innovation and efficiency under public ownership, these economists conclude that privatization is both necessary and sufficient for the realization of significant economic benefits.

The critique of public ownership that was part of the argument for privatization was both conceptually and empirically based. Under public ownership, it is in no-one's particular self interest to ensure that consumers' wishes are defined and met, that there is a constant search for new and improved products and processes, or that production takes place at least cost. Quite the reverse: public monopolies often seem to offer consumers the products they think they ought to have; the interests of politicians and trades unions lead to pressures that tend to increase costs and stifle innovation (particularly when it leads to changes in working practices or unemployment).

A particular problem exists in relation to the evaluation of investments, which are very important in the light of the capital intensity of the major utilities. Because there is no clear and direct link between the outcomes of investment programmes and the pay and prosperity of the managers who formulate them, while investment seems usually to be regarded as a good in itself by public utility managers, investment planning tends to be over-optimistic and investment turns out to yield low returns. The procedures for bureaucratic scrutiny of investment plans *ex ante* do not appear to have provided an effective substitute for the capital market in imposing discipline on the investment of management. Both this, and the tendency to excessively high operating costs, are encouraged by the softness of the financial constraints to which public enterprises were made subject.

The evidence on the economic performance of British public enterprises through the 1970s does not contradict these views.[3] There is certainly room for debate as to how responsibility for this performance should be allocated among management, unions, government officials and politicians, but to the outside critic the question of such an allocation is not really relevant: it is the system within which all of them operate that is seen to be the problem. An important fact about the privatization programme was that it was not electorally unpopular. At least part of the reason for this was the public perception of the poor performance of the public enterprise sector throughout the 1970s.

The counter-arguments made by the critics of the privatization programme amount essentially to the statement that privatization is neither necessary nor sufficient for improving the economic performance of the major public utilities, and holds out the possibility of economic consequences inferior to those that could be achieved under state ownership. I take these points in turn.

*Necessity*

It can be argued that improvements in the economic performance of public enterprise are perfectly possible without a change in ownership. The introduction of an efficiency auditing mechanism; tighter financial constraints; appointment of managers with private sector experience; introduction of incentive payments for managers; organizational restructuring with greater emphasis on decentralization and profit accountability; and distancing from political intervention, are all measures that have been advocated and discussed throughout the 1970s, as ways of making public enterprise work. There is a very interesting paradox here. Supporters of privatization rejected these proposals on the grounds that they were unlikely to be effective. Yet they were adopted by the government that also carried out the privatization programme, and have been shown to work extremely well.

Consider Figures 2.1 and 2.2, which show the trends in labour productivity and total factor productivity for the nine major public utilities as they existed in 1980 – British Airways, BAA, British Steel, telecommunications, gas, electricity, coal, water and postal services – over the period 1981–90, and also those for the economy as a whole.[4] The improvement in relative performance is striking. From 1981 productivity in these industries has grown much faster than in the rest of the economy. Yet British Telecom was not privatized until 1984, followed by British Gas and British Airways in 1986, BAA in 1987, British Steel in 1988, and the remaining utilities were public enterprises throughout this period.

Of course, a major part of the drive for efficiency that underlies these trends was the need to prepare the industries for privatization. It should also be noted that, in addition to the measures listed above, an important aspect of the transformation of the efficiency of these industries was the willingness to confront the relevant trades unions – in particular those in the coal, rail, posts and telecommunications industries – and if need be to fight long and damaging strikes.[5] The irony, then, is that it

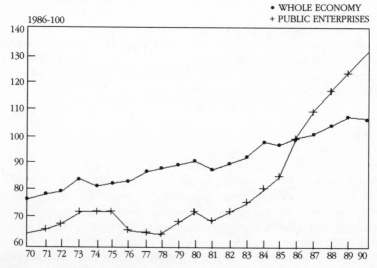

**Figure 2.1**  UK: labour productivity
*Source:*  Bishop and Thompson (1992).

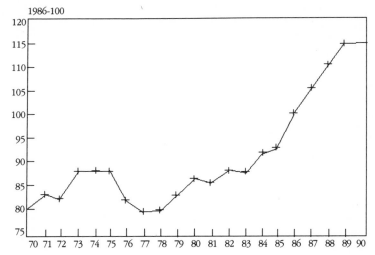

**Figure 2.2**   UK: total factor productivity
*Source:*  Bishop and Thompson (1992).

is probably only the drive to privatize the industries that created the political will to carry through the changes necessary to make the industries efficient. Had this drive not existed, it is probable that we would have seen the history of the 1970s – a decade of lost opportunities for public enterprise reform – simply repeated.

In one sense, therefore, the evidence shown in Figures 2.1 and 2.2 proves that privatization was not strictly necessary for improvements in efficiency – this could be achieved under public ownership. But in the absence of the privatization policy there is considerable doubt that the required measures would have been taken.

## Sufficiency

The dispute over whether privatization alone is enough to achieve the predicted economic benefits turns on the distinction between privatization and liberalization, and also on the concept of managerial capitalism. The Austrian view of individual profit maximizing entrepreneurs eagerly seeking out opportunities to gain sales and make innovations is not a good description of the reality of modern business enterprise. This is characterized by a separation of ownership from control. The large corporations that dominate economic activity are controlled by managers; ownership is dispersed among large numbers of shareholders and it is not at all clear *a priori* that the control mechanisms available to shareholders – primarily take-overs and profit-based incentive schemes – are sufficient to make managerial capitalism equivalent to the Schumpeterian model of entrepreneurial capitalism. In that case market structure does become relevant. There is no presumption that managerially controlled firms in markets that are protected from actual or potential competition will be efficient and innovative. They may be just as inefficient as public enterprises that are similarly insulated from competition, while they can use their market power to charge high prices and maintain satisfactory profits for shareholders.[6] In other words, efficiency gains have to be achieved by opening up the public utilities to the forces of competition as much as possible – that is by liberalization – rather than just by changing ownership, or privatization.

These points were well known and quite widely discussed[7] at the time of the sales of the first utilities to be privatized, British Telecom, British Gas and British Airports Authority (BAA). However, not until the privatization of the electricity and water industries at the end of the decade do they seem to have had an impact on the structuring of the enterprises before sale. Telecommunications, gas and the south-east airports were sold off as single enterprises with their monopoly powers more or less intact (although in the case of telecommunications it could be argued that there was an element of potential competition, at least in some markets, in the form of Mercury plc). Some reasons for this are considered in the next section. Here we note that the force of the argument that creation of a private monopoly cannot be presumed to be necessarily in the best interests of consumers was implicitly recognized by the creation of a new regulatory framework to control abuses of monopoly power as far as possible. For Professor Littlechild, these were seen as devices to hold the fort until competition arrives,[8] but in fact, even in the case of telecommunications, where technological developments hold out the most hope of some elements of competition, the regulatory framework has hardened and tightened, and seems to have become very much a permanent part of economic environment in which these industries must work.

Although, in my view, belief in the economic benefits that would stem from private ownership was the main driving force behind the privatization programme, other objectives have also been identified and have certainly played a role in tactical decisions taken in the implementation of the programme.

The two objectives most widely mentioned are:

(i)  the achievement of wider share ownership among the British public;
(ii) reducing the Public Sector Borrowing Requirement (PSBR).

We can consider these in turn.

Achieving wider share ownership can be seen as a political end in itself. As with the sale of public housing to tenants, an increase in the proportion of the population with significant wealth-holdings in the form of property or shares could be considered likely to increase their predisposition to vote Conservative. There is however a further very important motive for widespread share ownership in the privatized utilities, and this is, simply, to make it more difficult for a subsequent Labour government to renationalize them. Any government is aware that its hold on power cannot be guaranteed beyond the next general election, and it cannot place legal constraints on the ability of a later government to reverse its policies. The wider the shares in the utilities are held, it could be argued, the greater the political unpopularity of a policy to renationalize them. It is significant that the Labour party appears to have dropped the threat of renationalization from its manifesto, with two exceptions: the electricity bulk supply grid and the water industry. Thus, wider share ownership could be viewed as placing a political constraint on future governments to ensure the permanence of the outcome of the privatization policy.

It could be argued that this will also have a beneficial effect on the performance of the privatized enterprises. In committing themselves to long-term investments, the enterprises would want to be reasonably sure that the returns to that investment will not be expropriated, say by renationalization on terms which fall short of the capitalized value of future investment returns. Anything that reduces the probability of renationalization could therefore be regarded as improving the climate for investment in these enterprises. It could even be argued that perception of this effect at the time of privatization could lead the demand for an issue price of shares to be higher than would otherwise be the case, but this link seems tenuous in the extreme.

The significant underpricing of shares in the privatization issue has often been commented upon. At least one important reason for this was to make the shares more attractive to the wider public: small investors who are typically reluctant to take on the risks of equity investment would be attracted by the virtual certainty of an immediate capital gain. This of course does not imply that the shares will continue to be held, and indeed it has been the case that typically many small buyers of the initial issues have sold their holdings. Nevertheless, aided by such inducements as discounts on purchases of gas for shareholders in British Gas, the numbers of small shareholders in the major utilities have remained quite high.

The PSBR can be thought of loosely as the difference between the government's revenues from taxation and profits from sale of public outputs on the one hand, and its total expenditure on the other. It represents a financial requirement which is met by some combination of borrowing and expansion of the money supply. Privatization will in general reduce the PSBR, since the privatized enterprise's investment will cease to be part of government expenditure, and this usually exceeds its profit, which falls out of government revenue. However, simply because of a not very rational accounting convention, privatization had a more dramatic effect on the PSBR figures throughout the 1980s. The proceeds of privatization are classified in effect as government revenues (negative expenditures) with the result that the measured PSBR is reduced accordingly. This is in fact a nonsense: asset sales are a means of financing a given deficit of expenditure over revenue, rather than a real reduction in that deficit. The government is able to reduce its requirement for bond finance by the precise amount of the privatization proceeds. For the economy as a whole this simply represents a change in the mix of fixed interest securities and equities available to investors as a means of saving. The overall pressure on the demand for borrowing remains broadly unchanged (except for second-order effects due to the change in the economy-wide debt-equity ratio).

It is probably the case that privatization represented a more expensive form of financing than issuing the equivalent amount of government debt would have been. This is because, due to the discounted issue price, the effective rate of return on the shares (a measure of the cost of this means of funding to the government) has been well above the interest rate on government securities. However, to the economy as a whole, this essentially represents a transfer of wealth, away from taxpayers (or more generally, whoever can be thought of as owning public enterprises) and towards the buyers of the privatization issues (some proportion of whom were foreign) .

However, because of the accounting convention, privatization proceeds were reflected in a lower PSBR. This was of considerable political advantage to the government, because its short-term macroeconomic policy placed great weight on controlling and reducing the PSBR. In the absence of privatization proceeds, simply because of the effect of this on the published PSBR figure, the government would probably have had to have undertaken more unpopular measures to reduce expenditure and increase tax revenue, or to have accepted a less dramatic rate of fall in the published PSBR. It is hard to reject the view that awareness of this did influence the pace and timing of the privatization programme.

## Constraints on the privatization programme

It is worth repeating that one factor which did not place a constraint on the programme was political opposition. Privatization was not an unpopular policy with the electorate, and part of the reason for this may well have been the favourable prices – available to all – at which the assets were sold. The first and most fundamental constraint was the need to ensure that the enterprises were sufficiently profitable to make sale (at positive prices) possible. This very much influenced the timing of the privatization of particular enterprises. For example, it could be argued that the coal industry is in many respects a better candidate for privatization than gas, water and electricity, since it can quite readily be structured as a competitive industry and, in the absence of protection, would in any case be subject to international competition. However, the elimination of unprofitable capacity and improvement in productivity and profitability of the remainder have taken time.

On the other hand, profitability was not really a problem with privatization of the other major utilities – telecommunications, gas, electricity and water. The main issue here was the need to decide upon:

(a) the structure of the entity to be privatized;
(b) the framework of regulation of the enterprise(s) once privatized.

In each case there were a number of options, which centred upon one question: should the public monolith be preserved as a private company or should it be broken up in some way? In the case of telecommunications, gas and airports the choice was to preserve the monolith, in the case of the (later) privatizations of electricity and water the break-up solution was chosen. The arguments on either side can be summarized quite succinctly: in the interests of reducing the extent of likely market failure post-privatization, some degree of restructuring was always desirable. Against this a number of arguments were set. Management and workers in the industries to be privatized were typically strongly opposed to restructuring, and in the period approaching privatization they had considerable bargaining power. The political desire to put a significant privatization programme in place in the lifetime of the first Thatcher government, and to reinforce and extend it in the lifetime of the second, put a tight time constraint on the administrative process of privatization. It was easier and quicker to privatize the monoliths, and even those who were fully aware of the lost opportunities for restructuring (for example, Sir Alan Walters) appear to have accepted the argument that it was better to privatize with a sub-optimal structure than to risk losing the opportunity to privatize because of loss of office at an election. Finally, privatization proceeds were likely to be higher and the sale more easily made if less restructuring – in the interests of generating a competitive environment post-privatization – rather than more was undertaken. In the mid-1980s, when the PSBR was perceived as a very strong constraint, this argument is likely to have had some force.

The issue of the design of a regulatory framework was particularly acute at the time of privatization of British Telecom, but the solution adopted then was the one applied, with some adaptation, to the later privatizations, and so this became less of a problem. The clear perception of the problem of an abuse of monopoly power in telecommunications made some kind of regulatory framework imperative. The first proposal was to create a 'rate-based' price regulation scheme of the kind common in the USA. As a result of criticism from some of the economists involved (again Sir Alan Walters was very influential), who could draw upon a large theoretical and empirical literature on the failings of this type of regulatory framework in the USA, the so-called RPL–X framework was in fact introduced. This differs from rate-based regulation, at least in principle, in that it places a constraint on the future rate of growth of the prices of an enterprise, but allows it to retain any profits it can earn by reducing costs to a greater extent than was envisaged when the constraint was set. Thus, in contrast to rate of return regulation, the enterprise has an incentive to increase its efficiency and productivity.[9]

Note finally that what might have been expected to be a constraint on the privatization programme, the ability of the capital market to provide the funds required by the privatization issues, in fact turned out not to be a problem. With only one exception, the issues were heavily over-subscribed, though measures such as payment by instalment for the very largest issues undoubtedly helped. The exception was of course the sale of the government's shares in British Petroleum (BP), which took place shortly after the great stock market crash of 1987. For once the underwriters had to earn their money, although they were extremely reluctant to do so.

## Conclusions

For anyone who shares the view that private ownership is both politically and economically preferable to public ownership, the privatization programme must rate as an unqualified success, particularly if, as we might expect, the next few years see the sale of rail, coal and postal services to the private sector. From the economic standpoint, however, what is of importance is not the form of ownership *per se*, but rather its effect on the economic performance of the enterprises concerned. The results shown in Figures 2.1 and 2.2 must support one favourable conclusion. Whether or not the same achievement could have been made under public ownership, the privatization policy has certainly produced a major improvement in the efficiency and productivity of these industries.

A major question at the time of privatization was whether the proposed regulatory framework would be strong enough to control monopoly abuses and secure the predicted economic benefits of privatization. In fact, largely because the regulators concerned seem to have been active and energetic in challenging the enterprises, and have used their powers in more interventionist ways than was perhaps expected by the 'framers of the regulatory constitution', while using the opportunity for review to tighten the constraints on the firms, regulatory policy has been more effective than many critics thought it would be. This is not to say that everything is perfect: the economics of regulation look certain to be a fruitful field for economists for some time to come.

## Notes

1.  For a description of the timing of the sales of the various state-owned enter-
    prises and the amounts realized see Tables 1–3, Chapter 3.
2.  By the term market failure is meant the failure of the market mechanism to
    achieve an efficient allocation of resources. For example, given the existence
    of a monopoly, or of environmental damage ignored by the firm(s) creating
    it, it can be shown that changes can be made that would make everyone in
    the economy better off.
3.  See in particular R. Pryke (1981), *The Nationalised Industries: Policies and
    Performance since 1968*, Oxford, Martin Robinson; and R. Pryke (1982), 'The
    comparative performance of public and private enterprise', *Fiscal Studies*, **3**
    (2): 68–81.
4.  These figures are taken from M. Bishop and D. Thompson (1992),
    *Privatisation in the UK: Internal Organisation and Productive Efficiency*,
    Centre for Business Strategy, London Business School, March. I am very
    grateful to David Thompson for letting me see this paper in advance of pub-
    lication.
5.  This was also important in respect of other enterprises that were privatized,
    such as steel and shipbuilding, though they are not included in the group
    of industries on which Figures 2.1 and 2.2 are based.
6.  There is a huge literature on the comparative performance of public and pri-
    vate enterprise. One conclusion seems to be that owner-controlled private

firms are more efficient than managerially-controlled private firms and state-owned enterprises (A.R. Vining and A.E. Boardman (1992), 'Ownership versus competition: efficiency in public enterprise', *Public Choice*, **73** (2): 205–40). However, there is no clear evidence to suggest that managerially-controlled private firms in non-competitive and regulated environments are more efficient than public enterprises in similar circumstances.

7. See, for example, D. Heald and D. Steel (1982), 'Privatising public enterprises: an analysis of the government's case', *Political Quarterly*, **53**; J. Vickers and G. Yarrow (1985), *Privatization and the Natural Monopolies*, Public Policy Centre; R. Rees (1986), 'Is there an economic case for privatization?', *Public Money* **5** (4):19–26; among others.

8. See S. Littlechild (1983), *Regulation of British Telecommunications' Profitability*, Department of Industry, London.

9. Unfortunately, space precludes a full discussion of the regulatory framework that now surrounds the privatized enterprises. For a recent discussion of this, see R. Rees and J. Vickers (1991), 'RPI–X Regulation', (unpublished), Institute of Economics and Statistics, University of Oxford.

# Reference

Bishop, M. and Thompson, D. (1992), *Privatisation in the UK: Internal Organisation and Productive Efficiency*, Centre for Business Strategy, London Business School.

# CHAPTER 3

# THE POLITICS AND PRACTICE OF PRIVATIZATION IN BRITAIN

## Jeremy J. Richardson

### Introduction: government and public sector industries in Britain

*The importance of policy communities and policy networks*

In any policy area a well practised set of policy actor relationships and interactions already exists. Thus, when a new issue arrives on the political agenda – whether as a result of an indigenous or exogenous stimulus – we might expect policy actors to resort to 'standard operating procedures' (Richardson and Jordan, 1979) for the processing of the issue into formal policy proposals.

Policy style theory (Richardson *et al*, 1982) would suggest that privatization, as an issue, would be processed according to norms and values of the policy system as a whole. In the British case, these norms and values have generally emphasized the accommodation of key interest groups – what the British call the 'affected interests'. In practice, the word 'affected' has been interpreted in an exclusive rather than an inclusive way, and has tended to mean those interests directly involved in the running of that policy sector (or public service) rather than all of those affected by it – such as consumers or clients. Moreover, there has been a tendency for the affected interests, as defined by government, to become part of what we have elsewhere described as 'policy communities' – namely a group of policy actors (public and private) who regularly interact over a long period of time in such a way that shared values and even a common language develops. Policies in Britain were, we argued:

made (and administered) between a myriad of interconnecting, interpenetrating organisations. It is the relationship involved in communities, the policy community of departments and groups, the practices of co-option and the consensual style, that perhaps better account for policy outcomes than do examinations of policy stances, of manifestos or of parliamentary influence (Richardson and Jordan, 1979, p. 74)

Apart from 'policy communities', there are other (related) ways of characterizing the patterns of interaction between policy actors. One alternative model is that of 'issue network'. The concept of 'issue networks' was originated by Heclo in rejecting the conventional, rather ordered (iron triangle), view of politics in the USA. He argued that 'looking for the closed triangles of control, we tend to overlook the fairly open networks of people that increasingly impinge upon government' (Heclo, 1978: 88). With this increasing complexity, it has become even more difficult to identify leaders of policy areas.

In theory, there is no conceptual reason why a particular example of the policy-making process should not conform to a number of models – at different stages. Looking at the case of water privatization, for example, we found that a certain model could be applied to a particular phase of the policy process, but that no one model adequately captured the totality of the process. At times there was a strong policy community at work with an inner core of groups closely involved in negotiating outcomes. At other times there was a shift of power, away from those groups historically granted the 'franchise' for policy, towards an issue network of groups not usually influential over the main lines of water policy. The process became less predictable and for a brief period of 'internalised policy-making' (Jordan and Richardson, 1982) even excluded the ultimate 'core' group itself – the water industry.

A new stimulus can upset existing patterns of policy-making, posing new questions and challenges. The arrival of privatization as a concept had at least the potential to cause a destabilization of existing policy communities and networks, particularly as public ownership had had an unhappy political and economic history in Britain. By 1979 there was considerable dissatisfaction with the existing system for managing the publicly owned industries and it could be argued that the policy area was, therefore, ripe for change.

*The problem of controlling public sector industries*

In Britain there has been a long history of public ownership of industry. This was given an enormous boost by the programme of post-war nationalizations introduced by the 1945 Labour government. The principles underlying that major policy innovation were perfectly clear. Public ownership was based upon two key premises. First, that government departments were not the appropriate organizational structure for running publicly owned industries and that they should be run by public corporations. Second, that ministers should decide the broad lines of policy and should leave the administration of policy and the day-to-day running of the industries to the public corporations – the so-called 'arms-length relationship'.

Whatever the actual economic results of these post-war nationalizations, this experiment in political control (the so-called Morrisonian doctrine, named after Herbert Morrison, its inventor) was judged by most observers to be a failure, on a number of counts. It certainly did not remove the industries from political controversy. Despite the consensual nature of much of British politics in the 1950s, 1960s and most of the 1970s, the debate about public or private ownership remained the most divisive in terms of party conflict. (Indeed, the debate may be the only major instance of the alleged 'adversary model' of British politics at work in the post-war period up to 1979.) More importantly, the nationalized industries did not escape political 'interference'. Successive House of Commons Select Committee Reports highlighted the degree to which ministries did interfere in the day-to-day running of the industries and the extent to which the industries lacked an effective and clear policy framework in which to operate. As Heald suggests, there was already a vacuum into which 'privatisation as a solution to the problem of control' could be inserted. However, he also notes that it did not follow, necessarily, that the problem of control had to be solved by abolishing the public enterprises, rather than by designing new systems of control. (Heald, 1985: 8). Indeed, Helm and Yarrow argue that privatization was as much a reaction to the failure to design appropriate regulatory policies in the public sector, as it was to the ideological stance of Thatcherism (Helm and Yarrow, 1988: xxviii).

A particular difficulty was that the industries' borrowing was included in the Public Sector Borrowing Requirement (PSBR). As that in itself became a central part of the political and economic debates of the mid- to late 1970s, so the debate about the nationalized industries and their performance intensified. Essentially, post-1976 it became the conventional wisdom that the PSBR was too high and that it had to be subject to more effective control. This meant that the nationalized industries were themselves subject to increasingly strict financial controls and to a somewhat tighter regulatory framework. For example, external financial limits (EFLs), controlling the amount a nationalized industry could raise from external sources in any one year, were introduced in 1976 as part of a general control over public expenditure. Also, the performance of the industries within the financial framework began to be monitored more regularly, with monthly returns submitted by them to their sponsoring Departments and to the Treasury. Whether by accident or design, this tightening of financial control had the effect of edging the industries' managers towards a recognition that the only way to avoid the new irksome burdens was to escape from the public sector altogether. As Heald notes, the government had covertly cultivated the support of management in public companies generally through a process which made 'life unnecessarily unpleasant for the nationalised industries [and] this became a convenient spur to a change in management attitudes to denationalisation' (Steel and Heald, 1984: 17). Moreover, new senior managers were brought in to run some of these industries post-1979 (e.g. in British Airways, British Steel, the water industry, telecommunications) and they began a process of changing the organizational culture of their industries. It would be wrong, however, to see increased financial controls, the introduction of tighter regulation (e.g. by the use of the Monopolies and Mergers Commission), and the introduction of a new breed of senior managers as a planned process of preparing the industries for privatization. Nevertheless, these changes were (with hindsight) important preconditions for privatization, especially as they turned the managers (a key 'affected interest') of these industries into converts – always the most enthusiastic reformers.

Not only had a process of changing organisational cultures been set in train, but various publicly owned industries had been subject to structural changes. For example, the water industry had been radically restructured in 1973. These reforms produced a shift in perceptions as well as in structures. As Sewell and Barr suggest, 'the 1973 (water) legislation not only introduced some major innovations in the administrative framework, it also provided for some radical changes in the approach to water management. Water was now to be regarded as an economic good' (Sewell and Barr, 1978: 342). More importantly, since the creation of the new integrated Regional Water Authorities, water was considered less of a 'service' and was seen more and more as a 'commodity'. In telecommunications also, structural reforms prior to privatization were important. For example, in 1981 the government introduced a Telecommunications Act which took the telecommunications function away from the Post Office, thereby creating British Telecom (BT). It also introduced a measure of liberalization into the provision of domestic and commercial telecommunications services and a rather lesser measure of liberalization into the supply of telecommunications equipment. The split was made in order to free the telecommunications industries from its 'service' function of running the Post Office (Moon *et al*, 1988: 343). Also, the newly appointed Chairman of BT, Sir George Jefferson, had the reputation of a more business-orientated view. For example, he created individual profit centres, recruited new sales staff, revised the tariff system to reflect real costs more truly, and put the accounting and management systems more in line with commercial practice. Similarly, the appointment of an American, Ian McGregor, to run the British Steel Corporation (BSC) in 1980 marked an intensification of restructuring plans already started under a Labour government (Dudley and Richardson, 1990). Of particular note were the special conditions attached to Mr McGregor's appointment. The government agreed to pay his American employers (the bankers Lazard Frères) a basic fee of £175,000 for his services during the first three years of his contract, and Lazard would receive a fee of up to £1,150,000 depending upon the performance of BSC during McGregor's chairmanship.

By 1979, not only was there ample evidence that the Morrisonian concept of the public corporation had solved neither the question of public accountability nor the question of efficiency, but also the general political and economic climate had changed in two key aspects. First, monetarism had taken hold in both main political parties. It was not a Thatcher invention as is often believed (see Richardson, 1989). Second, there was a growing realization that Britain had to tackle at last the very long-standing problem of low productivity and overstaffing in its key industries, many of which were publicly owned. Put simply, when privatization finally reached the agenda, there were already several preconditions for policy change – a perception by policy-makers and policy-watchers that 'something was wrong' and an electorate ready to accept more radical action in the economic sphere, after the so-called 'winter of discontent' under the Labour government in 1979 in which public sector unions had disrupted the provision of essential services.

Such situations are ripe for the emergence of new intellectual fashions in the policy process. Just as monetarism became the new intellectual fashion in response to continued economic crises in many Western democracies (Damgaard *et al*, 1989), so privatisation gradually took hold as a concept which promised to solve a number of long-standing problems with which policy-makers had been grappling unsuccessfully. Think tanks such as the Adam Smith Institute had developed a coherent intellectual justification for a privatization programme, and managed to by-pass existing policy communities in gaining access to Conservative politicians, both in opposition and later in government. Even so, it could not be claimed that the Conservative government of Mrs Thatcher, elected May 1979, arrived with a clear set of ideas and

policies to underpin what eventually became an accelerating programme of privatization. As in the case of water privatization
(Richardson *et al*, 1992), the reality is of a rather stumbling government
on a learning curve of radicalism. Water may be an extreme example
of the privatization process being nearer to the chaotic end than to the
rationalist end of the policy spectrum, but it is worth quoting a few ministerial statements on water, prior to its eventual privatization in 1989,
in order to underline our argument that privatization was generally a
pragmatic process.

We have absolutely no intention of privatising the water industry. The
Government have no plans to urge that upon the water industries. There has
been some press speculation about it in the past, but there is no intention to
do so (Mr Neil McFarlane, Parliamentary Under-Secretary of State for the Department
of the Environment, HC Debates, 20 December 1984: col. 457).

The Government would welcome new ideas on privatisation. However, the water
industries are natural monopolies for many of their functions and we need to be
particularly careful when considering replacing a public monopoly by a private
one (Mrs Margaret Thatcher, Prime Minister, HC Debates, 31 January 1985: col. 292w).

my right hon. Friends and I will be examining the possibility of a measure of
privatisation in the Industry (Mr Ian Gow, Junior Environment Minister, HC Debates,
7 February 1985: col. 1142).

In the last six years we have made the water authorities fit and ready to join
the private sector ... Privatisation is the next logical step. It will bring benefits
to the customers, to the industry itself and to the nation as a whole (Mr Kenneth
Baker, Secretary of State for the Environment, HC Debates, 5 February 1986: col. 287).

As David Kinnersley has argued, water privatization was characterized
by a 'long period of confusion and false starts' (Kinnersley, 1988: 136).
The National Audit Office later commented that the lesson of water
privatization was that 'privatisations should be planned in simpler and
more discreet stages or, if this is not always possible ... then the full
degree of complexity and its implications ... should be as clearly set
out as possible at the beginning of the exercise for the benefit of
Parliament' (NAO, 1992: 10). This case was not untypical of the privatization process as a whole.

## The ambitions and objectives of privatization

*Specific objectives or muddling through?*

In a recent review of the implementation of Thatcherism, Rhodes and

Marsh have identified seven aims for privatization, as follows:

1. to reduce government involvement in industry;
2. to improve efficiency in both the privatised companies and what remained of the public sector;
3. to reduce the Public Sector Borrowing Requirement (PSBR);
4. to ease problems in public sector wage bargaining by weakening the unions;
5. to widen share ownership;
6. to encourage employee share ownership;
7. to gain political advantage (Rhodes and Marsh, 1992: 37).

Looking back, however, it is all too easy to see the process as rational in terms of identifiable objectives. As they note, the 1979 Conservative manifesto did not even mention the term privatization, and the commitments to asset sales and deregulation were dwarfed by the general commitment to monetarism as policy objectives (Rhodes and Marsh, 1992: 37). Abromeit argues that it is possible to see privatization as 'one of the components of the comprehensive settlement of Thatcherism with the intervention of the welfare state; within the monetarist concept, with its strong belief in the benefits of free markets, privatisation was one of the signals for the return of the minimalist state'. Yet she reminds us that it was only later 'that members of the government ... styled it the key element of their policy' (Abromeit, 1988: 70). We must be careful, therefore, to set the process of privatization in Britain in the context of the strong traditions of British policy-making as a whole – more muddling through than conscious and well-planned action. Privatization may have turned out to be the almost tangible evidence of the Thatcher revolution (Gamble, 1988). But as Mitchell argues:

what emerged in the late 1970s was not so much an intellectually coherent package of ideas waiting to be implemented by a radical Conservative government, but a combination of growing doubts about aspects of social democratic consensus which coincided with, and was partly caused by, an economic crisis (Mitchell, 1990: 16)

Official statements of the objectives of privatization were not made until 19 November 1983 (Mitchell, 1990: 19). As he comments 'it was a programme which the Conservatives staggered towards as they encountered difficulties in financing capital expenditure programmes, albeit with a recognition of the potential of the populist nature of privatisation' (Mitchell, 1990: 21). The former Prime Minister, Harold Macmillan, put it more brutally when he accused Mrs Thatcher's government of selling the family silver. To a significant degree, the proceeds of privatization have assisted the government in disguising the fact that it consistently failed to control (let alone reduce) public expenditure, despite its claimed commitment to monetarism.

In contrast, the supporters of privatization both within and outside government are inclined to paint a picture of a more coherent and planned set of legislative actions. For example, Gerry Grimstone, now a director of Schroders merchant bank and a former Assistant Secretary in the Treasury responsible for privatization policy, has argued that, post-1983 at least, the programme 'had an intellectual coherence that it had previously lacked, and it became increasingly clear that a well organised programme could bring political as well as economic success' (Grimstone, 1990: 5). Similarly, in 1986, the Adam Smith Institute was claiming that 'nowhere has privatisation been undertaken, as it has in Britain, as part of a *systematic* programme' (Adam Smith Institute, 1986: 15, emphasis added).

## The role of ideology

Before turning to the actual privatization programme, we need to address the question of whether political ideology was a specific motivating factor. Many authors see ideology of primary importance in the process. For example, Wolfe argues that:

The Thatcher privatisation programme provides an instance of government success in reorganising relations between state and society in accordance with its ideological goals ... Ideological motivations prompted cabinet ministers to reshape the state itself, shifting many formerly state-run productive enterprises and services to the private sector (Wolfe, 1991: 252).

Similarly, Vickers and Wright also emphasized the role of ideology, as follows: 'the first series of motives may be described as ideological. For the right, especially in Britain and France, privatisation is part of the general strategy to shift the boundary between public and private in favour of the latter. It is nourished by deep-seated anti-State sentiment' (Vickers and Wright, 1989: 5). A variant of this ideological motivation is identified by Dunleavy, who sees similarities between the privatization 'boom' and other UK policy 'booms'. He sees one of the factors bringing about the privatization boom as:

a firm ideological belief in the efficacy of the central innovation in tackling governmental problems. This faith is buttressed by the absence of detailed cost-benefit analyses, a characteristic lack of attention to non-tangible or non-quantifiable indices of policy effectiveness, and a systematic neglect of transition costs involved in the innovation (Dunleavy, 1986: 15).

There is no doubt that broad ideological factors were important in the development of the privatization programme in Britain and elsewhere. However, it would be difficult to sustain an argument that privatization represents a case of an ideologically driven government riding roughshod over established interests in the pursuit of a coherent programme of reform. A number of qualifications need to be made to such a thesis. First, the ideological leap had already been made by the previous Labour government which had sold a portion of British Petroleum (BP) as part of its response to the IMF rescue package in 1976. This was a small but significant step in response to sheer financial need. Second, the post-1979 privatization programme was, as suggested above, developed pragmatically – it did not really get going until after the 1983 election. Third, ideology had to be tempered by the political need to mobilize consent and support from key interests – hence our earlier emphasis on the significance of policy communities and policy networks as heuristic models of policy-making in the UK. Ideology was important, but its implementation was subject to significant constraints in the form of policy-making traditions.

## Constraints on privatization

### The importance of 'interest'

The most obvious constraint was, of course, lack of knowledge on the part of policy-makers. Now that the massive programme of privatization is in place it is easy to forget that policy-makers had relatively little experience of the technical, logistical and political problems in the transfer of these huge public corporations (including public utilities) from the public to the private sector. As we have emphasized, the Conservatives did not arrive in office in 1979 with a detailed legislative plan. The thinking by the New Right and by leading Conservative politicians such as Nicholas Ridley was a long way from solving the many practical problems that privatization presented. (In any case, as Heald suggests, the so-called Ridley Report, leaked to *The Economist* in 1978 'indicates that the seeds of the privatisation programme were sown by hostility to the public sector unions after the humiliation suffered by the Heath Government' Heald, 1985: 11.) As a primary objective of privatization was a reduction in the PSBR, as Heald notes, 'the PSBR argument has been rehearsed so frequently that it sounds like a jammed record' (Heald, 1985: 11), it is perhaps unsurprising that in practice it proved difficult to produce legislative proposals that also met other conflicting objectives such as increased competition. As Grimstone concedes, 'mistakes have been made and lessons have had to be learnt by experience. In the early days of the programme, sales were treated as one-off individual market transactions and no real attempt was made to co-ordinate the programme nor to capture the public's imagination' (Grimstone, 1990: 11).

Of particular concern was the question of whether there would be effective mobilization against privatization by key interests and whether there would be public opposition to the concept of privatization. In terms of the latter, the government could take some comfort from the fact that there was a long-standing lack of enthusiasm for nationalization. Yet, equally, there was no evidence that privatization was about to tap any reservoir of electoral enthusiasm for the alleged benefits of the market economy. The attempt to shift a large block of the economy from the public to the private sector did not rest on any populist demands. Thus, several observers have commented that survey data do not confirm that privatization captured the public mood (see Crewe and Searing, 1988, and McAllister and Studlar, 1989). Indeed, Dunleavy goes further in arguing that privatization can be seen as an example of the class interests of bureaucrats being advanced at the expense of rank-and-file workers and service recipients (Dunleavy, 1986). He argues that privatization can take place even if it does not advance social welfare (what he terms 'inappropriate privatisation') because 'there may be quite large differences between the 'internal' and the 'social' costs of public service provision being undertaken by a government agency' (Dunleavy, 1986: 22).

We do not necessarily have to accept this argument for us to recognize that intensity of interest is important in the process of policy change. The public at large has a general interest (the so-called public interest) in the ownership of industry, its financing, and its efficiency as this affects the nation's economic performance. Also the public has an interest as consumers and recipients of services, for example, rail transport, hospital provision. Yet these interests are difficult to articulate in ways which can impinge directly upon the policy process. The sheer intensity of interest by key actors in the policy process – in this case particularly the managers of the industries concerned and the city interests who stood to gain by involvement in the privatization process – was not balanced by an effective opposition from, for example, the unions representing the workers in those industries to be privatized. In practice the government developed its rolling privatization programme with a keen eye on the need to accommodate those organizations who had a very direct interest in the process. It also had a keen eye on the need to make privatization financially attractive to the public at large – on the principle that if the public had no general interest in or enthusiasm for privatization, it might be made more enthusiastic if there were likely to be direct financial rewards without much risk. 'Squaring the interests' was perfectly compatible with the government's main aims – to raise finance and thus reduce the PSBR and avoid tax increases; to move the economy to a more private, enterprise-driven model, consistent with its ideological beliefs; and to shift responsibility to private managers as the ultimate solution to the hitherto intractable problems of steering and control of the nationalized industries. It was also compatible with the norms and values of the policy process, as described earlier. Above all, the government was constrained by the need to privatize in such a way that there was a market for the shares in the industries. If a market failed to emerge, not only would the extra finance not be delivered to the Exchequer, but the political and electoral costs would have been considerable.

*Making the flotations attractive*

In the event therefore, most privatizations were underpinned by the need to make the flotations attractive to the market. Considerations of competition and efficiency were a long way down the list of objectives, simply because the more the industries were returned to a competitive environment (and therefore in terms of the government's own ideological beliefs to a more efficient system of resource allocation), the less attractive the industries were to the existing managers of the nationalized industries and to the big investing institutions, such as the pension funds, and to City interests which had to underwrite the sale of shares. The short-run benefits of getting the institutions out of the public sector and getting the revenue into the Exchequer were more important than the long-term aim of increasing competition and efficiency. The commonest model (electricity was the main exception and this was much later in the programme) was to keep the industries with their present form of organization (that is, they were generally not broken up), and essentially to turn public monopolies into private monopolies, with occasionally more competition at the edges (for example, in telecoms).

One notable exception to this general rule was the National Bus Company (NBC), where the Transport Secretary, Nicholas Ridley, imposed a privatization structure on an unwilling industry. Prior to NBC privatization, Ridley had already pushed through the highly controversial policy of deregulating local bus services (outside London) in 1986.

The senior management of NBC, compelled to adjust to one major upheaval, lobbied strongly for the privatized company only to be split into a few component parts. Ridley, however, was equally determined to promote competition and once again won the day (despite Treasury opposition) when NBC was fragmented and sold off as 72 separate companies (see Dudley, 1989).

In 1987 Ridley was once again able to demonstrate his ability to impose policy solutions on a recalcitrant community when, as Environment Secretary, he created a regulatory National Rivers Authority against the wishes of the senior management in the water industry (see Richardson et al, 1992). Ridley's ability to outwit vested interests, and his apparent disregard of any personal political consequences, was not copied by the government as a whole, however, and the majority of ministers were unwilling to antagonize the relevant policy community.

Since 1979, therefore, Britain has seen much more privatization than deregulation, simply because to have a large measure of deregulation alongside sudden privatization would have weakened the market for shares in the privatized companies. This gave the existing policy communities enormous influence most of the time, apart from in those cases – such as water – where the privatization process clashed with more important political priorities. Thus, in the water case privatization became more problematic, not only because water was perceived by the public as somewhat special and therefore less 'privatizable', but also because, by the mid-1980s, the environmental issue had regained its high political salience. This enabled the policy process to be shifted from one dominated by a tightly drawn policy community (essentially the industry itself and the government) to a much more extended issue network of actors not usually influential in the water policy sector. Both industrial users (as represented by the Confederation of British Industry) and the environmentalists (headed by the Council for the Protection of Rural England) made great play on the environmental regulatory issue. In particular, the environmentalists were able to play the European card quite effectively, by demonstrating that the European Court might well rule as illegal any post-privatization structure for the water industry that did not set up a genuinely independent environmental regulatory authority. In this case, the government finally imposed a solution on the industry. Having imposed a regulatory solution, however, it immediately brought the industry back into the consultation process and made major concessions in order to maintain its overall support for privatization (e.g various financial incentives to cover the costs of tough EC pollution controls and conceding generous cost-past-through measures relating to water charges).

To characterize the privatization process as 'privatization by negotiation' is, therefore, not unreasonable. For example, the strong advice for the water industry from the managers of previously privatized industries was that pretty well everything was negotiable, the closer they got to the planned flotation dates. The overriding need for a successful flotation meant that a little known interest – the professional financial advisers to the government and to the industries (i.e. merchant bankers, accountants, pensions experts) – played a very influential role in the process. The water case, where interests external to the existing policy community played a brief but significant role, is probably atypical of the privatization process as a whole. In general, privatization policies were processed within the confines of existing policy communities – a fact that helps to explain why regulatory conflicts have arisen more recently, as other interests have come to recognize that they are bearing the cost of the regulatory bargains which were struck between the government and the narrowly defined affected interests.

Having decided to accommodate the managers of the industries and the influential City and banking interests, the government also designed the privatization packages to be attractive to the employees (by generous preferential share options and discounts), to the consumers of the industries and to the public at large. In virtually every case the price to the public was set at a level which meant that, although the government's revenue was not maximized, it ensured (a) successful flotation in the City; and (b) an enthusiastic response from consumers and the public. Employees and public alike were offered risk-free capital gains if they invested in the privatized concerns. The general political weakness of the unions in these cases was exacerbated by new legal restraints on trade union action which limited the scope of attempted disruption of the privatization schemes. Also, union members were being offered a very generous share package (which many if not most accepted), and this meant that union opposition, which existed in principle, was of little consequence.

The various potential constraints were, therefore, negotiated away by resort to the norms and values of the British policy process – namely the accommodation of those interests judged to be directly affected by the proposals. At times the range of interests could be quite narrowly defined, allowing the government to operate via traditional policy communities, and at other times new interests had to be admitted (e.g. bankers and other professional advisers), thus extending the network of interests involved.

**The programme so far**

By March 1990, 29 major companies had been privatized, with receipts to the Exchequer of £27.5 billion and future sales projected to produce £5 billion per year. Almost 50 per cent of the 1979 state sector and 800,000 employees had been transferred to the private sector (Treasury, 1990: 8). The number of shareholders in Britain trebled after 1979 and approximately 90 per cent of eligible employees became shareholders in their companies. A detailed breakdown of proceeds from privatization is provided in Tables 3.1, 3.2 and 3.3, from which it can be seen that the big corporations such as British Telecom (£1358 million in 1984–5, £1246 million in 1985–6, and £1081 million in 1986–7); and British Gas (£1820 million in 1986–7, £1758 million in 1987–8, £1555 million in 1988–9), produced significant reserve gains for the government. The only major privatization since 1990 has been the electricity supply industry in England, Wales and Scotland. This produced £1400 million for the government in 1990–91. Girobank was sold to the Alliance & Leicester Building Society in 1990 but the proceeds of £112 million went to the Post Office, as it was a wholly-owned subsidiary.

In the 1990s scope for further privatization is much more restricted, while those few undertakings which remain in the state sector are proving highly problematic candidates for transfer to the private sector. Consequently, the government has encountered enormous financial and political problems in attempting to fragment and privatize British Coal and British Rail. After numerous crises, by the end of 1993 both privatizations remain in the pipeline, although, in the circumstances, the government could only be highly grateful that the July 1993 sale of its remaining 22 per cent stake in BT raised £5 billion for the hard-pressed Exchequer. One further privatization during 1993 involved the sale of Northern Ireland Electricity for £360 million.

The process by which the transfer from public to private ownership has occurred has been in three broad stages. First, a corporation was identified as a privatization candidate. Second, it was prepared for the market – often by writing off debt, slimming down the labour force and generally addressing long-standing structural problems. Third, an attractive package was devised to ensure that there would be a market for the shares. As suggested earlier, the 'flotation test' was crucial. Indeed, as Abromeit points out, the privatization process has been a policy of cheap sales. For example, BT shares were five times oversubscribed and went up fifty per cent on the day of issue (Abromeit, 1988: 77). She characterizes the whole process as 'not so much an instance of a radical programme of structural change, but rather ... a short-term

**Table 3.1**  Britain: privatization proceeds, net of costs (£ million), 1979–80 to 1982–83

| | 1979–80 | 1980–1 | 1981–2 | 1982–3 |
|---|---|---|---|---|
| Amersham International | | | 64 | |
| Associated British Ports | | | | 46 |
| British Aerospace | | 43 | | |
| British Petroleum | 276 | | 8 | |
| British Sugar Corporation | | | 44 | |
| Britoil | | | | 334 |
| Cable and Wireless | | | 181 | |
| National Enterprise Board Holdings | 37 | 83 | 2 | |
| National Freight Consortium | | | 5 | |
| Miscellaneous | 64 | 84 | 189 | 75 |
| Total[2] | 377[1] | 210[1] | 493[1] | 455 |

[1] Excludes certain advance oil payments which net out to zero over the three years 1979–82.
[2] Excludes proceeds from sales of subsidiaries; these are retained by parent industry. The main sales in this category were:

| | 1982–3 |
|---|---|
| International Aeradio (BA) | 60 |
| British Rail Hotels | 30 |

programme, put up for practical and fiscal considerations' (Abromeit, 1988: 83).

The question of the so-called 'golden share' has, at times, been a significant element in the political debate about privatization. The government recognized that 'in certain cases, there is a clear need to protect a business from unwelcome take-over, for example, on national security grounds, or, as a temporary measure, to provide an opportunity for management to adjust to the private sector' (Treasury, 1990). To this end, the government retained special shares in a number of the privatized companies – typically preventing any one person or group of persons acting in concert, from controlling more than 15 per cent of the equity of a privatized company. In some cases the 'golden share' provision was timeless and in others it was for a specified time period. There is little evidence that the ownership of the golden shares has been significant and it seems more of a political response to Opposition criticism than a device for facilitating the continuation of governmental 'steering' of the privatized industries.

**Table 3.2**   Britain: Privatization proceeds, net of costs (£ million), 1983–4 to 1986–7

|  | 1983–4 | 1984–5 | 1985–6 | 1986–7 |
|---|---|---|---|---|
| Associated British Ports |  | 51 |  |  |
| British Aerospace |  |  | 347 |  |
| British Airways |  |  |  | 435 |
| British Gas |  |  |  | 1820 |
| British Gas Debt |  |  |  | 750 |
| British Petroleum | 543 |  |  |  |
| British Telecom |  | 1358 | 1246[1] | 1081 |
| BT Loan Stock |  | 44 | 61 | 53 |
| BT Preference Shares |  |  |  | 250 |
| Britoil | 293 |  | 426 |  |
| Cable and Wireless | 263 |  | 577 |  |
| Enterprise Oil |  | 384 |  |  |
| National Enterprise Board Holdings |  | 168 | 30 | 34 |
| Miscellaneous | 39 | 45 | 20 | 3 |
| Total[2] | 1139 | 2050 | 2707 | 4460 |

[1] Includes some third instalments (worth £87 million approx) paid early.
[2] Excludes proceeds from sales of subsidiaries: these are retained by parent industry. The main sales in this category were:

|  | 1983–4 | 1984–5 | 1985–6 | 1986–7 |
|---|---|---|---|---|
| British Rail Hotels | 15 |  |  |  |
| Jaguar (BL) |  | 297 |  |  |
| Sealink (BR) |  | 40 |  |  |
| Wytch Farm (BGC) |  | 82 |  |  |
| Warship yards (BS) |  |  | 54 |  |
| Sealink (BR) |  |  | 26 |  |
| BA Helicopters |  |  | 14 |  |
| Unipart (Rover) up to |  |  |  | 52 |
| Leyland Bus (Rover) |  |  |  | 4 |
| British Coal subsidiaries |  |  |  | 0.5 |

## Privatization: achievements and problems

Any assessment of the achievements of privatization must be in the context of the objectives which the government set itself. From the government's perspective, three major successes can be claimed for privatization. First, it undoubtedly delivered large revenues to the Exchequer. Second, it did widen share ownership in the UK. Third, it has produced a dramatic reduction in the size of the publicly owned

**Table 3.3**  Britain privatization proceeds, net of costs (£ million), 1987–8 to 1989–90

|                                          | 1987–8  | 1988–9  | 1989–90 |
|------------------------------------------|---------|---------|---------|
| BAA                                      | 534     | 689     |         |
| British Airways                          | 419     |         |         |
| British Gas                              | 1758    | 1555    |         |
| British Gas Debt                         |         | 250     | 400     |
| British Petroleum                        | 863[1]  | 3030[1] | 1,370   |
| British Steel                            |         | 1138[2] | 1,280   |
| BT Loan Stock                            | 23      | 85      |         |
| BT Preference Shares                     | 250     | 250     |         |
| General Practice Finance Corporation     |         | 67      |         |
| Plant Breeding Institute                 | 65[3]   |         |         |
| Rolls-Royce                              | 1028    | 3       |         |
| Royal Ordnance                           | 186     |         |         |
| Water plcs                               |         |         | 500     |
| Miscellaneous                            | 14      | 8       | 30      |
| Total[4]                                 | 5140    | 7075    | 3,580[5]|

[1] Total estimated net proceeds are £5,310 million, with 3rd instalment due 27 April 1989.

[2] Total estimated net proceeds are £2,420 million with 2nd instalment due 26 September 1989.

[3] The Central Government sector received £65 million, but only £27 million was paid into the Consolidated Fund.

[4] Excludes proceeds from sales of subsidiaries: these are retained by parent industry. The main sales in this category were:

|                                          | 1987–8  | 1988–9  |
|------------------------------------------|---------|---------|
| British Transport Advertising            | 40.5    |         |
| Istel (subsidiary of Rover Group)        | 47.6    |         |
| National Bus Company subsidiaries        |         | 36.0    |

[5] Estimated outturn up to 31 December 1989.

sector of industry and, therefore, a potential reduction in what was popularly termed 'governmental overload' in the 1970s. Put simply, the government has managed to export or hive off many of the day-to-day problems for which it was held responsible under nationalization. A fourth – and much more arguable – claim is that the privatized industries have become more efficient. Thus, the government has argued that: 'The economy benefits through higher returns on capital in the privatised industries, which can no longer pre-empt resources from elsewhere in the economy but must compete for funds in the open capital markets ... These advantages are borne out in the success of the privatised companies ...' (Treasury, 1990). There is little doubt that the performance of the privatized industries has improved. What is difficult to assess is whether this can be attributed to privatization as such. There does appear to have been a shift in organizational culture within the industries. This began in the run-up to privatization (for example, in British Airways) and has continued post-privatization, as the managers in the privatized industries have increasingly adopted private sector attitudes – for example, by becoming somewhat more customer orientated. Thus, Pitt argues that BT has witnessed a 'ramping up' of the organization – a cultural transformation given prominence in speech after speech by 'change champions' within the organisation (Pitt, 1990: 63). The organizational effects claimed to emanate from the liberalization/privatization phase in BT are listed by Pitt as follows:

First, management style is changing with the appointment of managers at the commanding heights who are acting as the carriers or 'champions' of an entrepreneurial risk-taking culture at variance with its predecessor the Post Office – bureaucratic and risk averse. Secondly, marketing style is becoming more aggressive with 'new look' sales promotions, advertising and the recognition of discrete marketing niches requiring service from 'dedicated' account managers. Thirdly, the organisation has become more 'results orientated'. Devolution and decentralisation have been accompanied by improvements in management information systems. The quality of information provided for effective management in a fast changing, competitive and commercial environment has improved. The use of techniques such as ARMOR has been specifically designed to reduce operating margins through a reduction in overheads. The introduction of profit centres has done much to make staff aware of 'profit' as a *sine qua non* of organisation viability in an open market situation (Pitt, 1990: 68–9).

The difficulty in assessing the impact of privatization on performance is that British industry as a whole was undergoing rapid change during the 1980s as the economy became more and more exposed to international competition and as new managerial values became fashionable. The typical changes in organizational structure and culture post-privatization could be seen elsewhere even in those organizations remaining in the public sector. In one of the few systematic attempts to evaluate the effects of changes in organizational status, Dunsire *et al*, argue that results on tests of performance in productivity, employment, and financial ratios against change in status, competition and internal management failed in most cases to support the thesis that change in ownership improves enterprise performance (Dunsire *et al*, 1991: 210).

The claim that privatization has achieved a major increase in share ownership also needs some qualification. Although the UK is now said to have a higher proportion of shareholders than the USA, it should be noted that there has been considerable selling of shares (profit taking) by ordinary members of the public and that the number of ordinary individuals still retaining shares is confined to one or more of the privatization issues (i.e. there has not been a significant extension of share ownership beyond privatized industries). In fact there have been quite drastic reductions in the number of shareholders in the privatized companies since the first flush of enthusiasm in the context of virtually guaranteed profits. For example, the number of shareholders in British Airways at privatization was 1,100,000 which by March 1990 had fallen to 347,897. Similarly, the number of shareholders in British Telecom has fallen from 2,051,373 to 1,236,870, and in British Gas from 4,407,079 to 2,780,813, and in Rolls Royce from 2,000,000 to 924,970 (Treasury, 1990: 7). A process of concentration of privatized shares in the key City institutions has taken place.

In terms of the evaluation of privatization, we should not ignore other forms which can loosely be termed privatization (i.e. the transfer of publicly owned industries to the private sector via the selling of shares). The spectrum of activity has been wide. As Hartley reminds us, contracting out was also an element of the privatization programme. The private supply of services funded by central and local government (and by public agencies such as Health Authorities) has, in part, been an important part of the government's programme. Typical examples have included refuse collection, catering and cleaning of offices, schools and streets, greater competition in tendering for construction projects in local government, and competitive tendering in NHS hospitals (for a review see Hartley, 1990). This aspect of privatization – often extremely controversial, for example in the NHS – should be seen as part of the government's strategy of 'loosening up' the public sector and of changing the organizational culture of public sector organizations, whether or not they are not to be privatized. Even the civil service has not been immune. The hiving-off of blocks of activities into executive agencies – the so-called Next Steps initiative – has accelerated and some 220,000 civil servants worked in executive agencies, just four years after the start of the Next Steps initiative (Price Waterhouse, 1992: 4).

Against these undoubted successes must be set a range of problems, more or less related to the difficulties caused by the relative lack of liberalization and competition in the privatized sectors. Essentially, problems which arose for the government because of public ownership of the industries have been traded for problems relating to the regulatory process governing the new public sector. These problems are having to be managed in the context of increasing public and élite concern about alleged abuse of monopoly position by some of the industries. For example, in March 1992, the Telecommunication Users' Association was reported as pressing the government to force Mercury Communications (the sole licensed competition to BT), to extend its services to most of Britain. (By early 1992 it was estimated that Mercury's share of the market was no more than 5 per cent and that this was concentrated on the more lucrative end of the market.) The Association was also pressing OFTEL (the regulator) to refer BT to the Monopolies and Mergers Commission in order to discover details of BT's pricing structure.

In the 1990s, however, it became clear that the telecommunications regulator was confronted with a dilemma. On the one hand, the encouragement of competition domestically required the weakening of BT's dominant UK position. On the other hand, fierce international competition, and the convergence of telecommunications, computing and entertainment networks, apparently required large units, or even international alliances, for success. Consequently, BT Chairman Iain Vallance feared that his company faced a 'utility trap' of detailed constraints on its pricing and development of technology, while hostile alliances formed against it within Europe (*Financial Times*, 6 December 1993). In particular, BT management feared a proposed link up between France Telecom and Deutsche Telekom, the French and German state operators.

Pitt's comments on the telecoms sector are equally apposite for other privatizations. Thus, he writes that 'BT is a useful reminder to the Government that the connection between policy formulation and policy implementation may be strewn with difficulties. The devil may be in the details ... privatisation does not reduce criticism, but to paraphrase Clausewitz, continues it by other means' (Pitt, 1990; 72–4). If privatization was the growth industry of public policy in Britain in the 1980s, the growth industry in public policy in Britain in the 1990s is undoubtedly regulation. As Veljanovski's review of the growth of regulation in the UK demonstrates, 'with over half a decade of experience, there is a growing demand for a fundamental reassessment of regulation "UK style"' (Veljanovski, 1991: 4). He highlights the fundamental issue post-privatization – namely, that:

on the one hand, the overriding purpose of privatisation was to propel the new entities into the private sector with new and greater freedoms to pursue commercial objectives and improve efficiency. Yet, unfettered, they have every incentive to charge customers high prices, reduce the quality of services and prevent competition (Veljanovski, 1991: 5).

Increasingly, the regulators have begun to respond to public criticisms and Britain is now experiencing a series of regulatory fights as the regulators begin to crack down on the privatized industries. Typical of such regulatory fights was the conflict between the privatized water companies and Ofwat over the differing calculations of the cost of capital and its relationship to pricing levels. There is also increasing conflict between privatized industries as they each try to maximize the freedoms granted by privatization. (For example, there is considerable conflict between privatized electricity generators and British Gas over the price and availability of gas for generating sets.)

The privatized gas and electricity industries have become highly complex policy networks, which can make the old arm's-length relationship between Minister and nationalized industry appear comparatively simple and straightforward. For example, in the 1990s gas has become a political minefield, with a number of the leading actors adopting a highly adversarial approach. Many of the problems have resulted from the government's decision in 1986 to privatize British Gas (BG) as a single entity and monopoly supplier, and since that time those charged with regulating the industry have persistently attempted to introduce a higher degree of competition. Thus, in 1991, the Office of Fair Trading recommended that BG should separate its pipeline and marketing operations from the supply business, and also that by 1995 BG's share of the industrial market for gas should be reduced from 90 per cent to 40 per cent. This radical restructuring was compounded when, in 1992, the industry's regulator, the Office of Gas Supply (Ofgas) compelled BG to implement a formula which kept price rises 5 per cent below inflation for 5 years. The already acrimonious relationship between Ofgas and BG then deteriorated rapidly, with the Director-General of Ofgas, Sir James McKinnon, taking every opportunity to criticize publicly BG management, particularly over the rate of return on its pipeline business. By August 1992 BG management had become so battle-scarred that it was quite happy to request a Monopolies and Mergers Commission (MMC) inquiry into the industry as a whole. It appeared that, in this case, the MMC was perceived by BG as being the lesser of two evils.

The Director-General of the Office of Electricity Regulation (Offer), Professor Stephen Littlechild, also became embroiled deeply in political controversy during the crisis over proposed coal pit closures in the autumn of 1992. The crisis began when British Coal (BC) made the dramatic announcement in October 1992 that, because of declining demand by the electricity generators, 31 pits would close by March 1993, with the loss of 30,000 jobs. After a massive political protest, the government was compelled to announce a moratorium on 21 of the proposed closures. Coal interests put particular blame for the crisis on the privatized electricity companies' newly found enthusiasm for building gas-fired power stations, and demanded that the regulator put an end to this so called 'dash for gas'. Professor Littlechild argued that he had no power to direct investment by the electricity companies, and that his job was to remove obstacles in the market so that competition could determine which types of fuel were best. Amidst great political controversy, however, Offer did produce a report which basically endorsed the 'dash for gas' (Offer, 1992), and so weakened still further the political strength of the coal industry. At the time of writing (December 1993) Professor Littlechild has still not decided whether to refer the electricity generators to the MMC in response to complaints from the big industrial users of electricity.

The experiences of Kinnon and Littlechild demonstrate the extent to which, in the 1990s, the regulators (in some cases against their will) were becoming politicized figures. Regardless of the political framework within which they operated, they could not avoid making statements which would antagonize at least one of the relevant interests. To this extent they appeared to be taking on increasingly the role of the Minister in the old arms-length relationship. At the same time, despite the regulators' undoubted authority, they lacked the basic accountability of the politician, with the result that a political void existed when an overall strategic analysis of the privatized industries was required.

Veljanovski characterizes the post-privatization regulatory process as follows:

- Regulation is evolving into an informal system of rule making which operates through negotiation and bargaining in the shadow of the law.
- This development has an economic explanation. Regulatory strategies are the predictable outcome of maximising behaviour by the parties involved subject to resource and institutional restraints.
- Economic regulation UK style is evolving into a system of controls which are at odds with the original intention of privatisation; namely, (a) that the 'regulatory bargain' struck between government and shareholders at the time of privatisation would remain the basis for the future commercial operation of the privatised utilities:
  (b) that for the most part the regulatory system would be a rules-based one with intervention along agreed lines. (Veljanovski, 1991: 9–10).

Of particular relevance to our earlier discussion of the importance of the UK policy style, it is important to note that the primary characteristic of implementation (regulation) is still bargaining. As Graham and Prosser claim: 'It is not too extreme to say that negotiations and bargaining are institutionalised in the regulation of privatised enterprises in Britain' (Graham and Prosser, 1991: 230). Bargaining and negotiation were inevitable once the government took the initial policy decision to achieve privatization at (almost) any cost. Where the objective of privatization conflicted with the objective of competition, the former won leaving the new regulators to 'confront a situation where the structure of the industry is fundamentally at odds with the goal of competition . . . as a result many of the regulators have found themselves railing against the implicit understanding – the "regulatory bargain" – struck between the utilities (read shareholders) and the Government at the time of flotation' (Veljanovski, 1991: 22). Only when this 'regulatory game', as Veljanovski puts it, has been played for several more years will we be able to judge the real effects of privatization. As Prosser suggests, while the lack of openness regarding decisions remains, 'it is unlikely that privatisation will resolve the problems which were so characteristic of British nationalisation' (Prosser, 1989: 158). Moreover, the fundamental problems of monopoly and externalities do not disappear with a change of ownership (Helm and Yarrow), 1988: xxcvii).

Just as the privatization process itself can be characterised as the government being on a learning curve of radicalism, so the regulatory process has not been static. As suggested above, the regulators have become more aggressive. For example, in telecommunications, gas and water, the regulators have become noticeably combative towards the privatized industries, no doubt encouraged by increasing public criticism both of the high profits of the privatized industries and of the very considerable salary increases of the managers of the industries. (In 1991–2 the electricity generating company, Power Gen, increased its profit by 30 per cent in the midst of a recession). Typical of this new style of regulation was the decision, taken by OFTEL in June 1992, to force British Telecom to reduce its prices by 7.5 per cent below the rate of inflation, compared with the previous figure of 6.25 per cent). Also, telephone connection charges were ordered to be reduced. In anticipation of similar regulatory action, British Gas announced in May 1992 that it was reducing tariffs by 3 per cent. Alongisde a tougher regulatory style, regulation is gradually becoming more transparent.

As more experience was gained and more public criticism emerged, the government also began to address the regulatory issue more vigorously in the policy design phase of later privatizations. As Vickers argues, this was especially so in the case of electricity (Vickers, 1991: 28). Thus, he contrasts the period 1983–7 where the drive to privatize was the overriding aim, with the post-1987 period where in electricity at least, 'the government displayed a much more vigorous attitude to restructuring and the separate regulation of activities than had been evident earlier' (Vickers, 1991: 28–9). More generally, he argues that in 'four areas – structure, entry, pricing, and quality and investment – policy has become more vigorous over time, notably in the last few years. This trend is evident both within industries such as telecommunications and gas, and from the fact that the government has given much more attention to structural and regulatory matters in later privatisations, such as electricity, than in some previous ones' (Vickers, 1991: 29). As he notes, the task is now to develop stable yet flexible incentive structures that promote efficient industrial performance. Regulatory economics in Britain is only at the beginning (Vickers, 1991: 29).

Finally, we may conclude by noting that privatization has certainly not solved the political problems of dealing with these large industries. Indeed, it has brought out into the open many of the conflicting policy objectives which, under public ownership, were internalized and hidden from public debate. Water policy is perhaps the most extreme example of this new transparency, where a public and almost bitter debate has developed between the two main regulators – OFWAT and the NRA. The Director General of OFWAT, Ian Byatt, has been vociferous in his public criticism of the costs of increased environmental regulation (particularly from the EU), whereas the Chairman of the NRA, Lord Crickhowel, has been equally forceful in his defence of higher standards. More generally, the question of the accountability of the regulators themselves is now on the political agenda (Butler, 1993). By raising the question of who should regulate the regulators, critics have demonstrated that the old questions of steering, control, and accountability have not been solved by privatization. If anything they have become even more difficult to resolve.

## Note

This chapter in part draws upon work conducted with Dr W. Rüdig, Professor M. Janicke, and Dr L. Mez in a project on water policy in Britain and Germany, and funded by the Anglo-German Foundation for the Study of Industrial Society. I should like to thank Geoffrey Dudley for his help in updating an earlier version of the chapter.

# References

Abromeit, H. (1988), 'British privatisation policy', *Parliamentary Affairs*, **41** (2): 68–85.

Adam Smith Institute (1986), *Privatization Worldwide*, London, Adam Smith Institute.

Butler, Eamon (ed.) (1993), *But Who Will Regulate The Regulators?*, London, Adam Smith Institute.

Crewe, Ivor and Searing, Donald (1988), 'Ideological change in the Conservative party', *American Political Science Review*, **82** (2): 361–84.

Damgaard, E., Gerlich, P. and Richardson, J.J. (1989), *The Politics of Economic Crisis*, Aldershot, Avebury.

Dudley, G.F. (1989), *Privatisation 'with the Grain': Distinguishing Features of the Sales of the National Bus Company*, Strathclyde Papers on Government and Politics, No. 59.

Dudley, G.F. and Richardson, J.J. (1990), *Politics and Steel in Britain 1967–1988*, Aldershot, Dartmouth Publishing Company.

Dunleavy, Patrick (1986) 'Explaining the privatisation boom: public choice versus radical approaches', *Public Administration*, **64** (1):13–34.

Dunsire, Andrew, Hartley, Keith and Parker, David (1991), 'Organisational status and performance: summary of the findings', *Public Administration* **69**, Spring: 21–40.

Gamble, A. (1988), *The Free Economy and the Strong State – the Politics of Thatcherism*, London, Macmillan Press Ltd.

Graham, C. and Prosser, T. (1991), *Privatizing Public Enterprises*, Oxford, Clarendon Press.

Grimstone, Gerry (1990), 'The British privatization programme', in J.J. Richardson (ed.), *Privatization and Deregulation in Canada and Britain*, Aldershot, Dartmouth Publishing Company: 3–13.

Hartley, Keith (1990), 'Contracting out in Britain: achievements and problems', in J.J. Richardson (ed.), *Privatization and Deregulation in Canada and Britain*, Aldershot, Dartmouth Publishing Company.

Heald, David (1985), 'Will the privatization of public enterprises solve the problem of control?', *Public Administration*, **63** (1): 7–22.

Heclo, H. (1978), 'Issue networks and the executive establishment', in A. King (ed.), *The New American Political System*, Washington, AEI: 87–124.

Helm, Dieter and Yarrow, George (1988), 'The assessment: the regulation of utilities', *Oxford Review of Economic Policy*, **4** (2): i–xxxi.

Jordan, A.G. and Richardson, J.J. (1982), 'The British policy style or the logic of negotiation?', in J.J. Richardson (ed.), *Policy Styles in Western Europe*, London, George Allen & Unwin: 80–110.

Kinnersley, D. (1988), *Troubled Water, Rivers, Politics and Pollution*, London, Hilary Shipman.

McAllister, Ian and Studlar, Donley (1989), 'Popular versus élite views of privatisation: the case of Britain', *Journal of Public Policy*, **9** (2): 157–78.

Mitchell, James (1990), 'Privatisation as myth?', in J.J. Richardson (ed.), *Privatisation and Deregulation in Canada and Britain*, Aldershot, Dartmouth Publishing Company: 14–37.

Moon, Jeremy, Richardson, J.J. and Smart, Paul (1988), 'The privatisation of British Telecom: a case study of the extended process of legislation', *European Journal of Political Research*, **14**: 339–55.

National Audit Office (1992) *Sales of the Water Authorities in England and Wales*, London, HMSO.

Office of Electricity Regulation (1992), *Review of Economic Purchasing*, London, HMSO.

Pitt, Douglas (1990), 'An essentially contestable organisation: British Telecom and the privatisation debate', in J.J. Richardson (ed.), *Privatisation and Deregulation in Canada and Britain*, Aldershot, Dartmouth Publishing Company.

Price Waterhouse (1992), *Executive Agencies*, London, Price Waterhouse.

Prosser, Tony (1989), 'Regulation of privatised enterprises: institutions and procedures', in Leigh Hancher and Michael Moran, *Capitalism, Culture and Economic Regulation*, Oxford, Clarendon Press.

Richardson, J.J. (1989), 'Britain: changing policy styles and policy innovation in response to economic crisis', in Damgaard *et al*, *The Politics of Economic Crisis*, Aldershot, Avebury.

Richardson, J.J. and Jordan, A.G. (1979), *Governing Under Pressure*, Oxford, Basil Blackwell.

Richardson, Jeremy, Gustaffson Gunnel and Jordan Grant (1982), 'The concept of policy style', in Jeremy Richardson (ed.), *Policy Styles in Western Europe*, London, Allen and Unwin.

Richardson, J.J. Maloney, E. and Rüdig, W. (1992), 'The dynamics of policy change: lobbying and water privatisation', *Public Administration*, Summer.

Sewell, W. and Barr, L. (1978) 'Water administration in England and Wales', *Water Resources Bulletin* **14**: 337–48.

Steel, D. and Heald, D. (1984), 'The new agenda', in D. Steel and D. Heald (eds), *Privatising Public Enterprises*, London, RIPA: 13–19.

The Treasury (1990), *Privatisations in the United Kingdom: Background Briefing*, London, HM Treasury.

Veljanovski, Cento (1991), 'The regulation game', in Cento Veljanovski (ed.), *Regulators and the Market: An Assessment of the Growth of Regulation in the UK*, London, Institute of Economic Affairs: 3–28.

Vickers, John (1991), 'Government regulatory policy', *Oxford Review of Economic Policy*, **7** (3) :13–30.

Vickers, John and Wright, Vincent (1989), 'The politics of industrial privatization in Western Europe: an overview', in Vickers and Wright, *The politics of privatization in Western Europe*, London, Frank Cass: 1–30.

Wolfe, Joel (1991), 'State power and ideology in Britain: Mrs Thatcher's privatization programme', *Political Studies*, **XXXIX**: 253–69.

# CHAPTER 4

## PRIVATIZATION IN FRANCE: 1983–1993

## Hervé Dumez and Alain Jeunemaitre

There are two dimensions to any analysis of privatization. The first has to do with the way in which a nation's policy attunes to the global momentum, witness the initial boost given to Mrs Thatcher's government at the beginning of the 1980s.[1] The second belongs in a wider perspective, within the historical substance of the country concerned.

How has it happened that France, a country with a renowned tradition of interventionism, stretching from Colbert to the Socialist governments of the Fifth Republic by way of Gaullist precept, has become a convert to privatization? And so spectacular a convert. In record time, between 1986 and 1987, a vast programme was drawn up, launched and carried through. Then it was put for a while in cold storage (relatively speaking, as will be seen), only to re-emerge in the autumn of 1993.

The answer to this question entails more than exploring the first dimension – the fact of privatization becoming fashionable and the manner whereby the 'fashion' caught on in France. It requires looking further back in time, to 1945 at least.

### The post-war French model

It is certainly not our intention here to give a detailed analysis of the French 'model' any more than it is to rewrite the history of the post-war period. Our purpose is to provide points of reference.

For France the aftermath of the war was a period of economic hardship, with the effects of mass destruction, and systems of production and distribution in disarray. Rationing had to continue in spite of the war being over. The mood was in favour of interventionism (Kuisel, 1984). The industrial bourgeoisie were relatively discredited and, more important, held to be resistant to expansionism. The path chosen was in pursuit of growth fed by a strong dose of state intervention.

Interventionism makes use of a whole range of implements to spur growth. These include price controls to curb inflation, exchange control to maintain stability in the balance of payments, and, in regard to industrial policy, forms of protection, subsidies, preferential treatment for French industry, advocacy of mergers between French firms, control over foreign investment in France, promotion and boosting of exports. But interventionism leads also to the socialization of welfare, with social security, distributive pensions and a guaranteed minimum wage. This structure was set up in France in the years immediately following the war.

Then also in 1945, with the main sectors of industry – energy and transport - already publicly owned, a new series of nationalizations was carried through, both in these sectors and in others (Renault for instance) while a major part of the banking sector was nationalized, giving the state the means to ensure the finance of growth. At the same time, individual cover against sickness, unemployment and old age came to be administered on a collective basis. Thus, a French model was set up which continued to function until the early 1980s. Governments of both the Fourth and Fifth Republics brought its criteria to bear on their management of the economy. The 1968 crisis, a kind of revolution but with no victims or political take-over, even reinforced the conviction that the model must be maintained more or less as it was if a volatile situation was to be averted.

But the model occasioned a number of costs. One effect was marked inflation that price controls failed to contain (Dumez and Jeunemaître, 1989), and for which a safety valve was found in devaluations to restore competitiveness, the prime example being that of 1969, or else to eliminate disparities with trading partners. Another was that the level of financial dealing passing directly through circuits of government or close to government was so high that the French financial market became atrophied. On several occasions government made an attempt to direct savings towards industry. In 1967 the Commission des Opérations de Bourse was set up, to act in an equivalent role to the US Securities and Exchanges Commission, with a view to bolstering confidence among small investors in the workings of the market. In 1978 the Barre government initiated forms of tax exemption for savings schemes in the form of shares. But even though the policy could be rated a success (between 1977 and 1982 the number of shareholders doubled from 1.5 to 3 million), the French financial market remained modest in comparison to London. A further aggravating factor was that financial circuits were compartmentalized because of the several sector-directed interventions on the part of government (i.e. some circuits financing agriculture, others housing, local authority investment and so on).

The election of a Socialist government in 1981, for the first time in the Fifth Republic, marked the model's apotheosis. A huge wave of nationalizations was carried through, embracing banks, insurance companies and industrial groups, at the same time as the retirement age was lowered to sixty, the basic wage increased and working hours reduced. Subsequently the model was drawn into crisis by degrees under the impact of its own inner contradictions and France's integration in the construction of Europe.

## The inherent crisis of the French model

The French system of social welfare gradually broke down, with unemployment surging from one million, to two, and then to three million at the start of the 1990s. The financial strain fell on wage-earners and on firms. The elderly population increased and the distributive pensions system was thrown off balance. A diminishing working population was obliged to pay for the growing numbers in retirement. A third element, (as in all the major industrial countries), expenditure on health, found its share of GDP growing with no apparent means of its being curbed.

The problems of social welfare combined with the financial problems of the government *vis-à-vis* state-owned concerns. The dilemma was to provide arms-length support for nationalized industries in difficulty (in 1985 Renault was saved from bankruptcy by means of a capital grant from the government) while meeting the financial needs of those that were expanding. Between 1982 and 1985, public sector concerns were paid Ffr50 billion in capital grants and Ffr6 billion in loans without obligation. Over a period of three years, from 1981 to 1983, government subsidies attained Ffr136 billion. It became rapidly clear that a ceiling had been reached, that the government no longer had the financial means to sustain the pace of its industrial policy. By an Act of 1983, a Socialist government, facing deep crisis in public financing, authorized nationalized concerns to call on private sector investment, and thus in a sense prepared the way for future privatization. The name by which this Act was known, public sector 'respiration', ironically points to the clear danger at the time of the public sector being financially asphyxiated.

Standard industrial policy too, apart from the problems of financing, becomes crisis-prone; not that it was written off as a failure. While its functioning became the subject of expert study (see for example,

Padioleau, 1981 and Cohen and Bauer, 1985), it would appear that the predominant assumption in government circles and of opinion at large inclined towards a statement of affairs being in balance, and preferably positive. The success stories, such as Airbus or the TGV, ran parallel to the failures in steel or computers. The source of crisis lay in another direction. The pace of the internationalization of industry was becoming more and more unstoppable. In this context, state-owned concerns face a double disadvantage. First, internationalization is expensive and returns us to the problem of budgetary constraints: the acrobatics involved in the nationalized company, Péchiney, finding the necessary funds to buy up American Can provide a good illustration. Second, the fact that the French government was a shareholder aroused deep suspicion and considerable reticence among likely foreign partners.

A case in point of a fairly dramatic nature occurred at the very beginning of the 1990s with the purchase of British companies by French state-owned concerns. The Secretary for Trade and Industry, Peter Lilley, twice referred the matter to the Monopolies and Mergers Commission (MMC)[2] for a ruling as to whether the purchase of a British firm by a French nationalized industry was not against the public interest. In the event, MMC authorized the deal, holding that the relations of state-owned concerns with their shareholder did not differ from those that applied in the case of private firms. But such incidents showed how state-owned concerns were at a disadvantage when it came to purchases and 'marriages' at an international level. The problem was further highlighted at the end of 1993 with the objections raised by Swedish and private shareholders in Volvo (especially those representing pension funds) to the Renault/Volvo merger, and with pressure in Sweden for Renault to be privatized sooner than expected. Whereas government had served public enterprise well between 1981 and 1985 by providing the resources needed for recovery, its role as single shareholder or referee constituted more and more of a handicap. With limited financial resources, it constricted public sector firms when they sought to expand, and its overbearing presence inhibited them in forming alliances that were necessary for survival and development. Superimposed on the internal crisis of the French model was the impact of European integration.

## The increasingly decisive influence of European construction

The momentum for the construction of Europe showed itself in two areas – competitiveness as a policy and the question of a single currency.

While the creation of the single European market was underway by the middle of the 1980s, with 1 January 1993 as a target date, the policy of competition inside Europe enjoyed a fresh surge, with the aim of removing any barrier that obstructed market standardization. Effectively, the public sectors of member sates constituted a problem. The Treaty of Rome (as is known), remains neutral on the matter of economic ownership, leaving each state free to nationalize or privatize. However, the pursuit of competitiveness within Europe brought ever greater constraints to bear on public sector firms.

Nationalized concerns operating within the competitive sector, when they enjoyed financial support, were increasingly subject to investigation by the Commission. The capital grants made to Renault in 1985–6, for example, were the cause of confrontation between the French government and Sir Leon Brittan, who in July 1991 also initiated an enquiry into capital provision made to Bull by the state. One after another, public concerns in France that were financed by this means were confronted by the Commission, asking whether such forms of finance were comparable with those of a private shareholder in a private firm, or whether they were in reality subsidies in disguise and, as such, to be counted as unfair competition within Europe.

Meanwhile the monopoly position of public concerns not operating within the commercial sector became increasingly precarious. The Commission's aim was to separate functions that constituted a natural monopoly from services that were appropriate for the market, so avoiding the possibility of cross-subsidization. The policy spread to all public services – telecommunications, postal services (with a distinction made between dispatching standard letters and parcels, express mail, and publications), energy and transport.

In other words, the European competitive norm obliged state-owned enterprise to perform in the same way as private enterprise in the context of the market. Therefore, any reason for keeping such concerns under state ownership vanished. In 1983 the French government itself urged them to strive to balance their accounts, present schemes for reorganization and to increase their efforts towards greater productivity.

The move towards a single European currency was also crucial to the problem. In 1979 the European Monetary System was set up, providing for fixed parities between currencies and with a type of realignment between parities that excluded competitively motivated devaluation. There again the French model showed itself irrelevant. Fixed parities within a European framework and in the context of the deregulation of financial markets (during the second half of the 1980s) and their being opened up worldwide assumed tight control over budgetary deficit, welfare expenditure and public sector indebtedness. The situation intensified with the guidelines for convergence set by the Maastricht Treaty in preparation for European Monetary Union. Budgetary pressure, which weighed heavily on the government in France, made any vigorous public service policy, with the likelihood of deficit budgeting and indebtedness, virtually impossible.

## The appearance in France of the theme of privatization

Four elements led to the appearance of privatization on the agenda. First, the sheer scale of nationalization in 1981–2 without question turned the public sector in France into an anomaly. In 1984 it represented six hundred concerns, a labour force of nearly two and a quarter million and an appreciably larger proportion of GDP than the public sectors in either Britain or Germany. In one sense, privatizations in France implied no more than a return to the international norm after the Socialist 'anomaly' of 1981–2 (Wright, 1990).

The second element is more central. Privatizations enabled the Gordian knot of public sector administration over the period of 1980–1990 to be cut. Sales of public assets enabled the budgetary deficit and level of public indebtedness to be reduced, so making it easier for the franc to maintain its level in the EMS; they enabled firms to tap new resources by making calls on financial markets and more readily to form international ties and agreements; they enabled them to develop the home financial market by drawing in new investors and to prepare the ground for privatizing the welfare system (notably in respect of retirement). The programme was a revelation since it appeared to contain only advantages. In 1986 the unspoken question was: why hadn't it been thought of before?

The third element was the product of political strategy. In 1981–2 the Socialist government initiated a major interventionist programme which set off a series of destabilizing economic effects, with the result that in 1983 it was faced with the choice either of withdrawing from the European mechanisms (EMS in particular) or remaining inside but adopting an altogether different economic philosophy. In their distress, the Socialist leaders chose to remain within the EMS, the corollary being necessary acceptance of budgetary constraint, the fact of indebtedness, and the need to put the public sector back on a sound financial footing and under strict management. Following the years of apprenticeship – to allude to the two parts of Wilhelm Meister – there came the time of renunciation (Dumez and Jeunemaître, 1990). The combined parties of the right-wing opposition chose as their platform the break with socialism. Hence the parliamentary election campaign of March 1986 was fought on the issue of economic liberalism. Friedrich von Hayek was invited to the Paris City Hall by Jacques Chirac, the Gaullist heir, amid much trumpeting from conservative papers such as *Le Figaro*, and *Figaro-Magazine*. One witnessed the spectacle of a Socialist government reorganizing the nationalized concerns as profit-making businesses, overhauling the financial markets and gradually dismantling price controls. Neo-liberalism characterized the mood of the time, and of a dogmatic kind as reflected in the policies of Margaret Thatcher and Ronald Reagan. Jacques Chirac himself, who once championed a form of '*travaillisme à la française*', adopted the Thatcherite philosophy.

The fourth and final element was the 'theory' of privatization properly speaking. Of the four it was probably the least important. In any case it would seem that ideological references from the privatization programme have their origin not so much in Anglo-Saxon theories (formulated on the basis of agency theory or theories of efficiency) as in the old Gaullist intellectual core, in particular in the notion of 'participation'. It was felt to be important to bring employees and wage-earners in general into industrial management so that, symbolically rather than in reality, they could share in the decision-making process.

Here again a long story lies behind the French privatization programme. In effect no actual 'conversion' was undergone by the French élite to neo-liberalism, rather was it a neo-liberal packaging of old Gaullist theory. Witness a statement by Jacques Friedmann, principal author of the privatization programme and at the time president of Air France, when he formulated the wish to keep back 1.5 per cent of the company's capital in the form of shares for its employees: 'The competitive spirit that we need to deploy requires our personnel to be involved, motivated, hence provided with a share in the firm's profits' (*Le Monde*, 23 July 1987). Witness also the nomination to the chairmanship of the Commission de Privatisation of Pierre Chatenet, conseiller d'Etat and President of the Commission des Opérations de Bourse, who, in the latter capacity, played an active part in boosting 'worker participation' at the end of General de Gaulle's presidency.

By the time the Right had won a majority of seats in the National Assembly and Jacques Chirac the premiership, the firms nationalized in 1981–2 had become profitable again[3] and the Socialist party was hard put to explain why these concerns and others should remain the property of the state. Hence, given all the advantages it promised, the privatization programme quickly got under way.

## Realisation – first programme 1986–7

To simplify matters, we shall begin with a brief summary of what was achieved in 1986/87. Then, somewhat differently from others who have made a retrospective study of privatization in France, we shall examine the programme from within the context of the time.

### Assessment

Assessment of the first wave of privatization in France has been made many times. It appears to have been a success, but two major problems are unresolved. Were concerns undersold (i.e. was the offer price set too low?), and did the core-controlling interests (*noyaux durs*) follow reasoning that was not so much economic as political (i.e. suggesting a seizure of the nation's assets by the conservative parties). For a good discussion of these points, see Cartelier, 1992.

One point needs to be made immediately. The programme took place over a very short period of time. President Mitterrand refused to sign the edicts in July 1986 authorizing the government to embark on the programme immediately, thus forcing the Chirac government to rush a bill through parliament, which it did on 6 August 1986. The process of privatization began in the early autumn and to all intents and purposes came to an end with the crash on 19 October 1986. Within nine months ten groups were privatized in one go, at a value of Ffr93,5 billion. Five million French people acquired shares in the companies concerned, taking the total number of shareholders in France to close on ten million in 1987.[4] Hence the programme was a considerable one and carried through quickly. It resulted in returning most of the companies nationalized in 1981 to the private sector, but went further by including the Société Générale, one of the major banks nationalized in 1945, and TF1, successor to the first television channel set up by the state and always very much under its influence. To have carried through so large a programme in a matter of months was in itself an achievement. Yet at the start nothing was known for sure.

### A programme open to every danger

In a book that appeared in 1987, Edouard Balladur describes how the programme was drawn up: 'Over several months, in advance of the parliamentary elections, the opposition parties of the time deliberated on what the future action should be ... [with the result that] a common platform for government was signed on January 26 1986' (Balladur, 1987: 75). The programme, that was mapped out in a few months designated 66 companies as '*privatisables*' (1454 including subsidiaries) – 42 in the banking sector, 13 in insurance, 9 industrial groups, 2 in the communications sector. The overall value of the programme fluctuated between Ffr275 and Ffr300 billion and affected 750,000 wage-earners. It corresponded to a 30 per cent increase in the capitalization of the Paris stock market (compared with only 10 per cent in that of the City, and a British programme spread over seven years).

The gamble of course, was on whether there was a larger reserve margin of untapped savings in France than elsewhere. The peculiarities of the French model, described earlier, revealed that capitalization in France represented only 10 per cent of GDP – against 59 per cent in the UK, 53 per cent in Japan, 52 per cent in Switzerland, 44 per cent in the USA and 41 per cent in Canada. Even so, the gamble remained a highly risky one. No one had any idea how investors would respond. Apprehensions at the time – in fact, while the programme was in the process of development, a year before it was launched – were well expressed by Lionel Zinsou-Derlin, then adviser to Laurent Fabius, the Socialist prime minister:

The French financial market can absorb the issue of about 10 billion francs worth of shares each year, added in part to which 8 billion worth of non-voting shares, which do not entirely correspond to full shares. This volume of funds constitutes a record. It is attributable to continuous efforts to revitalise the Bourse over the last three years, to favourable stock market conditions worldwide and to the rise in share values produced by lower interest rates. Before 1982, the volume of available resources fluctuated between 500 million and 3 billion francs, evidence of the French market being much more restricted than foreign markets. Even with the spectacular progress achieved, it only represents a quarter of the British market. Taken by itself, the sale of 51 per cent of Rhône-Poulenc capital is likely to call on 20 billion francs and cripple the French market's capacity for a year (Zinsou-Derlin, 1985: 252–3).

Thus the Chirac government chose to adopt a high-risk strategy. Other countries frequently sold their publicly-owned concerns directly to the private sector (as was the case in Portugal and in Spain, where SEAT was bought up by Volkswagen); only the UK adopted the method of large-scale flotations; but the French programme was on a larger scale than the British, and the stock market four times smaller.

*Setting up the machinery*

The government set up a Commission de Privatisation (Article 3 of the Act of 6 August 1986), its task being to evaluate the price of concerns to be sold and propose a floor price for the sales offer to the Minister responsible who was free to choose a price above. Having selected the price, the Minister had latitude to fix the number of shares offered for sale according to the number of investors he sought to attract. As regards publicity, the government received assistance from major French and foreign agencies – Publicis, Bélier, Dupuy, HCM and Saatchi. On legal matters it resorted to the major practices – Gide, Loyrette, Nouel, Jeantet and Klein. And it mobilized the know-how of the major London merchant banks – Lazard, Merrill-Lynch and Kleinworth-Benson. Nothing was left to chance.

*Marketing*

The programme's success centred on the government's setting the price of shares. Controversy raged: did the government deliberately undervalue the price to ensure the success of its programme, so despoiling the community at large to the advantage of first-time individual and institutional investors?

The fact that a majority of shares in the privatized concerns rose substantially above the selling price as soon as they were quoted and that the capital was subscribed several times over, so that the number of shares per shareholder had to be rationed, appeared to afford sufficient evidence to give an affirmative answer. In fact things were not quite so simple.

In the first place, a concern does not hold a price that can be determined objectively. The price must take account of the state of the market and contains a degree of conjecture (the updated forecasting of profits in the years ahead). As regards the groups nationalized in 1981–2 a reference existed, namely the Bourse prices applying before that date, which afforded an indication. The trickiest case was that of TF1, a firm operating in a special field (i.e. television, which had never in its existence been the subject of quotation).

Concerning the upward movement of shares on the first quotation, there are a number of comments to be made. First, private firms that raise capital generally – at least where they are sound – follow this pattern. At the same time, settling for too low a price also presents risks, in the sense that shareholders rapidly resell and open the way for a series of takeover bids. Second, in the French case market premiums were lower than in the British.

But above all assessment must take account of the dynamics of the process. The first complete privatization was that of Saint-Gobain.[5] The market premium accompanying its introductory price was 19 per cent. The success of the operation reflected on those that followed. With Paribas the premium was 18.6 per cent, with CCF 16.8 per cent, Havas 8 per cent, Société Générale 6.1 per cent, TF1 7 per cent. The gap between the offer price and the first quotation therefore narrowed considerably as time went on, seeming to testify to an element of learning from experience.

*The core-controlling interests (noyaux durs)*

This was the nub of the second criticism. Politicians were worried by the size of the French groups. At the time a figure was much quoted: Siemens finances would allow it to buy up the entire capital of CGE (Compagnie Générale d'Elecricité). In other words, fear of hostile takeover bids from foreign groups hung over the privatization programme. In his own way, the Head of State echoed the fear in refusing to sign the edicts:

I am not only entrusted with ensuring that the Constitution is respected but, in regard to certain particulars written in the Constitution, I am answerable for the independence of France. Hence I cannot accept that these assets, assets which belong to the nation, are sold in such a way that in the future items, products and commodities vital to France's independence may end up in foreign hands . . . For me it is a matter of conscience (François Mitterrand, press conference, 14 July 1986).

The Act finally passed on 6 August 1986 specifies in three Articles how the national interest is to be protected. Article 9 allows the Minister, should he so desire, to restrain any individual or legal entity from acquiring more than 5 per cent in a concern to be privatized. Article 10 forbids the state to sell more than a 20 per cent stake in a firm to be privatized to foreign capital. Further, if it is deemed to be in the national interest, the Minister may convert a firm's shares into specific shares and grant an interest in excess of 10 per cent to one or more participants. Such types of interest in specific shares cannot be disposed of within five years unless the Minister, acting by decree, reconverts the same specific shares into ordinary shares.

Such was the legal basis on which the strategy of *noyaux durs* was built up. Making use of his prerogatives, the Minister sought to secure the capital of privatized firms within a close mesh of cross-interests. First, with each privatization, certain firms were picked out and allocated a number of shares not exceeding 5 per cent. Together, these firms were to hold up to 30 per cent of the capital of the privatized concern. These 'blocks' of shares could not be sold for two years, and over the following three years the privatized concern had a preemptive right over their repurchase. Second, a number of these firms and banks participated in the various stages of privatization. Through this system of controlling blocks, it was thus hoped to cement a form of national heritage capital that could stand in the way of any attempts at take-over from abroad. It was further hoped that even if such a take-over bid were to succeed, the operation would not be to the detriment of the small shareholder, the controlling block selling its stake at a high price. Employees were allocated 10 per cent of the capital.

Twelve of the largest industrial conglomerates and twelve main banks and insurance companies were invited to participate in the capitalization of the privatized concerns. The majority were approached for one transaction, sometimes two, never more (except in the case of public investors). Indeed, however real the threat from outside France, there was probably more apprehension about possible take-over bids from other French firms. The main concern was to ensure that the capital resulting from privatization was evenly spread across as much of French industry and banking as possible, and the close-knit complex of cross-interests was supposed to afford protection against this happening.

There was no lack of criticism. Distribution of the controlling blocks was carried out off-market, by mutual agreement, under the supervision of the Minister for the Economy, Edouard Balladur, at the market price raised by a block premium. The procedure led to an incredible dispersion of the capital involved in privatization, as well as to a degree of self-regulation in most of the groups. Using their subsidiaries as an expedient, firms got possession of part of their capital (see Hamdouch, 1989). Besides, the opposition parties persisted in claiming that the procedure had resulted in a significant part of the nation's capital assets being undersold to the government's political friends and allies. In fact, there too, circumstances obtaining left the government with very little margin for manoeuvre. In the absence of pension funds and large-scale private institutional investors, the list of companies in a position to subscribe to the capitalization of those privatized was a limited one. Political considerations made it unacceptable to entrust control of a company in the process of being privatized directly to one or two shareholders. Then, as in most countries, business circles clearly have a closer connection with the parties of the Right than the Left. Bearing in mind the constraints, it is difficult to see how a substantially different appreciation of the situation to that made in 1986–88 could have been reached: the one represented by diagram after diagram published in French newspapers depicting a few large French conglomerates joined by a jungle of arrows pointing in all directions and symbolizing the cross-interests involved (see, for example, Morin, 1993). Was the system, then, with all its drawbacks, an effective one? In spite of the fears often expressed, it has to be granted that it has thus far (end 1993) succeeded in protecting the companies privatized.

*The end of the experiment*

Taking into account the risks run, the privatization programme went off remarkably well. There is no question that the Minister for the Economy and those round him, who were given far greater responsibility in the matter than is customary in governments of the Fifth Republic, demonstrated a high degree of skill. The culmination of the process was reached with the privatization of Paribas in January 1987. The advertising campaign that extended an invitation to the public to join the bank's directors in the boardroom is vividly recalled. There was a record number of subscriptions, 3.8 million individuals bought shares, often as a family; the number of shares per person had to be limited to four. Then in October 1987 came the crash. On the night of the crash, Edouard Balladur, speaking on television and radio, exhorted small investors not to sell. Effectively, they generally resisted doing so and made a show of passiveness, while the institutions gave their sales orders. On 9 November after having been turned away, the Suez share was introduced on the Bourse. At the first session it was down 17.6 per cent on its introductory price, and spirits fell. Matra was privatized in January 1988, after which the privatization programme went into hibernation. The result of the presidential election of 1988, assuring François Mitterrand of a second term, interrupted it – for a while.

*'No more . . . no more'*

The presidential election was fought on the issue of change, and the verdict of the electorate was against change. In his Open Letter to the French – in effect, his programme – François Mitterrand set out his position: there would be no more nationalization and no more privatization (the formula became known as 'no more . . . no more'). It was an implicit recognition that nationalization no longer constituted an option for the Socialist party and that it would not be politically appropriate to go back on the privatizations realized, an implicit recognition, in other words, that they had been a success. It was also a means of reassuring the electorate. The Left now stood for conservatism in the face of the parties of the Right whose reforms threatened to disturb the equilibrium of French society.

In an initial phase beginning in 1988, the Socialist government tried to break the *noyaux durs*. Extraordinarily, the first attempt to take over a privatized concern was initiated by the government. The raid failed lamentably, and ended in an investigation by the Commission des Opérations de Bourse into insider practice. It meant a return to the 'no more . . . no more' logic.

If it was politically adroit – and it certainly convinced the electorate – the formula made no economic sense; it would be an obstacle to growth on the part of the state-owned sector, condemning it to stagnate. Until the general election of March 1993 and the return of the Right, the Socialist governments led by Michel Rocard, Edith Cresson and Pierre Bérégovoy were obliged to resort to acrobatics (a '*gymnastique compliquée*' in the words of Roger Fauroux, Minister for Industry in the Rocard administration), paying token regard to the President's 'no more no more' and ignoring it in practice.

Every prescription was tried: sales of a minority of stock, setting up joint public/private enterprise subsidiaries, and capitalization of public enterprise subsidiaries. The biggest operation involved the cross-acquisition of holdings between Renault and Volvo in April 1990. Effective adherence to the principle of creeping, partial, disguised privatization was made explicit in the Decree of 4 April 1991, which laid down that in the case of an agreement for co-operation being signed between a public and a private concern, the opening of public enterprise capital to a public share issue might be contemplated on a case-by-case basis by the Minister responsible, provided the state kept majority control. Again, as in 1983, it was a case of seeking a desperate remedy for public concerns whose financial needs the state could no longer supply. The decree enabled Bull to sign an agreement with NEC and IBM, and the BNP to realize a link with the Dresdner Bank.

Between December 1991 and January 1993 the Socialist governments sold altogether Ffr8 billion worth of public assets, involving Elf-Aquitaine, Crédit Local de France, Péchiney International, Total and Rhône-Poulenc. The sales provided an illustration – if one was needed – of the impossibility for the state to maintain a large public sector, given the budgetary pressure imposed by the policy of maintaining the stability of franc/mark parity. And they are evidence of the continuation – above and beyond political choice – of the privatization policy in France. The 'socialist' decree of April 1991 is in direct line with the so-called 'respiration' act affecting the public sector in 1983. The complete privatization of Crédit Local de France, the Balladur government's first privatization in 1993, was the sequel to the partial privatization undertaken by its Socialist predecessor.

## Resumption of the programme in 1993

The March 1993 elections saw the rout of the Socialist party and the return of the right wing. This time, Edouard Balladur, Minister for the Economy in 1986–8, became Prime Minister. The privatization programme published in the summer of 1993 comprised 21 concerns, including pivotal components of the French financial system – two of the largest banks, BNP and Crédit Lyonnais, and the largest insurance companies, UAP, AGF and GAN. A dozen experts called on by the economic journal *Expansion* assessed the combined value Ffr500 billion (Bentégeat, 1993).

As in 1986 the launch of the programme was painstakingly prepared. French institutional investors had complained on the previous occasion of being disadvantaged by some of the methods used (a tranche was reserved for foreign institutional investors, also some confusion about the offer on the French market with priority for small orders), hence the rules of the Conseil des Bourses de Valeurs were changed. In line with the British system, a tranche was to be reserved for institutional investors on the French market. In this way, if the small investors failed to appear, the process of privatization could still be completed because of the backing of French institutional investors. A further innovation was that the Commission de Privatisation, while retaining the function of fixing the floor transfer price of the companies in question, acquired the added one of deciding the composition of the *noyaux durs*, with the Minister's agreement.

Again a gamble was taken on the French stock market's capacity to absorb privatizing. In 1991 the market had seen the issue of Ffr43 billion worth of stocks and shares. In 1992 the figure fell to Ffr25 billion, and for the first half year of 1993, before the programme was properly launched, it was Ffr16 billion. With the privatization of the BNP and Rhône-Poulenc the government set its sights on a proceeds figure of Ffr43 billion. There was less of a risk here than might appear. In the first place, the publicity launch, the effort deployed throughout the banking system,[6] as well as a whole range of advantages for the small shareholder would count with new takers. Then, reserves of savings were high. Estimates of Ffr1000 billion were put on combined individual investments in unit trusts (SICAV), liquid investments indexed to interest rates. With rates inclined to come down, the investments would lose some of their appeal. Shrewdly devised tax measures could redirect some of this volume of savings towards the stock market when it mattered. Such a movement began to occur when the Balladur government launched a public loan in the summer of 1993. The response when it came was rational. Shares in Alcatel-Alsthom, Havas, CCF, TF1 or Matra yielded 150 per cent over 6 years (1986–7 to 1993), a much better return than any alternative investment. Finally, the French market had expanded, the share capital value of the Paris market more than doubled between 1986 and 1993.

In effect, the initial privatization – of the BNP – in October 1993 was highly successful. Individual demand more than five times covered the capital of Ffr46,4 billion. With 2.807 million shareholders the bank found itself second in line after Paribas, with 3,804 million. Clearly the risk strategy paid off, and the government considered itself to be on course to achieve its aim of arriving at investments of Ffr100 billion within 2 years. The selling price, as in the case of Saint-Gobain in the first privatization programme in 1986, was held to be very attractive. Whereas it was fixed at 240 francs, the BNP investment certificate (non-voting shares already invested and covering at the time of privatization somewhat more than 17 per cent of the capital of BNP) rose to 280 francs on the Paris Bourse on 14 October 1993.[7] The proceeds for the government amounted to Ffr28 billion.

The privatization of Rhône-Poulenc affords an opportunity to look at the whole process in detail. First, given the success of BNP's privatization, the date was brought forward, the public offer opening on 16 November 1993 and closing a week later, after which began the sales to French and foreign institutions. The government anticipated a figure of Ffr13 billion in proceeds from the sale of its 43.4 per cent stake. Second, there was the question of the price. The Privatisation Commission had set the base price at 131 francs. The government selected 135 francs, thus making it clear to opinion at large that national assets were not being underpriced. The closing price the day before had been 153.6; hence in settling for 12.1 per cent below, the government in fact allowed itself a safety margin. Would-be shareholders were held to 60 maximum (5 minimum). The tranche offered initially to the public represented 47 million certificates (Ffr6.345 billion). The government reserved the option of increasing the tranche to 52 million, if it

looked as if it would be oversubscribed, thereby reducing the institutional share, French and foreign. The institutions came in when the public offer ended. They paid a price higher than 135 francs but lower than
that quoted on the market, given the way the book list was made up,
the price being made known late on 25 November.

The make-up of core-controlling interests was announced by the
Minister before the public offer started. It included Crédit Lyonnais,
AGF, Société Générale and BNP plus three newcomers, Axa, Fiat and
Crédit Suisse. Hence no surprises. They would pay a price 2 per cent
higher than that agreed for institutional buyers, the pact binding them
was felt to be sufficient guarantee of their core stability. It laid down
that no share block transfer could be made within the first 3 months;
during the 15 months following, every member was to retain a minimum of 80 per cent of its stake (with the exception of transfers being
made within the *noyaux dur*); during the three years following, members would enjoy mutual pre-emptive rights. In addition, it was provided for new shareholders to be invited to vote on a proposal to
establish the right to two votes for those who had held registered shares
for more than three years, a move to further strengthen the *noyau dur.*

So, apparently, history repeated itself. The process was the same, as
were the actors (Lazard was appointed as the bank to counsel the
government with the BNP privatization, Indosuez with Rhône-Poulenc),
as were the methods used; in both cases the operation was a success.
In fact, in three respects the cases were different.

First, the state of the stock market: between January and October 1993
the Paris Bourse rose by 17 per cent in the context of recession. The
problem was one of liquidity. As we have seen, movement took place
from unit trusts to the Bourse, while other investments, in particular
property, were depressed. The government's fears centred on a repeat
of the October 1987 scenario; not so much a market crash, properly
speaking, as a sharp reversal of the trend, at the outset technical, which
would again interrupt the process of privatization. Hence, in order not
to overvalue the transfer price of the concerns due to be privatized
and to avoid allowing the mechanism to get out of control, the paradox
had to be faced that the concerns being privatized were performing
mediocrely, if not badly. BNP, the first on the list, announced for the
first half of 1993 profits of 552 million down by 60 per cent, a showing
for which the property crisis and the problems facing small businesses
were largely responsible (Petites et Moyennes Entreprises, PME).
Nevertheless, the level of funds was at a record high. The bankers'
concern was not to present a too favourable short-term situation.
Moreover, the Bourse had looked for a marked improvement in 1994

and non-voting preference shares rose by 35 per cent between January and September 1993, rising further, as has been noted, after the selling price of the shares was announced.

Rhône-Poulenc, coming second on the list, announced a drop of 30 per cent in its net results over the first nine months of 1993. The day before its privatization began, 15 November, it published half-yearly figures showing a loss of Ffr299 million, twice that for the third quarter of 1992 (the first nine months of 1993 remaining positive). The Banque Hervet had registered losses of Ffr361 million on 30 June 1993. It appeared to be better for a state-owned concern to record mediocre, even poor results, in order to be in a position to be privatized in 1993–4.

The second difference has to do with the use privatizations to which were put. In 1986-8 the proceeds of privatization went as a priority towards reducing national indebtedness. When they presented the second privatization programme in May 1993, the Minister for the Economy, Edmond Alphandéry, and the Minister for the Budget, Nicolas Sarkhozy, made it quite clear that the purpose was no longer to reduce the scale of indebtedness; the proceeds would be integrated in the budget and go to finance the government's employment schemes.

The third difference relates to the political and intellectual context of privatization. The election campaign in March 1993 centred round the debate about the entitlement to welfare ('*acquis sociaux*' in President Mitterrand's phrase). With the French economy in recession and unemployment rising inexorably to near the three million mark, neo-liberalism was scarcely reassuring. The Maastricht referendum revealed the underlying anxiety in public opinion. Hence the neo-liberal veneer to privatization had gone, and with it controversy; none accompanied the sale of BNP although it had been in the public domain since 1945.[8] The President of the Republic, expressing his views on the occasion of the customary press conference of 14 July and commenting upon the Balladur government agenda, voiced further reserves in the context of national independence. He exhorted the government to 'tread very warily where the defence of France is concerned, as in the area of research, the very heart of what constitutes our capability, our strength, our security and our intelligence'. And he cited four enterprises which, in his view, presented a problem. SNECMA, 'maker of aero-engines'; Aérospatiale, 'a paragon and not to be broken up'; Elf, 'the means to safeguard our purchasing capacity for energy production'; and finally Air France, 'for reasons of national prestige'. This suggests a process of reasoning not far removed from what David Henderson calls 'Do it yourself economics' (Henderson, 1986). Insofar as these four concerns, with the exception of Elf (which, it will be recalled, was partially privatized by a Socialist government), were experiencing major financial problems, François Mitterrand took no great risks. None of the firms mentioned stood much chance of being candidates for privatization in the immediate future. Even so there was no question of his not having put his finger on the major problem with the new privatization programme.

## Problems and perspectives of privatization in France

Until now only concerns that have shown themselves to be competitive have been privatized. There remains the problem of those with low productivity and monopolies. Privatization theory itself would say that they are the ones to be privatized in the first place in order to take up the slack and make them more market-orientated, since privatization necessarily involves deregulation and exposure to competition. But the key Air France strike in October 1993 probably marked a turning-point. After giving its support to the fairly modest restructuring plan of its chairman, Bernard Attali, a first step towards the contemplated privatization, the government disowned his action and backed down. Bernard Attali resigned. In mid-November 1993 the personnel of Air Inter took over from those at Air France, in the event protesting at the aim to open Air Inter's most profitable lines to competition (Air Inter, servicing lines within France, had been a subsidiary of Air France since 1992). Independently of any possible reversal on the stock market, the outlook for privatization was affected by these events. Resistance on the part of employees emerged as a factor strong enough to adjourn the process, and this in the firms which most needed restructuring (as a preliminary to privatization and in its wake). In addition measures to open public monopolies to competition, which were developed under pressure from Brussels, appeared to be unpopular both with their own workforces and with the public at large. Privatization and deregulation are closely linked in people's minds and opposition is growing.

But looking beyond the consequences of disaffection in regard to privatization, where the context is more social than economic, the juncture affords an opportunity to make two comments about the development of French society. The first concerns the role of the élite, their functioning and renewal. Since the change of political power in 1981 (the formation of a socialist government for the first time in the Fifth Republic), the public sector in France has been the arena for a kind of spoils system *à la française*. Every political change has been accompanied by a change in those heading the major state enterprises, not unlike musical chairs. To take an example, in the autumn of 1993 the government led by Edouard Balladur wanted to have people of its own persuasion at the head of the large groups due for privatization. Jacques Friedmann, who had been one of the architects of the 1986 programme, replaced Jean Peyrelevade, earlier one of the advisers to Pierre Mauroy, prime minister of the first socialist administration, at the head of UAP (Union des Assurances de Paris). Jean Peyrelevade replaced Jean-Yves Haberer at the head of Crédit Lyonnais; Jean-Yves Haberer replaced Yves Lyon-Caen, formerly deputy head of socialist prime minister Michel Rocard's private office, at the head of Crédit National. Earlier, Michel Pébereau had been appointed to the chairmanship of BNP and Philippe Jaffré to that of Elf. Movement such as this, not dissimilar to that affecting prefects on changes of government, is not in the least exceptional. Yet with the privatization of the major state-owned concerns it will no longer be possible. The process whereby the senior élite in France circulate and reproduce must certainly be affected. Will the *grands corps* system continue to vet and supervise appointments, across changes in political power, or will a new and different method for selecting the business élite emerge, one closer to models elsewhere? It is too early to know the answer, but this aspect of the effects of privatization will provide rewarding study. One significant detail: the representative of the German bank IKB (with a 5 per cent stake) on the board of Crédit National protested against Yves Lyon-Caen's dismissal on the grounds that he should have been consulted and that the change was the expression of a political decision and as such alien to business rationale.

The second comment is a more general one. The course of privatization is bound to throw light on the way that the structure of French society is developing. Indeed, as we have endeavoured to show in this article, for some years now France has hesitated between a model that is home-grown, interventionist and original, and one that is European. What is at issue with privatization is that very dichotomy. Is the eclipse of what Christian Saint-Etienne (1992) has described as the 'French exception' inevitable, or is it not? The fact that on 9 November 1993 the CNPF, the body which represents the larger employers in France, proposed the setting up of pension funds to organize for retirement through capitalization suggests that the movement towards privatization falls within a larger, all-embracing logic that implies the gradual disappearance of the extensive public sector in France, a more decisive role for financial markets, and the decline of the distributive system of welfare benefit and, more generally, of collective protection for individuals against sickness, unemployment and old age. As for industrial policy and policy in regard to public services, the French model is that of an expert in planning and organization. Methods and resources are centralized and subjected to control, value is attached to technical expertise, wastage is looked on askance (why let several firms perform the same function?), the goals set are long-term ones. Market mechanisms are not understood and little appreciated: the market is too myopic, too disorderly. It is not like the gardens of France where the paths are straight, the trees pruned and trim and the flowerbeds geometrical. And this is a model whose achievements are beyond dispute. Certainly there are some dark areas, but public services in France have kept pace with modernization and attained a high level of quality.

Is France ready to agree to its monopolies becoming open to competition, its social model being, in part at least, called into question, and to the process of restructuring getting underway again, all of this in the interests of closer European integration? Is France ready to 'relinquish' its traditional model for administering the economy and social welfare? For the moment the absence of debate surrounding privatization obscures these fundamental questions. But it will open up again before long. The fate of the privatization programme will be a good indication of the choices finally settled on.

## Notes

1. Results accruing from privatization in the world in 1992 put at 300 billion dollars (Mentré, 1992–3).
2. In the matter of the purchase of Woodchester Investments by Crédit Lyonnais as in that of a subsidiary of British Aerospace by Thomson. In neither case did the Director General of Fair Trading consider there to exist any threat to competition. The Secretary of State, disregarding the DGFT's opinion, referred directly to MMC (Dumez and Jeunemaître, 1991).
3. The five main industrial groups nationalized in 1981 – CGE, Saint-Gobain, Thomson, Rhône-Poulenc & Péchiney moved from a deficit of Ffr4.5 billion into a profit of Ffr4.6 billion in 1986.
4. Estimations vary with sources. Baring Securities supplied the following figures: Ffr130 billion collected, of which 42 billion from public sales offer on French market, 27,5 million in mutual investment (*noyaux durs*) and 11 billion from international tranche.
5. Sale of a part of Elf-Aquitaine capital took place on 19 September.
6. Half the 2.8 million who bought shares in the BNP privatization were clients of the bank. The bank's marketing section made a great effort to attract investment from account holders.
7. Following privatization, BNP shares rapidly reached 280 francs on the Paris Bourse, i.e. a market premium of 16.6 per cent.
8. BNP resulted from the merging of BNCI and Comptoir National d'Escompte, both nationalized in 1945.

# References

Balladur, E. (1987), *Je crois en l'homme plus qu'en l'Etat*, Paris, Flammarion.

Bentégeat, H. (1993), 'Privatisations: un magot de 500 milliards de francs', *L'Expansion*, 19 mai–2 juin: 71–76.

Cartelier, L. (1992), 'L'expérience française de privatisation: bilan et enseignements', *Revue Internationale de Droit Économique*, **3**: 375–402.

Cohen, E. and Bauer, M. (1985), *Les Grandes manoeuvres industrielles*. Paris, Belfond.

Dumez, H. and Jeunemaître, A. (1989), *Diriger l'économie. L'État et les prix en France (1936–1986)*. Paris, l'Harmattan.

Dumez, H. and Jeunemaître, A. (1990), 'A style of economic regulation. France 1969–1989', *Government and Policy*, **8**: 139–48.

Dumez, H. and Jeunemaître, A. (1991), *La concurrence en Europe*, Paris, Seuil.

Hamdouch, A. (1989), *L'État d'influence. Nationalisations et privatisations en France*, Paris, Presses du C.N.R.S.

Henderson, D. (1986), *Innocence and Design: on the influence of economic ideas on policy*, Oxford, Basil Blackwell.

Kuisel, R. (1984), *Le capitalisme et l'État en France. Modernisation et dirigisme au XX^e siècle*, trad. franc, Paris, Gallimard.

Mentré, P. (1992–3), 'Les privatisations. Bilans et perspectives', *Commentaire*, **60**, hiver: 861–9.

Morin, F. (1993), 'L'onde de choc', *Le Monde*, 1 septembre: 14.

Padioleau, J.G. (1981), *Quand la France s'enferre. La politique sidérurgique de la France depuis 1945*, Paris, P.U.F.

Saint-Étienne, C. (1992), *L'exception française. Pour un nouveau modèle démocratique de croissance*, Paris, Armand Colin.

Wright, V. (1990), 'The nationalization and privatization of French public enterprises 1981–1988: radical ambitions, diluted programmes and limited impact' *Staatswissenschaften und Staatspraxis*, **2**: 176–201.

Zinsou-Derlin, L. (1985), *Le fer de lance, essai sur les nationalisations industrielles*, Paris, Olivier Orban.

# CHAPTER 5

## GERMANY: SYMBOLIC PRIVATIZATIONS IN A SOCIAL MARKET ECONOMY

### Josef Esser

As in other Western industrial societies of a liberal-capitalist nature, social and economic discussions in the Federal Republic have been dominated since the mid-1970s by the neo-liberals. However, the latter had to wait until the autumn of 1982 before they could begin to think about implementing their strategies. It was the conservative-liberal government, comprising the Christian Democrats of the CDU-CSU (its Bavarian sister party) and the liberals of the FDP, which was the first to include in its programme its intention of reducing state influence on the private economy and of strengthening market forces. The new government also clearly defined its position on the privatization of public property: it underlined in its 1983 annual economy report its desire to work for a policy that would reduce the activities of the state to those that were appropriate, to transfer as far as possible public services to the private sector and to privatize public goods whenever possible without harming the interests of the state.

Since that date however the liberal conservative government has carried out its promise only to a very small extent in spite of an uninterrupted period of office. This has created increasing disappointment amongst neo-liberal theorists who have complained that the privatization and deregulation measures promised by the government have remained insignificant (Woll, 1987).

The debate on privatization was again reactivated in Germany in 1990 following the collapse of communism in East Germany and the process of reunification which was thereby triggered. A new policy emerged and this concerned the vast public sector of the eastern part of the country. The declared intention was to convert into competitive private enterprises the 9000 firms and holdings which were 'the people's property' under the Germany Democratic Republic (GDR). This new debate on privatization was also completely dominated by neo-liberal thinking. There was certainly no question of defining as a priority strategies of industrial and structural policies to strengthen the key elements of the East German economy. Emphasis was placed on the need to bring about a rapid, brutal and effective break with the past, in line with Schumpeter's concept of 'creative destruction'. However, since the spring of 1991 this crash programme has been abandoned, and privatization is no more than one objective amongst many others to improve the situation of non-profitable firms with the help of the state.

In this chapter we shall attempt to explain the clear reluctance of the State to pursue a radical privatization programme in spite of the demands of the mass media and of the neo-liberals. We shall begin by giving an outline of the West German nationalized sector, its significance and its structure. This will be followed by an analysis of the privatization policy of the conservative liberal government. Then, having briefly explored the causes of the 'symbolic privatization' and of the limited deregulation of the telecommunications sector we shall describe the policy that has so far been carried out by the Treuhand (the state body which has been given the task of privatizing the East German economy). It will be shown that after an initial hard-line policy characterized by neo-liberalism the policy has increasingly approximated the traditional West German social market model.

## Size and structure of the public sector in West Germany

When describing the public sector in West Germany it is important to distinguish between property which belongs to the Federation, that which belongs to the Länder and that of the towns and other local authorities. Naturally, a detailed study of the public sector (which cannot be undertaken here) would be necessary in order to show the extreme variety of situations concerning the public sector since the position changes from Land to Land and from one town to another. There is a similar situation in the local and regional level policies of privatization which differ markedly across the country. However, the following point should be observed. Very often the following duties are carried out at Länder or local level: rubbish collection, public health and public housing, gas and electricity supply, education and training, transport and road systems. Functions relating to rubbish collection, slaughterhouses, swimming pools, schools, and local transport systems are carried out at local level, whereas the Länder look after the energy supply, universities, and credit organizations. The German Federal Bank put at DM370 billion the value of the enterprises belonging to all the public authorities. In 1988 the shares of the Länder in the capital of these enterprises amounted to some DM12.3 billion, those of the Federation to about DM6.5 billion – in other words about half of the value of that belonging to the Länder (*Wirtschaftswoche*, 1988: 15).

Without doubt the twelve Länder banks constituted, both from an economic as well as a social viewpoint, the most important element in the sector belonging to the sub-national authorities. The four major Länder banks were the Westdeutsche Landesbank with assets worth DM141 billion, the Bayerische Landesbank with DM115 billions, the Norddeutsche Landesbank with DM69 billion, the Hessische Landesbank with DM69 billion. These banks have been transformed into universal banks. One would find nobody in the Federal Republic and especially in the governments of the Länder or in the councils of the major local authorities who would envisage the privatization of such effective credit bodies. Politicians of all political persuasions consider these banks to be vital instruments of structural and regional policies. Indeed, at the moment the principal issue concerns the possible merger of these banks so that they may remain competitive in financial markets which are increasingly liberalized and internationalized. When (as in the case of Hesse in 1988) a Christian Democratic Land government decided to give up its shares in the Land bank they were bought by savings banks which belonged to the local authorities within the same Land.

The privatization ambitions of the neo-liberals initially targeted local services. They have come to very little. No doubt the occasional town has privatized a local service such as rubbish collection or street cleaning. Several towns have also sold some of their properties to reduce their debt. However, on the whole, and irrespective of the political persuasion of the local authority local services have remained firmly in the public domain. Indeed, when the Federal Government does decide upon very limited policies of deregulation and privatization either the policies have no impact at Land or local level or the local and Land authorities buy what the Federation has decided to sell.

Consequently, when analysing the policy of privatization in Germany it is essential to exclude large parts of the considerable public sector belonging to the towns and to the Länder. At this sub-central level, the public sector is underpinned by a complex and widespread network of economic, political and social interests, and has become a significant means to pursue specific objectives in the field of infrastructure, transport, training, social and industrial policy. Until now, this system has remained perfectly intact. In other words, at the local and Länder level there is a wide consensus on the need to respect the social market economy. There is a feeling that public enterprises are needed to compensate for market failures – in both social and infrastructural terms. Naturally, these enterprises have to be competitive and efficient. But to the extent that they fulfil these conditions and are unlikely to improve their social and economic performance, local and Länder interests see no point in calling into question the current consensus. Nevertheless, there is a debate, which is just beginning in certain localities, on the virtues of public-private partnership inspired by the British and American models. This debate may give rise to practical policies.

In the remainder of this chapter we shall be discussing the industrial public sector of the central government, since it is only there that privatization on an appreciable scale is envisaged. It is worth recalling that this sector dates from the Weimar Republic or the Nazi period. It is embedded in political will, being advocated by both the pre-war Right and Left, and rooted in the ambition to industrialize the country rapidly in order to catch up with Britain and the USA (Himmelmann 1986, Knauss 1986). After World War II there was no nationalization in West Germany, either of major sectors or of firms in difficulty. As a result, the central government's public sector remained smaller than that of many European countries where powerful working-class movements were able to impose extensive nationalization programmes. The Germany working-class movement advocated nationalization in its early post-war programmes, but it was too weak politically to have it implemented. On the other hand, there was no one in West Germany who wished to denationalize the existing public sector. And the West German Constitution even protects, in Article 87, the state monopoly in the Federal railway system, in the postal and telecommunications sectors, and inland navigable waterways. A two-thirds majority in both houses of the German Parliament is required to break up the monopoly.

Christian Democrat governments of the 1950s and 1960s, which were far from being neo-liberal, fully exploited the public sector, inherited from Weimar and the National Socialists, in order politically to support the economic reconstruction of the country. And the Social Democratic-Free Democrats coalition government of the 1970s mobilized it to back its Keynesian-inspired mixed economy model. Andrew Shonfield rightly described West Germany during these decades as a market economy which was both free and organized (Shonfield, 1965), a combination of a class of unshackled entrepreneurs, effective professional organizations, a banking and public industrial sector anxious to further industrial policy, and a state willing to intervene in any social or economic area if a perceived 'national interest' dictated such intervention.

During the 1970s the industrial public sector controlled by the central government grew sharply. The reason was clear. The most important public sector groups included steel, coal and shipbuilding, which internationalization rendered increasingly competitive. In these circumstances, all such firms attempted to widen their industrial base by buying shares in companies which were involved in downstream activities. As a result, the number of firms in which the Federation held at least 25 per cent of the shares increased from 697 in 1970 to 958 to 1982.

Table 5.1 enables us to assess the size of the Federation's public sector when the Christian Democrats regained office.

**Table 5.1**   Germany: size of Federations's public sector

|  | Revenue | | Net Value Added | | Workforce | |
|---|---|---|---|---|---|---|
|  | 1982 | 1983 | 1982 | 1983 | 1982 | 1983 |
| *Majority shareholding* | | | | | | |
| Salgzgitter | 9,391 | 9,474 | 3,270 | 2,342 | 55,455 | 51,491 |
| VIAG | 5,877 | 5,900 | 1,705 | 1,857 | 24,869 | 24,435 |
| Saarberg | 6,165 | 6,594 | 1,971 | 1,695 | 32,599 | 31,963 |
| IVG | 580 | 600 | 294 | 323 | 4,001 | 4,133 |
| Total | 22,013 | 22,568 | 7,240 | 6,217 | 116,924 | 112,022 |
| *Minority shareholding* | | | | | | |
| VEBA | 50,533 | 49,189 | 6,689 | 6,662 | 80,474 | 77,157 |
| VW | 37,434 | 40,089 | 9,161 | 9,.831 | 239,116 | 231,710 |
| Total | 87,967 | 89,278 | 15,850 | 16,493 | 319,500 | 308,867 |
| Total | 109,980 | 111,846 | 23,090 | 22,170 | 436,514 | 420,889 |

*Source*: F. Knauss (1986: 227).

Compared with the situation in other European countries these figures are rather modest. In 1978 the major public sector enterprises comprised 13.7 per cent of the turnover of the 269 biggest companies in the country: with 3.9 per cent of total turnover, the West German public sector was the smallest in Western Europe a long way behind Austria (with 82 per cent), which had the biggest public sector, France (24.9 per cent), Great Britain (12.5 per cent) and Italy with 51.8 per cent (Czada, 1983: 256; Dunning and Pearce, 1981).

Table 5.2 provides data relating to the share, by industrial sector, belonging to the Federal Government, in terms of the percentage of domestic production. The over-representation of the public sector in problem-ridden industries – coal, steel, shipbuilding – emerges clearly.

**Table 5.2**  Germany: Share of industrial Federal sector in different industries (in % of national production)

|              | 1982 | 1983 |
|--------------|------|------|
| Coal         | 12.4 | 12.2 |
| Lignite      | 5.2  | 5.4  |
| Steel bars   | 9.8  | 8.7  |
| Rolled steel | 11.1 | 10.2 |
| Oil          | 9.9  | 9.9  |
| Aluminium    | 48.7 | 50.3 |
| Electricity  | 28.0 | 28.9 |
| Car industry | 36.8 | 36.3 |
| Shipbuilding | 10.6 | 14.1 |
| Glass        | 21.0 | 21.3 |

*Source*: F. Knauss (1986: 227).

The most important direct stakes of the central state in 1983 involved the Salzgitter steel group (100 per cent owned), Lufthansa, the national flag carrier (74.3 per cent), the mines of the Saabergwerke (74 per cent), Vereinigte Industrirunternehmen, a holding company with interests in electricity, gas and aluminium (86.5 per cent), Industrienerwaltungs – GMbh, which is active in industrial share buying, property deals, transport and oil (100 per cent). The central state has important minority holdings in powerful German companies such as VEBA, the energy and chemical group (43.8 per cent). In 1982, through its stake in the Deutsche Bundesbank, (excluding the central bank) the federal state held a significant place in the country's banking system – just behind the Deutsche Bank and Westdeutsche Bank (itself a public bank since it belongs to the Land of Rheinland-Westphalia). The most important part of the Federal state's banking arsenal is the Kreditanstalt für Wiederaufban, which specializes in providing financial aid for industrial development and export guarantee loans. The Lastenausgleichsbank falls within a similar category of central state interventionist mechanisms: it was initially set up to finance the programmes for integrating political refugees from the East. This body, together with the Credit Institute for Reconstruction, has become the major instrument for managing the European Recovery Programme. Mention should also be made of the Deutsche Siedlungs-und Landesrentenbank (which provides aid to the agricultural sector), the Berliner Industriebank (which financed help for the West Berlin economy), the Deutsche Pfandbriefanstalt, together with its subsidiary the Bau-und Bodenbank (which is involved in local government financing), and the Deutsche Verkehrs-und Kreditbank (which serves its sole shareholder – the German Federal Railways).

In the scientific field, too, the central state has considerable leverage. The Federal Ministry of Research and Technology controls fourteen research institutions, often together with the Land in which an Institute is located. These research institutes are charged with ensuring technological innovation, in close collaboration with the private sector (Hohn and Schimank, 1990). Finally, we should note the Treuarbeit, which plays an important role in structural and industrial policy by examining the balance sheets and potential of firms which apply for Federal aid. The Treuarbeit belongs to the Federal state and 5 Länder, each of which has an 11 per cent stake in the body.

## The privatization programme in West Germany

The first privatization measures taken in West Germany date from 1959–1965 with the denationalization of Preussag and the partial denationalization of VEBA and of Volkswagen. The failure of these privatizations was to play an important role in shaping the perceptions of governments involved in later privatization programmes. At the time, there was no question of making privatization an integral part of a wider programme of pushing economic policy in a different direction. Rather, the programme was designed to widen ownership as part of a policy of giving people a share in the country. The campaign in favour of popular capitalism was linked with the socio-political programme of the social market economy: its purpose was to make each citizen a committed manager-owner who was economically autonomous. However, this programme of redistributing national wealth was not a success. The major reason lay in the reluctance of large sections of the German population to invest their savings in equity: they preferred to put their money into investment with guaranteed returns. This situation has not changed since that time. The average German has little confidence in shares: only 11 per cent of West German wealth in 1990 was in equity. Financial investment is almost entirely related to guaranteed savings plans, life insurance or plans linked to housing.

When the liberal conservative government in 1983 committed itself to an overall privatization programme, it was reacting to the increasing pressure, largely ideologically inspired, exerted by neo-liberal circles and professional investors, and by the Free Democrats who belonged to the government coalition. There was no real economic necessity, but there was a need to underline the break with the immediate Social Democratic past. It must be emphasized that the pressure for a radical programme was largely symbolic. The industrial sectors that were of long-term strategic significance in the international marketplace were already in the private sector, and the public sector, as already noted, was not very extensive. Moreover, when the privatization programme was being defined, governmental circles became aware of the important role played by public bodies, banks, research institutes and infrastructure such as the postal services and telecommunications, railways and air transport in underpinning the social and political bases of the export-driven West German model. Apart from its largely symbolic aspect, the new privatization programme was expected to help state finances by the sale of some of the jewels in the national industrial crown.

Although the principle of privatization was decided in 1983, the Federal Minister of Finance waited two years before presenting his general programme. This prolonged period underlines the divisions over privatization within the government coalition and within the interest groups close to the coalition. In the meantime, and as a sop to an increasingly impatient Free Democratic Party, it was decided partially to privatize the apparently problem-free VEBA company. In the first place, the Federal government reduced its stake from 48 to about 30 per cent, and decided not to take part in the recapitalization of the company – which had the effect of reducing its stake to 25.6 per cent. This stake was later sold to private investors. The attempt to privatize through a policy of widespread share ownership was, as in the past, a failure. Over 4 million shares were sold but to only 521,000 new shareholders.

When the Federal Minister of Finance eventually outlined his general privatization programme in 1985, he announced that only thirteen companies were in a fit state to be privatized. All the other public firms were either financially not viable, were in deep crisis (the steel, coal mining and shipbuilding companies) or had to be kept in the public sector for industrial policy reasons (the case, for example, of the state-controlled banking sector, the research institutes, the railways and the postal and telecommunications services).

Furthermore, the Minister announced that in the thirteen cases of proposed privatization he intended to retain a stake in line with the strategic needs of the Federation. In the majority of cases this involved retaining a 51 per cent stake. In others a 25.1 per cent holding was deemed adequate. What is striking, therefore, is that the privatization programme was far from radical. Nevertheless, it triggered a wave of protests, even within the government. As a result, the cabinet decided, in March 1985, to reduce the list of thirteen to five: VIAG, Volkswagen, Prakla-Seismos, Deutsche Pfandbriefenstalt, Deutsche-und Landesrentenbank. In the other cases it was agreed to explore the matter further or to postpone to the following legislature (1987–1991). Since then, other public sector firms, including the telecommunications and transport sector have been placed on the policy agenda.

How far has the privatization been implemented? In 1988 the Federal state got rid of its remaining stakes in Volkswagen and VIAG. In both cases, it is interesting to note that the two Länder which also partly owned the companies did not follow the central government's example: Lower Saxony retained its 20 per cent stake in Volkswagen for regional industrial policy reasons, and Bavaria, for the same reason, sought through Bayernwerk A.G., in which it had a holding, a 15 per cent stake in VIAG. Once the steel crisis had abated, Salzgitter was also privatized. On the other hand, Bavaria increased its stake in Maxhütte, a steel-maker, just before it was to be declared bankrupt.

The central government also reduced its stake in Deutsche Verkehrs-Kredit Bank (to 75.1 per cent), in Deutsche-und Landesrentenbank (to 55 per cent) and in Deutsche Pfandbriefanstalt (to 81 per cent). The part-privatization of the DSL was greeted with considerable opposition. The crucial role played by this bank in the state financing of agriculture pressured the Minister of Agriculture to intervene in the privatization debate. The compromise which was finally reached involves the DSL remaining a public law institution with administrative functions. The private banks that favoured the privatization of DSL were far from happy.

The privatization of Lufthansa has also provoked several disputes, notably between Bavaria and the Federal government. The initial plan was to reduce the central government's stake from 79.9 to 55 per cent. The CSU, the Bavarian sister party of the CDU, was opposed to such a proposal, arguing that it would be unwise to undermine the national role of the airline by introducing foreign capital into the company. The state had to remain the dominant owner. The CSU also raised the vexed question of national defence, since Lufthansa was obliged in the case of armed conflict to place its aircraft at the disposal of the armed forces. Behind this appeal to national interest there lay the real reason for Bavarian opposition, and it was rooted in the industrial policy of the Land. For it is in Bavaria that German aircraft and aerospace industries are concentrated (with Messer-Schmidt-Bölkow-Blohm, MBB, now inte-grated into Deutsche Aerospace, a subsidiary of Daimler-Benz). The German parts of the European Airbus programme are also located in Bavaria. Franz Josef Strauss, Minister President of Bavaria, was chairman of the board of Airbus. The fear of the Bavarians was to see a privati-zation of Lufthansa leading to an undermining of the close links which had been established between Lufthansa, MBB and Airbus through the judicious use of state procurement policies. In the controversies within the government coalition the Free Democrats lost ground to the CSU. In spite of repeated accusations of advocating state capitalism, the latter maintained its opposition to the privatization of the national flag carrier. After lengthy debates in the cabinet, it won the day; it was decided to retain the Federal stake in Lufthansa. Nevertheless, Bavaria was unable to prevent the 'passive privatization' of the company, since it was agreed that it could raise new capital on the private financial markets, thus effectively reducing the public stake. However, Bavaria reacted by increasing its own shareholding. When Daimler-Benz took control of MBB, with the massive backing of the Bonn government which was keen to strengthen the German aerospace industry, the Länder of Bavaria, Hamburg and Bremen refused to sell their stakes in MBB, thus becoming minority shareholders in Deutsche Aerospace, the subsidiary of Daimler-Benz.

On the whole, it must be concluded that the 1985 privatization programme has been only partially implemented – even though the Free Democratic Party, a key coalition partner of the CDU, had denounced the timidity of the 1985 programme.

The only point on which the coalition appeared to be united was the need to sell certain parts of the family silver in order to raise money for the state budget. Nevertheless, the supporters of privatization were content with the measures taken. They were, it was argued, symbolic in character, and suggested that a Germany which appeared stuck in the mire of corporatism had finally decided to smash some of the taboos surrounding denationalization. Eventually, one might even envisage a more radical neo-liberal economic policy.

Vast changes in the telecommunications sector at international and European level have pressured West Germany, and many other countries, to call into question its status as a state monopoly – a status hitherto sacrosanct in nature. German neo-liberals have demanded its outright privatization, as in the USA, Britain and Japan. However, once again the Bonn government has so far refused to follow the neo-liberal path in spite of considerable pressure from the Free Democrats. Nevertheless, Bonn recognizes the key importance of the role played by the Federal postal system in creating the new telecommunications technical infrastructure (notably the Integrated Service Digital Network or ISDN), as well as the increasing importance of telecommunications for German competitiveness. It has, therefore, accepted that new organizational structures are required to enable quicker and more flexible reactions to technical, economic and political change.

Hence a governmental advisory commission was set up in 1985 for the purpose of examining the problem. It included, in addition to scientists and legal and business experts, senior representatives of professional associations concerned, delegates from all parties represented in the Bundestag, representatives from the Länder and a representative of the postal union, Deutsche Postgewerkschaft (DPG).

Following wide-ranging discussions lasting two-and-a-half years, the commission reached a broad compromise on the future of telecommunications, a compromise that provides the basis for the Act of 1 July 1989 on the structure of postal services, whereby Germany telecommunications have been reorganized.

What is remarkable about the changes proposed is that, in spite of obvious conflicts of interest between manufacturers of transmission equipment and information and communication technology industries, as between users, constructors and installation engineers, the commission achieved a compromise that was 'broadly capitalist' in character, yet resulting less in privatization than in 'mild deregulation'. The administrative function is distinguished from the strictly business functions and transferred to a reorganised Ministry for Postal Services and Telecommunications, which is now the central regulatory authority in this sphere. Federal postal services – Deutsche Bundespost – are subdivided into three relatively autonomous state-owned enterprises responsible respectively for postal services, financial services linked to the post office and telecommunications, each having at its head a newly-created managerial body. Cross-subsidization on the part of the profitable sector by way of compensation has authorization only for a limited transitional period. Telekom retains its monopoly and has sole responsibility for setting up ISDN. Furthermore, a distinction is made between the 'network monopoly', which administratively is in the public domain, and the market domain. Transmission services of all kinds as well as terminal equipment may be manufactured and put on the market by private firms with whom Telekom must compete.

This measure of liberalization within services and in the manufacture and distribution of equipment came in response to the demands of the private sector. However, at the same time, the strategic function of the technological policy, that is the effective implementation of ISDN and the standardization and normalization of a unified obligatory form of technology, remains a federal monopoly. This arrangement takes into account the interests of the Länder for whom the monopoly position of Telekom provides a guarantee of equitable distribution of equipment as regards the network and telephone services. In fact, the agreement of the Länder was vital in any restructuring of post and telecommunications.

Although Telekom has not been privatized, its functioning is now more subject to market mechanisms. So as to be able to finance the considerable cost of setting up ISDN on its own, it will need to perform in the same way as a service concern in the private sector. Both management orientation and work practice have to be adapted to marketing objectives and methods; rationalization is essential, entailing job losses and new working conditions, with a view to both higher quality and greater efficiency. The agreement of the post office workers union was won only after fierce resistance; for a long time it opposed the compromise plan put forward, but, be.ng in a weak position, was eventually obliged to accept it as the lesser of two evils. Even so, the question was not finally settled until 1994, and debate continues in Germany in some circles over whether or not Telekom should be totally privatized. From the government's point of view, this would afford the possibility of further budgetary revenue to help finance the integration of the eastern territories. Further, Telekom would be rid of the constraints affecting it as a public service and free to negotiate problems of wage levels, working conditions and work categories. Telekom would also welcome the opportunity to compete internationally, since its present status as a public corporation denies it the right to do. Naturally, the whole debate goes back over the format of the wellknown corporatist model. There had to be agreement with the main opposition party, the SPD, in order to make sure of the two-thirds majority in the Bundesrat required to repeal the constitutional status of the postal services; and the agreement of the Länder to such privatization would need to be assured or they might well veto the measure. Lastly, the consent of the post office union (Deutsche Postgewerkschaft) is essential, as is that of the body representing government officials, if the two major parties – CDU and SPD – are not to find their hands tied.

To understand precisely why the privatization process in Germany has been so hesitant, it has to be appreciated that public ownership of industrial corporations is relatively insignificant, and that the sectors of industry which are crucial in the drive for exports – mechanical engineering, construction of industrial equipment, car manufacture, chemical and electrical industries, to name only the most important ones – are privately owned. Consequently, a highly sophisticated and effective financial sector based on private capital is in place, whose interests closely interlock with those of West German industry. Unlike the situation that applies in other European countries, a policy of privatization is not, from an economic standpoint, of paramount importance in making sure that Germany is competitive in world markets.

Then again – a factor closely linked to that just mentioned and one plain to observe – there is no significant political or social force in Germany to advocate a massive privatization programme, no professional business associations, no trade unions, neither of the two main political parties. On the contrary, there is an effective consensus, generally speaking among political parties, unions and business associations that public assets should not be privatized so long as they are considered essential for industrial and regional policy. This is true for the major research institutes, telecommunications, federally owned banks such as Kreditanstalt für Wiederaufbau, air transport (Lufthansa), or again, at regional and local level, energy distribution and a certain number of business concerns. In all these sectors, the view has not changed that federal government intervention, in either monopolistic or majority share-holding form, is perfectly right and proper. But it is also true that in general the view is for these concerns to be run in line with market criteria, as regards profitability, competitiveness and so on. Accordingly, the current debate on privatization at all levels is in the main taken up with the issue of whether and to what degree these concerns are continuing to satisfy the demands of an enterprise economy.

Politically speaking, the only discordant voice here is that of the FDP, which has been forced by growing interparty rivalry to take a more aggressive stance on behalf of the interests of its relatively wealthy clientèle, who want more investment alternatives. The CDU certainly needs to take account of its neo-liberal partner in government; at the same time it cannot afford to disregard sections among its own electorate who clamour for wider possibilities of share flotation. Herein lies the crux of the somewhat symbolic character that German policy has taken on in respect of privatization. While this category of voters needs to be appeased, it has to be made clear to them that their interests, justifiable though they are, have to be deferred for the time being.

However, the broad mass of the electorate do not see privatization and deregulation as self-evident political objectives. In the wake of the unhappy experience of the sale of Volksaktien, popular share-holding capitalism no longer holds vote-winning properties either for the major parties or with the electorate. People emphatically prefer to put their savings into low-risk stock or into property.

A third important factor to explain the reserve evident in privatization policy in Germany is attributable to the country's political system and institutions. Devolution of power at regional and local levels has resulted in extreme fragmentation of political decision-making, hence the need for a co-ordinating role at federal level in order for it to function properly (Lehmbruch, 1976), and a whole range of institutional and technical 'political interlocking' devices (Scharpf *et al.* 1976; Ellwein & Hesse, 1987). Hardly surprisingly, municipalities and Länder have not the slightest intention of parting with public ownership given the advantages that accrue to them in areas of local and regional policy. Their preference would be for what the FDP disdainfully terms 'state capitalism': having at their disposal the wherewithal to conduct an appropriate policy in terms of research, technology and industrial development, meanwhile retaining the option to subsidize research and innovation among smaller firms.

Consequently, local and regional authorities stand in the way of federal privatization plans and, moreover, are able to exercise their veto on issues such as railway privatization or telecommunications. For all these reasons the aims of privatization were early on focused on no more than a few concerns, which had been brought into public ownership for historical motives and had proved themselves profitable. The debate over the principle of privatization, and when, and how, involved not merely the interests of a small number of shareholders eager to enlarge their portfolios, but fiscal considerations, the urge to bring a measure of reform into the distribution of national assets, as well as the concerns of industrial policy. In other words, the key factors in the coalition government's privatization policy spring from fiscal considerations or its symbolic function.

## Privatization policy in East Germany following reunification

It remains for us, by way of conclusion, to examine the degree to which the ongoing process of privatizing concerns in East Germany that were formerly the 'property of the people' may affect the overall policy of privatization in the new united Germany.

The Treuhand was set up in March 1990 by the GDR, while still autonomous. Its task was to convert the 9000 nationalized firms and holding companies, representing at the same time some 7 million workers, into business companies and require them to be run in accordance with the economy of the market. Bonn then used its pressure to make changes in the Treuhand's management, placing its own managers of proven capacity in key administrative posts in what has been termed the 'largest industrial holding company in the world' (Frau Breuel, chair of the Treuhand).

After reunification, the Treuhand became a legally constituted entity under the legal and technical supervision of the Federal Ministry of Finance. The 9 members of its Board and the 24 members of its management enjoy a considerable degree of autonomy in defining which of the 9000 firms under their jurisdiction shall be candidates for survival, whether they are to be split up, and if so how, and whether they are to be sold off, and if so to whom and for what price, and what should become of the proceeds. Examination of these problems is divided among 5 specialized sectors for the various industries and 15 subgroups regionally based, their task being to 'municipalize' immovable assets and privatize small firms operating in a fairly local context.

After reunification, the West German trade unions won the right to have four representatives on the board of management. Given that the Treuhand is not a joint-stock company under German law, the possibility for joint management by the unions does not exist; nevertheless, constant pressure on their part led to their being granted minimal participation. In conformity with the market ideology destined to prevail in the economic transformation process of the ex-GDR's reintegration, the Treuhand began by announcing that its priority was to privatize 'competitive' firms in East Germany and liquidate the remainder. Moreover, it took the view that structural problems – just as industrial and even social policy – were not within its competence. Naturally enough, with such a drastic policy of closures, the Treuhand rapidly made itself extremely unpopular not only with the East German population but also with the elected local and Länder representatives in the ex-GDR. Mass demonstrations, organized by the unions, began vehemently demanding that priority should be given to industrial rehabilitation before privatization or liquidation were considered. The feeling expressed itself strongly that the prime objective should be to preserve the basic industrial core and thus prevent the eastern part of Germany from being radically deindustrialized.

When in spring 1991 the number of job losses began to mount sharply, politicians and unions in East Germany increased their pressure on the Federal Government to force the Treuhand to alter its priorities. Indeed within the ranks of the CDU protests grew more vociferous, even to the point of threatening the party's unity. Consequently, from that spring onwards the Treuhand gave greater consideration to the rehabilitation of non-profitable concerns and set about finding ways to consolidate key areas of industry, such as steel, chemicals, shipbuilding and engineering, even when private investors and purchasers were not forthcoming.

Furthermore and generally speaking, when a decision about a firm's future is taken, greater attention will need to be given to its combined repercussions on the industrial sector concerned, on the region and on the labour market. Anyway, regional authorities in East Germany have succeeded in acquiring more muscle. While the Treuhand is still alone entitled to pronounce on a firm's future, with the option of closure, expert 'economic cabinets' have now been set up in the five new Länder whom it is obliged to inform in advance of measures that are being considered. This requirement of prior notice has resulted in a kind of corporatist system of negotiation whereby the unions and municipal authorities concerned are brought in with the Treuhand and regional governments. In this way, the regional and union representatives on the Treuhand's management board find themselves in a considerably stronger position to put the case for specific local problems being taken into account.

It is too soon yet to say whether this new policy of rehabilitation and privatization is likely to be a fruitful one. What is clear from sales achieved and proclaimed intentions of buyers, from stop-gap measures for those left jobless and the level of investment required, is the fairly general prevalence of political intention. All that can be said is that the East German economy would by now have collapsed were it not for the West German taxpayer and the DM140 billion which are paid yearly in aid. It should be added that initial projects for radical privatization were abandoned early on. In the face of the threat of the eastern regions being deindustrialized wholesale, there was (nearly) general appreciation that market forces alone were incapable of carrying through the economic and social integration of the former GDR with the Federal Republic.

Now, and for a long time to come, the need for intervention and support on the part of the government is accepted, the only matter to be settled is how extensive such intervention should be. Is the answer an overall and systematic industrial policy with the setting-up of state-financed industrial holding companies (the view held by unions and SPD and to which certain areas of industry are sympathetic)? Or would the joint involvement of the Länder and private and publicly-owned banks in major developmental concerns within a region be sufficient (the view held by Federal Government and most professional associations)? At all events, which ever way the debate goes, it is now accepted that after the wave of neo-liberal euphoria opinion is moving back in the direction of the West German 'market economy' model.

## Interim conclusion

In regard to most political, economic and social problems, including those linked together at local and regional level, as they are because of the existence of the two major national parties, of the interlocking of federal system, region and locality, and of the strength and effectiveness of the more significant professional and social bodies, the solutions arrived at by the German 'social market' economy model continue to stand out in terms of the balance of economic success and social stability they achieve.

Efficiency and stability are, in fact, two sides of the same coin, one standing for continuing economic modernization, which meets with general acceptance because it succeeds, and which succeeds because it meets with general acceptance. The fact that an equation containing so many imponderables has so far regularly met with solutions would seem to be a vindication of the political and organizational resources of the social market economy. In the absence of any real urgency, why then abandon it in pursuance of a policy of privatization and deregulation, whose consequences are unforeseeable but whose pioneers – the USA and Britain – cannot boast of having achieved results as impressive as Germany's? When and if Germany resolves to embark on a wide-ranging and systematic policy of privatization and liberalization, it will be promoted neither by neo-liberal ideology nor by the need to take up some Thatcherite or Reaganite challenge, but by the urge to proceed with a radical restructuring of capitalism, in the direction of more all-embracing productive methods, greater internationalization of markets and greater regionalization of commercial forces. To seek now to estimate the consequences of such a development on the German social market economy model would be to indulge in fanciful speculation.

## References

Czada, R. (ed.) (1983), 'Nationalisierungspolitik', in M.G. Schmidt (ed.), *Westliche Industriegesellschaften*, Munich R. Piper.

Dunning, J.H. and Pearce, R.D. (1981), *The World's Largest Industrial Enterprises*, Farnborough, Westmead.

Ellwein, T. and Hess, J.J. (1987), 6th ed. *Das Regierungssystem der Budesrepublik Deutschland*, Opladen, West deutscher Verlag.

Himmelmann, G. (1986), 'Geschictliche Entwicklung der öffentlichen Wirtschaft', in H. Brede and H. Von Loesch, *Die Unternehmen der öffentlichen Wirtschaft in der Bundesrepublik Deutschland*, Baden-Baden, Nomos: 31–56.

Hohn, N. and Schiman, K.D.U. (1990), *Konflikte und Gleichgewichte in Forschungssystem*, Frankfurt-New York, Campus.

Knauss, F. (1986) 'Unternehmen in der Industrie', in H. Brede and H. Von Loesch, *Die Unternehmen der öffentlichen Wirtschaft in der Bundesrepublik Deutschland*, Baden-Baden, Nomos: 213–29.

Lehmbruch, G. (1976), *Parteienwettbewerb im Bundesstaat*, Stuttgart, Kolhammer.

Scharpf, F.W. *et al*, (1976), *Politikverflechtung: Theorie und Empirie des kooperativen Föderalismus in der Bundesrepublik*, Kronberg, Athäneum.

Shonfield, A. (1965), *Modern Capitalism*, Oxford, Martin Robertson.

*Wirtschaftswoche* (1988), 52–53, 23 December: 15.

Woll, A. (1987), 'Diskrepanz zwischen Worten und Taten in der deutschen Wirtschaftspolitik', *Neue Zurcher Zeitung*, 23–24. 8 (Fernausgabe); 11–12.

# CHAPTER 6

## ITALY: PRIVATIZATIONS ANNOUNCED, SEMI-PRIVATIZATIONS AND PSEUDO-PRIVATIZATIONS

### Sabino Cassese

This chapter is divided into four parts. The first contains a caveat lest the subject be taken too much to heart. The second and third set out the privatizations of the 1980s (the first phase) and those which began in 1990 (the second phase). The fourth part puts privatization into context and describes the factors which have accelerated or slowed down the process.

### Caveat

The caveat here is fourfold: the need to distinguish between areas affected by privatization in different countries; the contingency character of privatization; the relativity of the concepts of public and private; the importance of the historical setting and of the overall context.

First, in Britain and in France privatization has chiefly had to do with firms whereas in other countries, various sectors and not only industrial ones have been affected. For instance, in the case of Italy, two sectors that are traditionally the preserve of the state – the collection of taxes and the programming of public works – were long ago transferred to the private sector. Tax collection (taxes that do not need to be paid directly) is carried out by private tax collectors on the basis of a concession granted by the state. The procedure was initially determined by law in 1871, drawing on the model of the licence in force in the kingdom of Lombardy and Veneto at the beginning of the nineteenth century. The collection of taxes is entrusted to qualified individuals selected by competitive examination, who are required to pay the sum total of taxes to the state, even if collection falls short of this total (so-called principle of presumed collection). The private tax collector receives remuneration (*aggio*) in the form of a percentage of the sum received.

The second area that has long been privatized concerns public works programming. At the beginning of the twentieth century, with the development of a public works policy occurring at the same time as a crisis in public employment, it was remarked that, owing to the difficulty found in recruiting specialist engineers and surveyors, central government had no properly equipped research department for public works programming. This led to the task being consigned to private individuals by resorting to various procedures: invitation by tender (whereby the candidate is required both to develop the scheme and ensure construction); allocation of the programme in question; projects put out to open competition; concession to carry out the work, and so on.

Other activities that were traditionally the concern of the state have recently been privatized. Here are three examples, the first of which concerns law and order. A few statistics will convey some idea of the position. In 1970 there were 10,000 attested security guards (*guardia giurate*) and 300 attested security organizations; in 1991 the respective figures were 36,300 and 873, nearly four times as many as in 1970. Over the same period *policia di stato* (c.f. CID) numbers rose from 80,000 to slightly short of 90,000. Office cleaning affords a further example. Analysis of public sector employment statistics reveals that in central government administration cleaning services have been progressively passed to private contractors. A third example concerns periodic vehicle testing. The law passed in February 1992, containing 'provisions for the safety of road circulation and regulations in the matter of vehicle roadworthiness', and the 'highway code' of April 1992 enable this task (formerly the preserve of the Motorization Service in the Ministry of Transport) to be made over to properly accredited individuals. They have to be registered and to observe the technical standards applied by the Ministry of Transport in regard to the equipment they need to provide themselves with, safeguards to clients and rates. They are subject to public inspection and to penalties.

A similar development has taken place during the last twenty years concerning new activities such as the administration of computerized systems. Following the initial convention in 1976 between the Ministry of Finance and the Società Generale della Informatica (SOGEI), the running and organization of the principal state computer systems, relating, in particular, to the Ministry of Finance, the Treasury Ministry, the State Audit Office (corte di comti) and the Ministry of Education, were entrusted to private companies in which the state holds a stake.

The last example concerns the privatization of property (provided for by a decree of 5 December 1991, which became law on 29 January 1992, and which will be referred to later in another connection). Article 2 provides for the transfer of state property to private companies in which the state has an interest; they undertake to administer them or put them up for sale, and to supply the Treasury by way of an advance on profits with sums which may well be in the order of 3000 billion lire. The Comitato Interministeriale per la Programmazione Economica (CIPE) made provision on 1 April 1992 for the Istituto Mobiliare Italiano (IMI) to create a company of this type.

In the second place, privatization policies represent government positions that are relatively short-term, hence by nature reflecting a given set of circumstances. It should not be forgotten that the cycle of growth in the powers of government, allowing for differences between one state and another, belongs to the period that stretches from the Great Depression of 1929–33 (and/or World War II) to the end of the 1970s (a decade that witnessed the largest number of publications on 'big government', 'overloaded government', 'expansion of the economy' and so on). The trend towards privatization, on the other hand, occupies a relatively short period: 1979–93 in Britain; the two years, 1986–8, in France (though privatization is now back in favour again).

The question arises as to whether privatization represents a lasting change or an adjustment to a long-term trend involving marginal change in the dimensions of the modern state. It would require extensive statistical analysis to establish whether, despite the brevity of the privatization phase, its influence has been sufficiently marked to bring about radical transformation in the direction pursued by one country or another. Evidence available in specific cases inclines one to show reserve. Indeed, taking 1982 and 1986 as a reference, and comparing, for example, Italy and the UK, it is noticeable that the importance of state enterprise relative to the whole economy (measured by standard indicators) has remained stable at around 15 per cent in the case of Italy, while in the UK it has dropped from 15 per cent to 7 per cent.

A third point: privatization is usually understood to mean that a firm passes from public to private ownership. However, sale in itself does not imply total relinquishment on the part of the state. In the first place, privatizations have been carried through, as a general rule, by strong governments, capable of providing themselves with structures appropriate for administering complex procedures and imposing their will on the heads of nationalized concerns as well as on trades unions. In this sense, privatizations represent a show of force on the part of the governments that have realised them. In the second place, more often than not privatization has been directed at public utilities, which have passed from public ownership to public 'regulation'. And experience shows that state control exercised from 'without' can be wider and more effective than proprietorial control from 'within'.

A final caveat relates to the significance of the historical background and context. Here too comparisons are essential. The degree and character of privatization is a function of the historical background of states where it has been applied and of the context in which it takes place. Italy, for instance, in spite of its centralizing, Napoleonic tradition and the still accepted division between the private and public arenas, has never possessed a French-type administrative élite (*grands corps*), and has always been characterized by an administration that is weak and exposed to the most diverse partisan and economic interests; nor has it ever seen a clear demarcation between public and private enterprise (unlike many other countries, there has been only one nationalization in Italy, electrical energy in 1962). In the UK, on the contrary, public companies established themselves with a series of nationalizations, and the privatizations which took place at a time of strong government had the effect of reinforcing and consolidating the distinction, previously unknown, between public and private law.

To conclude, privatizations are not uniform in character. They occur within a short-term span of so far unreckoned intensity. They are not to be seen in ideological terms, indeed they may even result in a reinforcement of public authority; they have to be appreciated in terms of the context, historical or other, of the country in question.

Privatizations in Italy can be divided into two phases, one during the 1980s and the other beginning with the 1990s. Let us look at each separately.

## The 1980s

During the first cycle a number of privatizations were initiated, to which the method of organization of the state sector in industry lent itself. This is structured on three levels. On the first level – the base – are the operating (joint-stock) companies with their share capital wholly or partly owned by the state. On the second level – the middle – are the state holding companies, the *enti di gestione* (public entrepreneurial organizations) – IRI (Istituto per la Ricostruzione Industriale), ENI (Ente Nazionale Idrocarburi), EFIM (Ente Partecipazioni e Finanziamento Industria Manufatturiera), EAGC Ente Autonomo di Gestione per le Cinema). At the third or top level is the Ministero delle Partecipazione Statale (Ministry of State

Holdings), whose task is to define the general direction and policy of the *enti di gestione*. The initial privatizations, relating only to the first of these three levels, were realized through the sale of shares held by the *enti di gestione*; in some instances, this involved the transfer of the entire stock of shares, in others only a part.

Privatizations during the 1980s continued the policy of rapid share transfers undertaken by the *enti di gestione* of the state holding companies, in particular by IRI, the first one to have been set up (in 1933). Between 1950 and 1957 IRI arranged for the transfer of 210 companies, so shedding about 105,000 employees. Over the last forty years IRI has reduced its holdings in the steel and engineering industries, in shipbuilding and repair and in maritime transport, while increasing them in the sectors of telecommunications, air transport, television and radio, motorways, infrastructure, banks, the construction industry and electronics. In this way, transfers and new acquisitions have led to considerable changes in the group.

**Table 6.1**   Italy: Volume of transfers made between 1984 and 1989

|      | IRI   | ENI | EFIM | TOTAL |
|------|-------|-----|------|-------|
| 1984 | 378   | -   | -    | 378   |
| 1985 | 2,630 | 188 | 13   | 2,831 |
| 1986 | 1,017 | 268 | 92   | 1,377 |
| 1987 | 1,705 | 325 | 34   | 2,064 |
| 1988 | 1,884 | 450 | 17   | 2,351 |
| 1989 | 2,446 | 687 | 134  | 3,267 |

Among companies that have shifted from the public to the private sector special mention should be made of the following: Alfa Romeo, which IRI made over to Fiat in 1986; Lanerossi, the textile group, which ENI transferred to Marzotto in 1987; the commercial bank, Mediobanca, in which the three state-owned banks controlled by IRI had a majority share, and which IRI reduced to a half share in 1988; Cementir, transferred on the recommendation of CIPI (the interdepartmental committee for coordinating industrial policy) in February 1992 from IRI to the private sector group, Caltagirone. Over the same period again, further ventures of this kind miscarried. For instance, one might cite Maccarese, the agro-industrial firm that IRI made an attempt to sell to the Gabellieri group in 1981–3; SME, the food-producing firm, which again IRI tried to sell to the De Benedetti group between 1985 and 1988; and perhaps single out the vicissitudes borne by Enimont, a company in which ENI and Montedison, the private group, had an equal interest and in which they both merged their chemical operations in 1988, before it was dissolved in 1990 following the transfer by ENI of its side of the activity.

There are six chief characteristics in this initial phase of privatization. First, privatization never overtly formed part of government policy, whether in the Craxi (1983–5), Goria (1987) or De Mita (1988) administrations. Second, the choice of transfers to be made was agreed neither by government nor in parliament. The *enti* themselves, the holding companies, decided on the particular sets of shares to be sold, with a government authority subsequently coming in to ratify the decisions. Third, the sale was in every case carried out by the public sector company, not by the Treasury Ministry or by other ministerial bodies. Fourth, the *enti di gestione* had complete latitude in devising the procedure adopted. The single common element was the fact that privatizations were approved by CIPI; otherwise the transaction was conducted by the state holding company on its own terms. Fifth, the proceeds of privatization went not to the Treasury but to the holding companies themselves. And finally, in each instance privatization consisted in translating public ownership into private ownership, hence in increasing private shareholding, with the input of private capital.

## The 1990s

The second phase of privatization begins in 1990 and can be divided into three groups: privatizations announced, semi-privatizations and pseudo-privatizations.

To begin with those that were announced, the programme of the sixth Andreotti administration (1989) declared that it proposed to sell off a portion of the 'patrimony of the state' (hence shares), 'so contributing towards a significant reduction in the public debt and making a flotation of assets until now unavailable, for the purpose of encouraging the realization of new initiatives'. A ministerial commission in November 1990 established that the public banking, industrial and insurance sector had a value fluctuating between 100,000 and 200,000 billion lire. The programme of the seventh Andreotti government is more precise. It announced 'a rights issue' of 'a minority holding of shares' of public corporations, 'beginning with ENI and ENEL (Ente Nazionale per l'Energia Elettrica), and provides for these corporations to be turned into joint-stock companies, the aim this time being to make the Treasury beneficiary of the proceeds of privatization. But it was precisely this aim which met with resistance on the part of the *enti di gestione*, which in spite of their ties with the government majority, set out their own claim on the proceeds of privatization.

These difficulties account for the slow and tortuous progress of the project. The initial step was a parliamentary bill setting out 'norms for the conversion of the public economic corporations and the disposal of the public rights', which was introduced by the government in June 1991. With the realization that the bill was making no progress in parliament, the government approved a decree in October 1991, whose substance was in part similar and whose title identical. The decree did not become law. A further decree was adopted in December 1991. It even allowed for the disposal of national assets being subject to economic management and it became law without modification in January 1992. It pertains to the *enti di gestione* of the state holdings, other publicly-owned concerns and the so-called autonomous companies falling within the competence of the state. With its objective stated in the briefest terms, it applied uniform treatment to entities that are very different one to another, hence the initial difficulties. Provision was made for privatization to take effect in two stages. First, the transformation of public corporations and autonomous companies into joint-stock companies. The transformation is authorized following a procedure that lays down proposal by the Budget Ministry, deliberation by CIPE, the opinion of the relevant Commissions in the Lower and Upper Chamber, deliberation by the boards of the corporations concerned, and, finally, approval by the Ministers of the Budget and the Treasury as well as by the Ministers for the different sectors concerned.

The procedure does no more than change the legal form. On the one hand, it takes to its extreme an already pronounced tendency, that of reducing the three existing types of state enterprise – directly administered, public utility, and one in which state has an interest – into a single type, that in which the state holds an interest. On the other hand, it represents a step back by attributing a directly shareholding role to the state and thus reverting to a model in vogue in the earlier years of the present century.

This transformation was intended to enable the sale of shares to take place, thus constituting the second stage, itself divided into three sections: sale in the narrow sense, launch on the financial market and with institutional investors, and transfer of the proceeds of the sale to the Budget.

The Act draws a distinction between the sale of a quota of minority shares (for which the approval of CIPE is sufficient) and the majority quota, which entails loss of control and for which a parliamentary debate and a decision by the Council of Ministers are required.

Flotation on the market, and with institutional investors, is aimed at guaranteeing a 'large and lasting spread (of shares) among the public' and is conducted so as to prevent 'concentration and the threat of domination'. As a precondition both CIPI and the Treasury Minister must pronounce on the issue, and it is the latter's task to include the proceeds of the sale under budgetary revenue. The provisional budget for 1991 made mention of 6000 billion lire profit, which was in fact not forthcoming since objections were made to the Act. For 1992 provision was made for 9000 billion lire.

However, the problems and complications are not quite over. Following the adoption of a general model, applicable also to independent firms, the decree of January 1992 establishes (by Article 8) that in the case of the Impresa autonoma degli monopoli statali, conversion into a joint-stock company is to be carried out not simply on the basis of procedures mentioned above but also requires a proposal from the Minister of Finance and consideration by the Council of Ministers. On 24 February 1992 workers' representatives in the salt and tobacco monopolies asked the Minister of Finance for an undertaking that the emerging joint-stock company would remain under state control, a request corresponding with widespread opinion among trades unions that privatizations would endanger security of employment.

The *enti di gestione* immediately opposed the Act's application. The Istituto Nazionale delle Assicurazioni (INA) pointed out that in its own case it could not be applied since it did not dispose of the funds that could be converted into company capital. ENI and ENEL followed suit with the objection that as state enterprises they were entitled to enjoy special or monopoly status (ENI the monopoly in oil and liquid gas prospection in the Po basin, and ENEL in the generation and supply of electricity). Thus, further accomplishment of the project proved difficult. Indeed, if the government was anxious to obtain resources to meet state indebtedness, state enterprises held the view that the proceeds of privatization should go to finance their own investment programmes.

A further difficulty arose from the fact that some of the enterprises that should by rights be subject to privatization present no interest for the market. The state railways make a substantial loss each year and need to call on Treasury subsidies. IRI's situation is scarcely better. One wonders how privatization can take place if there are no incentives for individuals to purchase shares in state enterprises.

The operation made slow headway. In March 1992 CIPE adopted a directional measure requiring the self-governing bodies and companies each to draw up its own programme for conversion to joint-stock company. These programmes had to make a clear distinction between functions of a collective nature and those to be carried out in the form of concessions. They were further required to submit proposals for transfer, division of activity, and both demergers and mergers, not merely those dictated by a desire to rationalize the sphere of activities. Each programme had to be submitted to the Minister concerned, who would draw up plans for conversion into joint-stock companies and pass them to CIPE, who in turn would decide on the bodies and companies to convert and initiate the procedure. Thus the first stage was set in motion, the stage of conversion into companies, which the directive quoted above defines as the 'strategic objective *per se*'. Moreover one notes that the Act provided for a simpler procedure, since it was the interdepartmental committee that was to decide on the course to be followed in view of conversions. But the preferred solution was to require institutions to draw up their own programmes and subsequently decide on the course to be followed.

Perusal of the directive reveals some interesting aspects, both subjective and objective. It is addressed not only to the *enti di gestione* of the state holdings and to the state enterprises, to ENEL, to INA and to the state railways, but also to institutions that can hardly be categorized in the same way (*Istituto Nazionale per il Commercio Estero*, ICE; trade fair organizations; and the Società Italiana degli Autori ed Editori). From an objective point of view, these bodies are required to specify both details concerning conversion and plans for transferring interests they hold in their dependent companies. By this means the government is in a position to control internal privatizations or those involving groups (as in first phase of privatization), so prompting a still more negative response in the institutions to be privatized. (One could cite the case of ENI, whose intention was to float SNAM and AGIP, companies it controls, on the stock exchange and which was prevented from doing so by CIPE's decision).

By mid-June 1992 some of the institutions concerned had still not responded to the directive. Their justification was to insist on the need for preliminary legislative regulation of specific areas, or else to declare that the body in question was not a business enterprise and therefore not in a position to produce an income (as maintained by the company responsible for overseas trade fairs). SIAE appealed against CIPE's recommendation.

But even the groups that replied and submitted their programmes insisted on the need for specific legislation; or advanced the solution that companies should be set up to administer entrepreneurial activities while the group itself as a public body be maintained as such; or else they called for additional state financing, so reversing the terms of the relationship (privatizations should serve to bring additional revenue to the Treasury).

With the aim of resolving some of these problems, the decree of May 1992 stipulates that the public functions of the groups facing conversion are transferred to the state to be conceded in the form of thirty-year concessions; that, in the absence of funds, the capital can be constituted by the assets – properly assessed – of the group in question; that the groups undergoing conversion would enjoy tax exemption, already allowed for in the case of banks by the state-owned banks (of which more later). Even if the shares floated on the market found buyers, the privatizations announced would involve a loss in revenue before the Treasury saw anything.

Among the numerous problems were those thrown up by the unions and by the state audit office (Corte di Conti). In addition to the employees in state monopolies, mentioned above, there were those in the state railways who went on strike on 27 June 1992 to protest against privatization, public status representing for them a surer safeguard of their jobs and also, possibly, a guarantee of greater leniency in regard to methods of practice and terms of employment. The state audit office, for its part, in a resolution issued in June 1992 by the section responsible for the financial management of establishments indirectly owned by the state, declared it would need to exercise its control even over companies formed after conversion.

The final element related to decisions reached by CIPE on 12 June 1992, setting in motion the procedure for converting ENI and the state railways (FS) into joint-stock companies. But at that moment, following parliamentary elections, a new government was formed. The Prime Minister, Amato, when presenting his programme to parliament on 1 July 1992, declared his government's intention to 'pursue the course of action scarcely begun for the implementation of measures already decided in regard to privatization with the object of improving them and carrying them to a successful conclusion'. Improvements, in the government's view, related to privatizations which 'amount to more than a mere predetermined allocation of blocks of shares for the benefit of a restricted number of purchasers and intermediaries'.

With the new government the 'legislative ballet' started up again. On 12 July 1992 a decree was adopted, which became law on 8 August 1992, modified by a further decree on 14 August. The new norms enabled the problems which had arisen to be overcome. They made mandatory the immediate conversion of the four state-owned giants – IRI, ENI, INA and ENEL – into joint-stock companies. They further made provision for CIPE to apply similar conversion to other state-owned groups, independent of their sphere of activity. Curiously, there was no provision for such conversion in the case of other state enterprises, for instance the so-called autonomous bodies, the most important being the post and telecommunications administration. The legal provision came into effect with CIPE's decision on 12 August 1992 to turn the state railways into a joint-stock company. Added to this, the new measures provided for the Treasury Minister to acquire a stake in the four new companies (as well as the Banca Nazionale del Lavoro – BNLsPa – and the Istituto Mobiliare Italiano – IMIsPa) and for him to exercise his rights as shareholder in conjunction with the Ministers of the Budget and Economic Planning, Industry, Commerce and Independent Trades, and State Holdings. Hence the new Act had more restricted application than the earlier one since, as stressed above, it excluded the autonomous state bodies.

The second part of the project, dealing with privatization itself (i.e. entailing the sale of shares to the public), is governed by a procedure as follows. The Treasury Minister maps out the restructuring process, and then, in agreement with the same ministerial colleagues as before, submits it to the Prime Minister. The Prime Minister forwards the programme to the appropriate parliamentary commissions who make their report. As a last step, the programme is approved by the Council of Ministers. In the words of the Act, the purpose of the restructuring programme is to 'enhance the value of the interests as ... much by transfer of activities and sectors as by exchanges of interests, mergers, integrations and any other form of action necessary to the restructuring process'. Further 'the programme must provide for the stock exchange flotation of companies that emerge from the restructuring of present interests as well as for the total proceeds to be allocated towards the reduction of the public debt'.

Finally, the model adopted by the new government established that areas of activity that belong specifically to the public sector (since they come within the special preserve provided for by Article 43 of the Constitution), being entrusted by law to the establishments privatized shall remain within the competence of the newly-formed companies, but on a concessionary basis. This provision replaced the decree of May 1991.

Following their conversion into joint-stock companies, the four state-owned groups referred to above approved articles of association which included two important new features. First, membership of the board was limited to three (so excluding representatives from parties in the government majority). Second, the body of shareholders – in effect, the government – was given wide powers to sell or purchase companies and to determine mergers, demergers or conversions.

A recent ruling incorporated other decisions affecting various bodies.

For instance, the abolition and liquidation of EFIM (Ente Partecipazioni e Finanziamento Industria Manufatturiera) was decreed in August 1992 (countermanding an earlier decree.) In the same month a decree replacing two in January and June 1992 pronounced the conversion of the Impresa autonoma degli monopoli statali (state monopolies board) into a joint-stock company, but limiting it to purely commercial and productive activity while reserving more general functions for the state to exercise.

After so many comings and goings, which are by no means over, the situation is more or less as follows. In the first place, IRI, ENI, INA, ENEL and the state railways have become joint-stock companies. A similar decision applies to the state monopolies board. EFIM has been abolished and has gone into liquidation. In the second place, the decisions made are at different stages of realization. The decrees affecting EFIM and the monopolies board have not yet been ratified. In mid-September 1992 the decision was made to privatize Credito Italiano, a bank belonging to IRI, and also Nuovo Pignone, a steel and engineering subsidiary of ENI, the workforce expressing hostility in the latter case.

Third, confronted by this legislative turmoil, it is hard to tell which norms apply to what. In respect of the principal state enterprise so far unaffected by these rulings, (i.e. post and telecommunications), it would appear that privatization can proceed on the basis of criteria laid down by the Andreotti administration.

Fourth, current legislation is different in two respects from what has gone before: The transformation of state-owned establishments into joint-stock companies has been achieved by act of parliament; such acts make no mention of special provisions for the sale of interests whereby the state could lose its majority.

Furthermore, bearing in mind the Amato government's original formulation, legislation passed in August 1992 has backtracked in some respects. For instance, the Ministry of State Holdings, which was due for abolition, is pointedly mentioned in the text. Whereas provision was originally made for the immediate and compulsory sale of between 20 per cent and 45 per cent of capital, such sale is now made subordinate to the prime objective of restructuring. In the earlier formulation the decision to privatize was a matter solely for government, but the definitive version introduces a procedure for parliamentary approval which effectively applies conditions. Last, the original text provided for the setting up of one or more giant holding companies, which would have made the whole process of privatization easier. However, it was later decided that the shareholder of the newly-constituted companies would be the Treasury Minister.

In addition to the privatizations already announced, which have been discussed above, the second phase also includes what may be termed semi-privatizations. These relate, more particularly, to banking and the post. An Act of July 1990 followed by a decree of November 1990 provided for privatization in the case of the 6 major state-owned banking establishments, some 600 savings banks along with medium-and long-term credit institutions. Two phases were envisaged. The first involved merging several banks with a view to forming one joint-stock company, or to choose a bank for one such conversion, or to let a bank so convert its own banking function. This required a project being submitted to the Bank of Italy, its approval being sought as well as that of the interdepartmental committee for savings and credit, and the Bank of Italy being informed at each stage of the proposed plan to ensure conformity.

The second phase had to do with the sale of holdings. This was made subject to no control unless it involved a majority of shares, in which case the opinion of the Bank of Italy and parliament had to be sought prior to a proposal from the Treasury and a decision being made by the Council of Ministers.

The Act of January 1991 is still more explicit. It provides for the Minister of Postal Services and Telecommunications to authorize the administrative body of these services to acquire shares in business companies operating in these or ancillary areas. At the same time, it lays down that they must represent a majority shareholding. It is worth noting that even the decree of December 1991, which became law in January 1992, as mentioned earlier, had application to the postal services administration, the corollary being that it had the choice between converting itself into a joint-stock company or setting up companies over which it would have control.

With banks as with postal services, conversion of a state enterprise into a joint-stock company was made conditional on continued control being exercised. Individuals may acquire shares so long as they represent a minority interest (this restriction being absolute in the case of the post but elastic in the case of banks, since, armed with the authorizations mentioned above even a majority interest can be disposed of).

In this way publicly-owned enterprises become hybrid joint-stock companies, subject in part to general rules and in part not (for example, constitution as a company is mandatory but membership is limited to one). In addition, the mechanisms adopted fail to allow the Treasury to benefit from the proceeds of privatization (except where there is straightforward conversion of banks into joint-stock companies).

Let us now turn to pseudo-privatizations. These retain the form of privatization but not the substance. There are two examples. The first is that of the Cassa di Depositi e de Consignazione, a division of the Treasury, which can now sell prescribed numbers of its holdings in specialized banks. In furtherance of this ruling, the Cassa transferred its own holding in CREDIOP – Consorzio di Credito per le Opere Pubbliche – to the Banco San Paolo di Torino. The operation involved was purely a financial one, which entailed the transfer of control over CREDIOP from the Treasury Minister to the Banco San Paolo (the Banco, for its part, from having been a state-owned bank, became a joint-stock company subject to control by the Treasury). The institution in question remained in the public sector but the operation enabled the state to include the proceeds from the sale of these holdings in its provisional budget.

The second example of pseudo-privatization is furnished by the Act of 29 January 1992 which contained 'provisions for reforming the sector of telecommunications'. It provides for the abolition of the state-owned telephone company (established in 1925) and the formation by IRI of a company 'whose shares are owned in their entirety by the same establishment' (i.e. IRI). According to the terms of the Act, the Minister for Postal Services and Telecommunications, after consultation with the Minister of State Holdings entrusts the company – by exclusive concession – with the public provision of telecommunication services, and whatever accessories and installations are required, such services being at present administered by the state telephone company. In this instance, all that has occurred is transfer from one authority to another within the state. The state telephone company coming under the Ministry for Postal Services was converted into a company whose shares had by law to remain in IRI's control. Continuity between the situation previously prevailing and that provided for by law was emphasized by the fact that employees of the state telephone company were taken over as one body by the new company.

Privatization of the last type, in fact, neither procures revenue for the state nor transfers management to the private sector. The reasons for such change may vary: the need to escape accountability, or to recruit and administer personnel by the norms of civil law; a greater flexibility in management; avoidance of direct state control while maintaining the advantages of the protection it affords.

## The context

Privatizations in Italy, whether announced or carried through, are to be seen in the context of major changes in the structure and functioning of the economy and, in general, in the relationship between the state and the economy. These changes are of four types. First there are those brought about by the quickening pace with which the single market is being set up. Article 102A of the Treaty of Rome affirms that union is a guarantee of an 'open and freely competitive market economy'. Community measures relating to competition and subsidization mention state enterprise only to pledge that it will receive the same treatment as private enterprise. Hence they are measures which deny any distinction between public and private.

Second, there are the two liberalizing measures carried out in the second half of the 1980s, the one affecting currencies (1986 and 1990), the other credit (1985–90).

Next, there is the erosion of public monopolies and the introduction of guidelines relating to competition. To cite examples of the erosion of public monopolies one need go no further than television and electricity. RAI (Italian television and radio) enjoyed at the start a monopoly in its area, which came to an end with a ruling by the Constitutional Court in 1976. A 1984 Act provisionally cleared the way for private initiative; the Act of 6 August 1990 regularized the situation and 'codified' the so-called duopoly between RAI and Fininvest. In the matter of electricity generating, the authority concerned (ENEL) was granted a monopoly in 1962. The Act of 29 January 1992 broached it by authorizing the generation of electricity – privately, or for sale to ENEL, or, in the case of recognized business companies, for their own use; and further by authorizing its sale, exchange or production on behalf of a third party as well as the transport of electrical energy, undertaken on private initiative, on the basis of agreements made with ENEL.

In 1990 a principle was set down in Italy similar to that incorporated in the European Community Treaty on the subject of associations, misuse of a monopolistic position and merger transactions. It led to the establishment of an authority whose task it was to guarantee a competitive market. It also contained a clause similar to Article 90 of the Community Treaty by virtue of which the principle of competition applies also to state-owned concerns or those in which the state has a majority holding, with the exception of those that provide services of general economic benefit or act as monopolies as regards 'whatever is essential for the completion of the particular tasks entrusted to them'.

Finally, the significance of the (contemplated) abolition of the directorate of the most important part of the public industrial sector, the Ministry of State Holdings, should not pass unnoticed. A request for a general referendum in September 1991 and a government bill tabled on 3 October 1991 were an indication of this. However, the Act of 8 August

1992 re-established the Ministry of State Holdings by laying down that it was to be consulted by the Treasury Minister in the matter of the exercise of the shareholder's rights and of the transmission to the Prime Minister of the plan for restructuring state holdings.

If these are factors to accelerate the process of privatization, the main instruments in its delay also need mentioning. There are four.

On the one hand, the practice of concession introduces a fundamental ambiguity. It authorizes a person to perform a function which is by nature public and to do so in his own interest (since as beneficiary of the concession he performs the service it demands for gainful purpose). On the other, the practice enables the state to retain control of the sector concerned, by virtue of the agreement or contract, control over prices and so on.

The stock market raises problems that seem to introduce a vicious circle. Privatizations enable Treasury indebtedness to be reduced, but the extent of indebtedness is such as to call for high interest rates, and this in turn draws on a substantial part of savings. Moreover, the shares floated on the market cannot attract those who seek to acquire management of the firms in question since, as we have seen, the state almost always reserves for itself the right of control. Thus, indebtedness is the cause of privatization being more of a problem, not the reverse. It remains to be hoped that privatization conduces to strengthening the stock market, because with only 200 companies quoted on the stock exchange compared with around 2500 in Britain the scale of operations is small.

A third sizeable obstacle comes from the difficulties provoked by political parties for whom privatizations are seen as the loss of a considerable sphere of influence. It needs to be borne in mind that state enterprise has been made to serve very different ends – to rescue private firms in difficulty, to ease labour market pressures in this or that location, or to enable jobs to go to 'clients' of the parties in power without having recourse to the usual procedures; and there are others.

Finally, mention needs to be made of constant resistance and a general tendency to hold up proceedings on the part of the state-owned economic entities, now converted into joint-stock companies, for whom the sale of a block of shares implies a shrinking 'sphere of influence'. To assess the degree of resistance to privatization, to consider that the implementation of privatization in the 1990s is still provisional (in the sense that the decision to sell has still not be taken), is to be aware that the entire exercise may be no more than cosmetic, and that basically the power of the state remains unchanged.

# CHAPTER 7

## PRIVATIZATION IN SPAIN: THE ABSENCE OF A POLICY

### Oscar Fanjul and Luis Mañas

## Introduction

The state-owned company as a concept is on the defensive all over the world and privatization programmes are being undertaken by the great majority of countries. Indeed, such a widespread coincidence in economic policy trends, from one continent to another, has rarely been witnessed. The privatization process is under way from the East of Europe, where it is reaching a vast scale, to the Asian communist countries such as China and Vietnam, where the thrust of the private sector is such that it has become the motor behind economic growth; from Mexico, where telephones, banks and airlines have been privatized, to Argentina, which has even dared to take on gas, oil and railways; or from Sweden, pioneers in the welfare state, to the France of Mitterrand or the peculiar Italian case.

In the face of this tendency, we are going to defend the theory that, in the case of Spain, there has not existed a privatization policy in the sense understood by the aforementioned countries. It is undeniable that privatizations have occurred, as we shall see, but we would like to emphasize the fact that these have been brought about in the absence of a clearly specified policy.

In fact, Spain's recent economic history shows a considerable increase in the size of the public sector. Thus, public expenditure has progressively taken up a larger proportion over GNP, rising from 24.7 per cent in 1975 to 43.5 per cent in 1991. This growth has no equal within the sphere of the OECD, which has witnessed a tendency to the contrary since the beginning of the 1980s. It is not surprising, therefore, within the context existing in Spain, that the tendency towards a drastic redefinition and reduction of the public sector has not been widely considered either.

In the various sections of this chapter an attempt is made to answer the following four questions from a Spanish perspective:

1. What may be privatized? – describing the origin and current situation of the public sector in Spain.
2. Who is encouraging privatizations? – including comments on the traditional attitudes, showing scarce enthusiasm for privatization, held by the whole Spanish parliamentary and ideological gamut.
3. Why privatize? – studying the conditions that have a negative effect on the efficient performance of Spanish state-owned companies.
4. How is privatization carried out? – reviewing the natural difficulties encountered in the privatization process, with reference to the Spanish experience.[1]

## Autarky and nationalizations on request

As opposed to widely held ideas to the contrary, the Spanish public business sector is not exceptionally large in comparison to those of the main European countries. It is not easy to quantify with precision what is understood by this sector, but Table 7.1 sufficiently depicts that difference in size, be it in proportion with the whole economy or in relation to its participation in certain basic sectors.

**Table 7.1** The importance of the state-owned company in Spain and Europe (1985)

| Size | Spain % | Average EC % |
|---|---|---|
| Employment by state-owned firms/total Employment | 5 | 10 |
| Investment state-owned firms/total investment | 10 | 20 |
| Value added by state-owned firms/GNP (excluding agriculture) | 8 | 12 |
| Percentage value added by state-owned firms by sectors: Energy | 29 | 70 |
| Transport and communications | 45 | 70 |
| Banks | 10 | 30 |

*Source:* European Centre for State-Owned Company, *Yearly Statistics*, 1987.

The above does not imply that state-owned companies have little importance in Spain. On the contrary, they are most important: they suffer notable losses, whose financing accounts for a considerable part of the budget deficit; they form the basis of trade union strength; and they are an important point of reference for collective bargaining.

In order to understand the nature of problems relating to the privatization of Spanish state-owned companies, it is necessary to study their origins. These companies are mainly ascribed to two blocks: the Instituto Nacional de Industria, (INI), dependent upon the Ministry of Industry; and the so-called 'Empresa del Patrimonio', pertaining to the Ministry of Economics and Finance. Whether or not companies belonged to one or other of these blocks is in many cases the result of pure historical chance.

The basic group is that of the INI, created by General Franco in 1941, along the lines of the Italian IRI.[2] It was created, then, after a civil war which had lasted three years, in a country acutely in need of reconstruction, by a political regime for which the role of the State in the organization and intervention of economy was a basic element of its economic policy.

Throughout this period of over 50 years, the INI's objectives have suffered an evolution both in themselves and in their ideological justification. Initially, emphasis was placed on the strategic objectives, which justified the development of a domestic industry or of transport and energy companies, among others. The Spanish economic policy of that time was highly autarkic, being characterized by strong trade protection and a tendency to economic isolation. This was to encourage import substitution in order to develop a strong national industry. The creation of public sector firms was mainly geared to the fulfilment of this objective. The subsidiarity principle was an important element of this type of policy; the INI was made responsible for developing those projects that were not undertaken by private initiative, but were considered high priority by the government. These were frequently highly capital intensive projects, involving great economies of scale and long terms of maturity.

Once the companies had been created as instruments of a given policy, they took on a life of their own and widened their objectives. Moreover, and as happened in Italy, state-owned companies were given regional policy objectives, thus being entrusted with boosting the economic development of certain less developed areas. At one stage, the existence of some firms was also justified – somewhat ingenuously and not very credibly – by the desire to stimulate competition and for the state to be present in certain spheres of the economy deemed important for the country, although the reasons for this were not clearly defined.

In any case, the present configuration of the public business sector in Spain is to a large extent the result of a process whereby private companies with losses were transferred to the state. It has been this mechanism of 'nationalization on request' by the private sector, encouraged by coalitions between owners, workers, authorities and regional institutions, which has determined the present structure of the Spanish public business sector. This explains the low quality of many of its assets and, therefore, the difficulties that exist for its privatization.

The type of 'nationalizations' described above started under the dictatorship of General Franco – the most representative of these were the Asturian coal mines, which since then have incurred huge losses, although also of considerable importance during the first stage of the new Spanish democracy. The Spanish economy, which had undergone an important industrialization process and growth during the 1960s, witnessed a period of sharp inflation and stagnation over the following decade. The first oil crisis coincided with the end of the old political regime and the development of a noteworthy process of transition towards a fully democratic administration. Under the impact of the first oil shock, Spain had to set out a new political constitution, organize the development of trades unions and political parties and, overall, undertake the important process of substituting political classes and institutions.

Within this context, Spanish industry and the economy in general underwent a very sharp crisis between 1973 and 1985. Unemployment rose from 2.7 per cent to a maximum 21.6 per cent (first quarter of 1985), and the absolute value of aggregate investment fell by 10 per cent (not recovering its previous levels until the second half of the 1980s). This crisis had a particularly severe impact on industry and, in order to alleviate social pressures, centrist governments over the period 1976–82 agreed to nationalize a large number of companies embarked on the road to bankruptcy, which contributed considerably to the deterioration of the public deficit.

Table 7.2 shows us precisely some of the 'bail-out' nationalizations carried out over the period.[3] Apart from the extremely costly coal mining, shipyards, iron and steel works, not to mention others such as shoe or carpet factories, are examples of companies that became state-owned, but initially were private, until they ceased to be profitable.

At the end of the political transition period, the socialist party PSOE (Spanish Socialist Workers' Party) obtained the absolute majority in the October 1982 elections. This was the first time a party had ever achieved

**Table 7.2**   Spain: nationalization of loss-making companies 1976–83

| YEAR | COMPANY | SECTOR |
|------|---------|--------|
| 1976 | Barreras | Shipyard |
|      | G. Empresas Alvarez | China/porcelain |
|      | Mahsa | Services |
|      | Povisa | China/porcelain |
| 1977 | Textil Tarazona | Textiles |
|      | Astilleros de Cadiz | Shipyard |
| 1978 | Altos Hornos del | |
|      | Mediterraneo | Iron and steel |
|      | Diatlansa | Shipyard |
|      | Oesa | Foodstuffs |
| 1979 | SKF | Ballbearings |
|      | Soler Almirall | Ballbearings |
|      | Secoinsa | Computer systems |
|      | Aesa | Shipyard |
| 1980 | Figaredo | Mining |
|      | Babcock-Wilcox E. | Capital goods |
|      | Marsans | Travel agency |
|      | Seat | Automobiles |
| 1981 | Equipos Nucleares | Capital goods |
|      | Trasatlantica | Shipping |
|      | Altos Hornos de | |
|      | Vizcaya | Iron and steel |
| 1982 | Foarsa | Iron and steel |
| 1983 | Aluminio | Aluminium |
|      | Alugasa | Aluminium |

*Source*: Martín Aceña and Comín (1991).

such a result in the life of the young Spanish democracy. At about that time, the policy of nationalization and expansion adopted by the first socialist government of the Fifth French Republic was considered to have little chance of success. The economic policy introduced by the new Spanish government was then characterized by the search for macroeconomic stability and the de-regulation and liberalization of markets, on a microeconomic scale. Spanish government policy diverged progressively from the French secular influence and became more akin to that of its Australian and New Zealand political counterparts.

As a result of this, the public sector turned sharply away from the former policy of nationalizing private companies in bankruptcy so as to protect the interests of both owners and employees.

We may understand from the above historical description that the Spanish experience shows important differences from events in other countries, such as France and England, where the public sector originated in a nationalization process initiated by their governments.[4] A nationalization policy has never existed in Spain in the same way as in those two countries. The Spanish state today is basically in possession of businesses not desired by the private sector.

There is a special aspect to the Spanish character that will shed light on the above statement. As opposed to the general situation in other countries, private participation in companies that provide public services (public utilities) or in public monopolies has been, and is, most considerable – perhaps the greatest in Europe. This is easily understood if we study the philosophical line of thought followed: private initiative prepared to exploit a monopoly did, indeed, exist and the state accepted this and took advantage of it. This explains the high private participation in comparison to that in other European countries. Such is the case of sectors such as gas, electricity, telephones, even the running of the fiscal monopolies like tobacco or the distribution of oil products, which has now been de-monopolized. It is remarkable that many of those who oppose the policy of privatizing companies that work under competitive conditions accept, nevertheless, the existence of private monopolies.

## Attitudes towards privatization

In spite of the fact that the origins of the public sector lie in the era of Franco, particularly those of the INI, the existence and continuity of such a sector has been backed by democratic parties in a similar way to other countries such as Italy, for example. In fact, an important part of the socialist party[5] and the other left-wing formations have not only argued in favour of its existence but also of its enlargement under the banner of the great Spanish industrial group.

Apart from the regions and groups directly benefiting from the existence of state-owned companies, support for the public *per se* and for an active role of the state in the economy are the main reasons behind the movements that have opposed and do oppose the privatization of state-owned companies. The concept of privatization has been largely associated with conservative policies, to be precise with those developed by

Margaret Thatcher, and part of society has seen these as a mere attack on the role of the state.

Paradoxically, the enemies of privatization have thought to defend the state by retaining under its control two main types of company: those that the private sector had never considered attractive for development or those that it had exploited but which had been transferred to the state when they were no longer profitable. Be that as it may, a profound debate on the advantages and disadvantages of privatization has never existed here either. Over the last seventeen years, Spain has been obliged to undertake a fair number of political and economic changes, from the transition to a democracy to entry in the EEC and SME, setting up on the way an almost federal state. Perhaps for this reason political parties have avoided the discussion and definition of a privatization policy that would have been further cause for social and political confrontation. In fact, the parties that have governed in Spain never in the past included privatization as an objective in their election or government programmes.

The socialist government in power with an absolute majority since 1982 has, indeed, repeatedly insisted on not adopting a privatization programme and it may be stated that such a policy, as understood in other countries (for example, Britain, France and others within the OECD), has never been developed. In fact, the strategy followed in Spain has been very different from that practised by Thatcher's government.

The socialist government in Spain did not attempt to dismantle a welfare state that, in fact, did not exist. Rather it created one by approximating social service benefits to levels comparable to those accepted within the European Community. Nor did it attempt to reduce the power of trades unions, but rather contributed to strengthen their role and power through legal measures and economic aid. Finally, it refrained from using the sale of state-owned companies to finance a tax-cutting policy.[6] It is true that, during these years, the public sector has sold companies, but there are very notable differences between these processes and the privatization practices carried out by the aforementioned countries.

In the first place, it should be taken into consideration that an important part of the public sector has still been undergoing considerable growth as a result of the mere development of its most efficient companies, and this has, in a natural progression, frequently been accompanied by the acquisition of private firms. Although it is also true that over the last ten years significant sales of public companies were effected, the nature of these operations is worthy of study in order to understand the difference between these privatizations and those under-taken elsewhere in Europe.

An essential part of what was sold by the state during the period was the so-called Rumasa Group, nationalized in 1983 when on the verge of bankruptcy. The only purpose of this nationalization was, as emphasized by the government from the start, to avoid the effect that the bankruptcy of such a large group with widespread ramifications would have on various sectors of the economy, including the banking sector.

It was precisely in order to confirm this attitude, which differed greatly from the true nationalizing spirit, and to mark a clear difference from any resemblance to the French 'common Programme', that the Government lent top priority to this Group's rapid reprivatization. For this reason, in 1983, the government did not undertake a global analysis of the companies that belonged to it in order to decide which ones should or should not continue within the public sector, or to decide upon the best timing for their privatization. It did not consider, for example, that there were more reasons for some of the companies recently nationalized to remain within the public sector than for other government-owned companies not belonging to that Group. Clear priority was given to privatizing the newly nationalized Group and the process was set in motion without delay. This sale was, then, an attempt to demonstrate the lack of a desire to develop a programme of nationalization and was not indicative of an organized process of privatizations.

Other companies have also been sold – some of them important – but in general this has been as a last resort. Indeed, there have been cases of companies with a prolonged history of losses, the survival of which, through technological, scale or commercial reasons, could hardly be contemplated without an important budget allotment. Their future would, therefore, be better guaranteed by their integration within another large and well-established firm. In these cases, sales have been accepted by the trades unions and other social bodies as inevitable and the companies have been sold directly, frequently to important multinational groups. This has been the case of Seat to Volkswagen or Enasa to the Fiat Group.

There is a third type of company sale that in Spain has been more closely associated with the idea of privatization, but which contrasts with the circumstances normally covered by the term. To be precise, a series of sales has been carried out on capital markets, but only of stakes considerably lower than 50 per cent. In making these divest-ments, such as Ence, Endesa or Repsol, the government has emphasized its desire not to lose control, usually retaining even more than 50 per cent of the share capital. This is the greatest difference between Spanish and British or French privatizations.

In these cases, the operations have been undertaken as part of a policy to reinforce state-owned companies, extracting them from the 'public ghetto', providing access to new sources of financing and using this system to subject them to a financial discipline that is absent in the public sector. However, none of these cases has been justified as a way for the state to reduce its size or renounce control of the companies involved.

Nevertheless, it is true that this has been the first step, in some cases of great significance, of a gradual approach that will not produce very drastic reactions from those against privatization policies.

## Necessary conditions for an efficient performance by state-owned companies

It is useful to recount some of the major problems faced by state-owned companies because of their condition. We will concentrate on those that exist in most countries and are precisely of greater relevance in the case of Spain. Many of these difficulties have recently become more relevant as a consequence of entry in the EEC and the evolution of Community regulations which have forced state-owned companies to conduct their business within an increasingly competitive and neutral framework. In the case of Spain, we think the main problems are as follows:

### The lack of control exerted by the capital market

Government-controlled companies listed on the stock market were and are very few. When a company is listed on the stock exchange, this market subjects it to a permanent analysis and judgement as far as efficiency, perspectives and risks are concerned, expressed in the evolution of its share price. The more efficient the working of capital markets – by which we mean the greater access there is to information, the more accurate is this information and the more freely are prices fixed – the more correct is the market judgement. Undoubtedly, errors may be committed, but in a financially developed and internationally integrated economy, in which sophisticated institutional investors and an important community of financial analysts are present, market judgement of a company's performance may only be ignored at great risk.

Within a context of this type, when a company announces a change of strategy – for example, a decision to diversify its activity or make an acquisition – the market issues its judgement: positive or negative, raising or lowering its share price. The market's monitoring role is, without doubt, one of the basic mechanisms to evaluate and motivate management decisions. Management's main objective should be to achieve the highest capital value for the company and mediocre performance with respect to this goal may be considered an invitation for the company to be taken over, thus endangering their very jobs. It has not been necessary to emphasize this fear during recent years as an incentive for company management.

This type of control or pressure has never existed in companies owned entirely by the state and its absence greatly helps to explain many of the errors committed in the decision-making process, or the slowness in taking action to solve problems. How should one judge, for example, whether a purchase or sales price is correct?.

The problem is worsened by the fact that the state does not often check on the profitability of its investments in the way a private investor would. Nor does it compare the profitability of its companies with the rest of the sector or the economy. Normally, and this is undoubtedly the case of Spain, the state and its public administrators observe only whether the company is making a profit or a loss, that is to say, the state and even the general public, make only a 'binary analysis', of profit or loss, paying no attention to the yield on the resources which state-owned firms employ.

All the above eventually affect company culture, in that the concept of economic profitability tends to lose importance and the cost of shareholders' equity tends to be forgotten; the fear of bankruptcy or a hostile take-over disappears entirely, together with a whole series of factors which keep up tension within organizations and lead them to increase efficiency.

*Management stability*

International experience clearly shows the high rate of rotation in the management of state companies, with the inevitable difficulty that this implies for the conception and development of medium- and long-term strategy. The absence of a stable owner makes public-sector companies most dependent on the political cycle, on the groups and parties in power at any given moment. The importance of this dependence varies greatly from country to country and according to the structure of the state, the stability of governments, the type of coalition adopted by them or its absence. In Spain, especially up to 1982, change in public administrators was very frequent, not because the governing party or Prime Minister changed, but simply because the Minister of Industry did. This short-term horizon has weighed heavily in the sociological panorama of public institutions when drawing up priorities of action and policies, and when it came to determining the degree of personal commitment. Frequent changes in strategy, policies and even styles of management have borne faithful witness to this. In short, business behaviour has frequently been marked by short-term problems and a lack of the confidence, perseverance and continuity, upon which the success of any company management depends.

*Political interference*

There is one aspect that has an extremely negative incidence on the behaviour of the state-owned company, which is not often mentioned. Economic authorities strive – providing their behaviour is not affected by pressure groups – for the good of all: for example, the better working of a sector. When public and private companies co-exist, there arises a temptation difficult to resist to employ public-sector companies in order to achieve what could be considered an improvement in the overall situation, although this may lead to a deterioration in their economic position. The end result is usually that of worsening the situation of these public-sector companies, be it through variation in their market share, the acquisition or sale of certain assets, price or tariff fixing, and an improvement in the situation of private companies and the sector as a whole, in the view of the economic authority.

It so happens, then, that when something belongs to all of us, it really belongs to no one. It is easier to convince or give orders to the public business administrator than to allow the rules of the market to work freely. As a result of the above, many public administrators have adopted the aim of seeking private shareholders, allowing them to generate the type of coalition which would prevent attitudes of this kind towards the state-owned company.

Without going into the personal view of the authors of this chapter, the presentation of this problem does not imply a normative judgement, but is rather the description of a not infrequent practice. For some, this is no more than an example of the role that could or should be played by the state-owned company and, for others, is an undesirable practice from the point of view of an efficient allocation of resources.

Many other types of public intervention are also exercised. It is the custom of regional governments to consider that state-owned companies hold responsibilities towards their communities, as though they were an element of territorial compensation. The attitude towards them is usually demanding and forgetful of economic restrictions, showing a great difference from the way in which they treat private companies.

A similar attitude may also be observed on the part of trades unions. Indeed, Spanish trades unions consider state-owned companies as fair ground upon which to intensify social pressures, using them as the scenario of confrontation with the government. This is the cause of the high labour costs borne by many such companies and explains the undesirable working practices that have been introduced in collective agreements, negotiated and accepted by management that was just passing through the company and would not, therefore, have to suffer them.

*Earnings systems*

An essential part of running a company is motivating its human resources, furthering their professional training and creating an organization that takes full advantage of their personal capacities. It is difficult to over-emphasize the importance of doing this successfully with a defined and compact management body, that must be identified itself as a key resource.

In order to achieve this, adequate earnings or reward systems are an essential instrument, although they are not the only one, nor are they always the most important. The nature of their importance may vary with the economic cycle, the situation within each profession and with each sector.

Flexibility in ways and means of payment is most difficult to develop in the public sector and, precisely, in the state-owned company. This is not the case only in Spain, but is a general problem which is faced by the governor of the American Federal Reserve and the chairmen of the larger state-owned companies in practically any country, alike.

However, it has been a particularly acute problem in Spain over recent years, comprising one of the greatest obstacles to the survival of the state-owned company in this country. The government has used state companies as an example and a reference for the rest of the economy. In order to set a social example, it has introduced substantial limitations on management earnings which, for example, in 1983, suffered large reductions, thus provoking the flight of many members of management staff to the private sector. This concrete measure was meant to induce more moderate trades union behaviour in that year but with little success. On the other hand, the lasting effect has been to introduce a considerable limitation in the working of state companies where its employees are still the most highly paid and its managers the most poorly paid in the country.

## Problems presented by a privatization: the case of Spain

The transfer of a state-owned company to the private sector is not an easy task. Apart from the problems associated with the sale of any company, be it state or privately owned, there are complications inherent to privatizations that derive from the very nature of their owner and the objectives sought by the operation. Let us recount the main difficulties that may occur in the process of privatizing a company and the Spanish experience in this respect.

### Definition of a sellable asset package

Any privatization should begin by defining the assets that the public sector wishes to divest in order to decide upon the most attractive way to package them for the potential sale that, at the same time, fulfils government objectives behind the operation. For example, the state holding INH decided to divest its exploration, refining, distribution, petrochemical and gas assets in the Spanish hydrocarbons sector. The next step was to determine the best way of grouping the assets together. Of the many possible alternatives, it was decided to join them all in a single company (REPSOL) to act as a vehicle for their sale.

A similar problem is, at this moment, being faced by the Italian Treasury in that it must decide upon the most attractive way to combine the assets it possesses in the hydrocarbons sector (Agip, Agip Petroli, Enichem) in the eyes of the market and that will, at the same time, contribute to solve its problems. In the case of Spain, similar issues are being posed in the sphere of the INI (whether to divest participations in a conglomerate or in the companies of which it is comprised) and in the state banking sector grouped around Argentaria (whether to sell shares in the Group or in its affiliated companies).

A certain friction usually arises between government objectives and the demands of the market. In this connection, the stock markets' aversion to business conglomerates with a presence in differing sectors is well known, as is the discount that this implies on the price of the whole as opposed to the price of its constituent parts. This means that the easiest path for the public sector, the partial privatization of a holding company under which its portfolio of various shareholdings is grouped, could involve a considerable cost in terms of lower revenues because it does not best suit investor requirements.

## Asset package with a positive value

Arguments have sometimes been put forward in Spain to support the inviability of a far-reaching privatization process, particularly of the INI Group, because of the impossibility of transferring unprofitable companies to the private sector. This would infer that only profitable companies may be privatized, thus giving an argument to the opponents of privatization which could then claim that the government is selling the 'family silver'.

The premise that unprofitable companies cannot be sold is not correct. It would be correct, though, to state that one may sell only companies which possess a positive economic value. Within the public sector there are, however, numerous companies with a negative economic value that may be classified into two groups:

1. Companies in which the real value of their assets, as an on-going concern, is simply negative under any imaginable form of management or working conditions. An example in Spain would be coal mining. It is very simple economics: mining for diamonds in a place where there are no diamonds could never be profitable.
2. Companies that have taken expensive off balance sheet commitments, for example, in terms of working conditions (salaries, reduced working hours, pension plans) which make them economically inviable. That is to say, their current value under those commitments is just negative for any buyer but could be positive with some restructuring which restores conditions normal in the market. We believe that, in Spain, there may be an ample and varied group of state-owned companies which fall within this category. Those companies see their future threatened by past decisions that had small impact on the short-term horizons of those managers who took them, but which made the companies unviable in the long term.

For the first group of companies, the only choice available is not privatization but liquidation. For the second, in order to privatize, all the conditions that hamper the performance of the company have to be swept away so that viability is restored. If that is not the case, the company could only survive under the umbrella of continued public sector subsidies.

There is another case that borders on the latter, in which the company has a positive value under its present conditions, but, in order to develop its full potential, should undergo a traumatic adjustment. Under these circumstances, the company may be privatized. However, the optimal way to go is probably not through the capital market but rather through its direct sale to a 'restructurer': a firm who would put strong management in charge and with sufficient financial backing to affront a prolonged period of maturity of the readjustment decisions.

## Definition of the legal framework

Privatization sometimes implies the need to change radically the regulation by which a given activity or sector is governed. An obvious example is the privatization of a monopoly, be it a:

• natural monopoly, such as water or electricity distribution
• legal monopoly, such as tobacco or the former oil monopoly in Spain.

Other examples would be related to one type or another of potential market failure in the sector, such as public goods (for instance, in motorways which can be private in Spain) or externalities.

The need to draw up radically new regulation derives from the fact that the public sector ceases to have hierarchical control over company decisions. Small though the private stake may be, it nonetheless radically changes the objectives of the company. They should be centred, from then onwards, on the return the company should provide to the investors whose capital it administers. Consequently, in contrast to the former situation of absolute control by the administration over its decisions, it becomes important to design a new legal framework that establishes the necessary incentives for the company to take the right economic decisions.

As the British experience has shown, the drawing up of a new regulation has to take into account that: the fewer the limitations imposed on the company, the greater will be its profits and, consequently, the higher will be the selling price received by the public sector. On the other hand, a posterior change towards stricter regulations may be subject to legal claims and complaints from the shareholders who witness a change in the conditions under which they made their investment in the company.

In some cases, it is necessary to clarify fiscal aspects, for the way in which the public sector receives company revenues is no longer indifferent: profits are no longer paid into the same till as taxes. This also implies a significant change in company management, for attention must now be paid to seeking an optimum fiscal policy.

*Management continuity*

When privatizations are carried out through sale on the stock markets, the management team previously in charge usually continues at the head of the company. Evaluation of the management team's strategy and their capacity to carry it through successfully is an important factor for potential investors. This evaluation cannot be made unless the management team has had the opportunity to demonstrate its qualities over a considerable period at the head of the company. If this is not the case, investors will face high uncertainty as to the direction the company may take once it has been privatized and this will have a negative impact on the price at which they will be prepared to invest in it.

The political stability that Spain has enjoyed since 1982, under a socialist party which has held an absolute majority in parliament without interruption, has lent much greater continuity to the management teams of public sector companies. Consequently, the two main partial privatizations through flotation on the stock market (ENDESA and REPSOL) were carried out under these conditions of stability at the management nucleus and in the development of company strategy.

*Limitations in design of the operation*

It is true that privatizations in Spain have not been submitted to the intense public debate that have accompanied them in other European countries, such as the UK, France and Italy. As a result of this, those entrusted with their realization enjoyed great freedom in the method of their execution.

The situation, however, is normally quite the opposite. The exacting nature of public control and the need to make highly differing objectives coincide often makes the task of those responsible for the privatization more difficult, since they may not necessarily be able to follow normal market practices.

Certain limitations of this type were imposed on the two major Spanish privatizations carried out through flotation on the stock exchange (ENDESA and REPSOL). One of these was the need to grant pre-eminence to the Spanish market as far as the volumes initially allotted for placement were concerned. In the case of ENDESA, this was not corroborated by the real demand proportions, thus causing some problems of share re-allocation and lowering potential revenue from the sale.

## Lack of depth in the capital markets

Once a package of assets that is attractive for investors and possesses a positive economic value has been created working within a well-defined legal framework, under a prestigious top-quality management, and once the operation has been designed under normal market practices, it would seem that buyers should appear automatically and the success of the operation would be assured. This assumption is widely extended, with reference to direct sales and stock market flotations alike, but it is very far from the truth, as many cases of problematic placements have shown: British Petroleum (October 1987), Elf Aquitaine (December 1991), GPA (Spring 1992).

As for privatization through stock market flotation, recent history demonstrates that requirements in terms of volume to be placed and the increasingly complicated nature of the operations undertaken have clearly superseded capital market capacities. Many of the large privatizations (particularly in Britain) have forced the markets to try new placement structures – previously untested by private companies – or to attempt placement of volumes unprecedented to that date.

In this respect, the first step was to surpass local markets, progressing towards the concept of a global offer in which institutional investors from all over the world take part simultaneously. Secondly, as shown in Table 7.3, previous volume records were broken one after another (leaving aside the problematic offer of BP in 1987). The final point is that practices were gradually changed, with the adoption of new concepts such as transparency, which means that investors must identify themselves in order to facilitate allocation to long term holders; or the American-style generation of demand ('book building') by which the consortium of banks receives an indication of demand volumes from investors throughout a marketing period.

The globalization of markets and investment is still far from absolute. There still exists a clear tendency on the part of institutions to maintain

**Table 7.3** Main British privatizations through stock market placement
(volumes surpassing £500 million)

| Company | Date | Volume (million £) |
|---|---|---|
| Britoil | Nov 82 | 548 |
| British Petroleum I | Sept 83 | 565 |
| British Telecom I | Dec 84 | 3,916 |
| British Aerospace | May 85 | 550 |
| Cable & Wireless | Dec 85 | 933 |
| British Gas | Dec 86 | 5,434 |
| British Airways | Feb 87 | 900 |
| Rolls Royce | May 87 | 1,360 |
| British Petroleum II | Oct 87 | 7,240 |
| British Airports A | Jul 87 | 1,280 |
| British Steel | Nov 88 | 2,500 |
| Water Cos | Dec 89 | 5,240 |
| Elect. Dist. | Dec 90 | 5,180 |
| Elect. Gens | Mar 91 | 2,160 |
| Scot. Gens | Jun 91 | 2,880 |
| British Telecom II | Dec 91 | 5,350 |

*Source:* Treasury figures

the bulk of their investments in assets within their country of origin, over and above that indicated by any model for optimum diversification of the investment portfolio.

Table 7.4 illustrates this situation in the main European countries. Only the UK and Switzerland invest more than 10 per cent of their portfolio in foreign assets. The tendency of French (4 per cent) and German (2 per cent) institutional investors towards local investment is surprising, as it is to an even greater degree when practised by investors from countries with small stock markets which greatly limit their choice, such as Austria, Holland or Spain.

Table 7.4 also shows three other interesting aspects of the matter:

1. The small overall volume of institutional investment, except in the UK (and Switzerland in relative terms to the size of its economy).
2. The marked preference for fixed income assets shown by continental institutions: investment in equity makes up less than 10 per cent of the total for Germany, Italy and Spain.
3. The importance of the American market which stands out because of the vast size of funds managed by institutional investors, in spite of their as yet low level of internationalization.

**Table 7.4**  Structure of international institutional investment

|  | Total Assets | Equity | | Foreign Equity | |
|---|---|---|---|---|---|
|  | US$ | US$ bns | % | US$ bns | % |
| Spain | 60 | 1 | 1 | 0 | 0 |
| Austria | 29 | 4 | 14 | 1 | 3 |
| France | 920 | 170 | 19 | 34 | 4 |
| Germany | 705 | 58 | 8 | 11 | 2 |
| Holland | 418 | 67 | 16 | 28 | 7 |
| Italy | 362 | 26 | 7 | 5 | 1 |
| Switzerland | 762 | 204 | 27 | 119 | 16 |
| UK | 1432 | 900 | 63 | 276 | 10 |
| USA | 5890 | 1618 | 27 | 107 | 2 |

*Source*: Deutshe Bank and own calculations for Spain.

For our purposes, the overall conclusion that may be drawn from these figures is that placements on continental markets are made more difficult because of the low institutional investment in equities. This leads to an increased dependence on retail investors – always less sophisticated and in need of greater incentives as far as return prospects are concerned – or on demand from foreign institutional investors.

If we turn our attention to Spain, Table 7.4 shows that the lack of institutional investment on the continent is exacerbated: there is very little institutional investment in absolute terms. What there is is not diversified internationally and it is almost entirely directed towards fixed income and real estate.

Consequently, the privatization of companies through the stock exchange must be directed towards foreign investors and demand from the domestic retail holder. In addition, the latter suffers a further de-motivation because of the negative bias in the taxation applied to direct shareholding, investment through mutual funds, both in terms of the taxation of dividends and capital gains.

## Loss of national control

Finally, one of the main factors limiting the spread of privatization or flexibility in its execution is the fear that the nation will lose control over privatized companies. The state-owned company is, by definition, submitted to control by nationals from within national territory. A change in ownership structure as a result of privatization also implies change in the control structure and, consequently, there exists an immediate or future possibility that this may pass into the hands of foreigners or be controlled from outside the country.

The concern that this possibility excites is manifest and widespread: the measures taken to avoid loss of national control by France (*noyau dur*), Britain ('golden shares' or the KIO-BP issue) and, recently, the limitations set by Portugal on its privatization programme are examples enough of this attitude. As far as Spain is concerned, although the arguments that justify the retention of control packages in large state-owned companies (Telefónica, REPSOL, Endesa or Tabacalera) are not explicitly mentioned, the fear of absorption of this large companies by foreign groups would come at the top of the list. This fear would be underscored by the widespread feeling that there has been a massive sell-out of Spanish private firms to foreign investors. However, this is hardly the occasion to discuss this important issue

For our purposes here, however, it is significant to evaluate the effects that the above may have upon a privatization programme. In the first place, it must be taken into account that, although national control has certain positive effects, these must be counterbalanced by the multiple effects of a different nature that are brought to bear in a privatization. For example, in the case of SEAT, the fact that there was no national partner capable of undertaking the restructuring of the company was rightly considered more important than any 'headquarters effect', when it came to deciding upon the group of possible buyers.

Second, the concession of a state-owned company to a determined national economic group gives rise to considerable political problems insofar as the objectivity of the state in its adjudication and the concentration of economic power are concerned. For example, the latter would be an important issue in Italy where there are a few family groups who exert control over an important share of the economy. However, in Spain, the main problem at present would probably be the opposite, that is to find groups which are strategically inclined and have sufficient financial and administrative resources to take charge of controlling stakes in privatized companies.

The third possibility to be taken into account is that the company be floated on the stock market, with share ownership widely dispersed and with an independent management who does not have a controlling stake. This by itself does not permanently maintain the company's national identity, as take-overs may occur at a later date. Consequently, this choice is usually accompanied by protective measures to hinder take-overs, which, in turn, produce the undesirable effect of weakening incentives for management to procure the maximum value of the company for its shareholders.

All three alternatives lead us to the conclusion that the wish to retain national control is an added complication of great importance to privatization, especially in a country such as Spain where there is neither a core of institutional investors that could support the 'management' of independent companies, nor powerful business groups that could take up controlling stakes in the privatized companies.

## Conclusions

We have seen that the Spanish public sector may be considered a special case within the European context. On the one hand, its creation was not the result of a consistent policy, which determined the areas of the economy that would be subject to public or private control. On the other hand, there has not been a privatization policy during the last decade either, but rather a series of privatizations which did not follow a clear set of principles.

In this respect, then, Spain is a somewhat unusual case. The reasons behind this situation may probably be found in the prudent attitude of recent governments that should be interpreted as the desire to avoid opening new breaches for discussion, be they between parties or internal, before completing the development of other aspects of the Spanish political and economic system that were considered more urgent. This attitude, fleeing ideological debate of the scope of public and private sectors, was most clearly expressed in the total and urgent privatization of companies belonging to the RUMASA Group and in the sale of emblematic companies, with no future in the public sector, to foreign groups, as in the case of SEAT or ENASA.

Nevertheless, in the future, budgetary problems resulting from the economic recession, the fulfilment of stipulations arising from the Maastricht agreement and, above all, the fact that Spain cannot remain an exception in a world trend, should lead to a more aggressive action in the field of privatizations. The aim will not be to return to the private sector that which, ideologically, corresponds to it, but rather to relieve the public sector (and consequently the Government) of a weighty responsibility from which it obtains neither political nor economical benefit.

## Notes

1. In this chapter the word 'privatization' will be used in the narrow sense of what Vickers and Wright (1989) have called 'industrial privatization' (i.e. the sale of public industrial assets to private individuals or gramps).
2. The interesting work by A. Espina (1991) argues that another model for INI was the 'Reichswerke', created by Hermann Goering in the Nazi Germany.
3. In addition to the firms listed in Table 7.2 (which were absorbed by INI), the "Departmento del Patrimonio" absorbed several major loss-making textile firms (Intelhorce, Hyatasa, Gossipium) and motorways (Autopistas Astur Leonesas, Navarras y del Atlántico).
4. In France six of the ten largest and most important companies are state-owned (this figure does not include public entities such as Electricité de France or Gaz de France, which formally are not companies). In every case this is the result of decisions taken upon state initiative as opposed to salvage operations on companies in crisis.
5. Gilmour (1992) shows how a similar process took place in England. English companies owned by the state were firstly developed by Conservative governments, but, following the Labour party's annual conference in 1944, the British socialists took them over as an important part of their political programme.
6. Separate mention should be made of a new element that has recently appeared: state-owned companies promoted by regional governments. Indeed, a cross-section analysis shows that there is no correlation between political ideology and the role that regional governments are adopting in the economy. These are governments with few years behind them that are setting out on the road to expansion within the economic arena that national States travelled many decades ago. Peculiar circumstances occur when strong nationalist parties are in existence, since for them public intervention in the economy is rather the result of a desire to achieve national strength than of an ideological position on the role of the State in the economy.

## References

Espina, A. (1991), 'Recursos Humanos y Política Industrial', en *España ante la Unión Europea*, Madrid, Fundesco.

Gilmour, I. (1992), *Dancing with Dogma. Britain under Thatcherism*, New York and London, Simon & Shuster.

Martín Aceña, P. and Comín F. (1991), *INI. 50 años de Industrialización en España*, Madrid, Espasa-Calpe.

Vickers, J. and Wright, V. (1989), 'The Politics of industrial privatization in Western Europe: an overview', in Vickers & Wright (eds), *The Politics of Privatization on Western Europe*, London, Frank Cass: 1–30.

# CHAPTER 8

## LOOKING REALITY IN THE EYE: THE POLITICS OF PRIVATIZATION IN AUSTRIA

### Delia Meth-Cohn and Wolfgang C. Müller

**Introduction**

In the mid-1980s Austria had the largest nationalized sector of all the West European countries (Parris *et al.* 1987: 27). The nationalization had less to do with ideology than with the peculiar circumstances of Austria in the immediate post-war period. Although the Socialist Party (SPÖ) was ideologically in favour of wide-scale nationalization, the all-party government, led by the conservative People's Party (ÖVP), supported a more limited version of the programme largely because of the need for reconstruction and 'Austrification' (Langer, 1966: 173–97). Consequently, rather than nationalizing whole sectors as the SPÖ wanted, the 1946 law affected only former German property, which under the treaty of Potsdam belonged to the Allies as war reparations, and those companies that had suffered serious damage during the war and were therefore unable to find private investors. In addition, only the shares of these companies were nationalized, leaving the private company structure intact. Although the ÖVP occasionally brought the issue of privatization on to the political agenda, there was little popular backing, and those measures that were introduced soon ran out of steam. By the early 1970s the issue of industrial ownership had lost its political importance.

Before privatization re-emerged as a political issue in the mid-1980s, the nationalized sector consisted of three major parts: the ÖIAG, a holding company of industrial shares; the two state-owned banks, the Creditanstalt and the Länderbank, with their own industrial concerns; and the electric power industry. The ÖIAG at this time comprised firms within the iron and steel industry (VOEST, VEW), the chemical industry (Chemie Linz), the electrical industry (Elin, 42.6 per cent of Siemens Austria), the aluminium industry (Austria Metall), the oil industry (ÖMV), the vehicle and machine industry (SGP) and the mining industries. In 1984 the ÖIAG employed about 18 per cent of the total industrial workforce, was responsible for 22 per cent of industrial production and 14 per cent of industrial investment (having decreased from about 30 per cent between 1970 and 1980).

The Creditanstalt was the second largest owner of industrial assets, held as a rule in the form of majority shares rather than total ownership. Following the partial privatization of mainly non-voting shares in 1956, 60 per cent of the bank was state-owned. Until 1985 it included the two largest industrial firms outside the ÖIAG: Steyr (motor industry) and Semperit. Other important industrial firms were located in the machinery (Andritz, Heid), glass, paper and textile industries. The Länderbank, with the same history of nationalization and privatization, also held numerous assets of which those in the construction industry were the most important.

In addition to these manufacturing industries, most of the electric power industry belonged to the public sector: about 60 per cent was state-owned, the rest belonged to the nine Austrian provinces.[1] Other nationalized companies were Austrian Airlines, the largest Austrian travel agency and numerous smaller firms in a variety of sectors. The public sector also included the traditional state monopolies of salt and tobacco, the federal railways, the post office and a considerable number of locally owned service industries. In 1990 the public sector as a whole employed 340,000 people; this amounts to 11.7 per cent of the entire Austrian workforce, down from 13.3 per cent in 1983 and 12.2 per cent in 1988. In 1990 some 18.7 per cent of total investments (or AS81 billion) were accounted for by the public sector, a drop from 21 per cent in 1983.

In the next section, we shall discuss the emergence of privatization as a political issue in the mid-1980s, leading to its acceptance as a potential strategy by both parties. Then we analyse the development of a concrete privatization policy by the SPÖ-led grand coalition government that assumed office in 1987, with particular emphasis on the changes which made this possible within the SPÖ. In the next section, we follow the implementation of the privatization programme from 1987 to 1991. Eventually it became clear that it was not succeeding; in the penultimate section, we give an account of the policy's failure in 1992 and 1993 and map out the privatization programme that then emerged. In conclusion, we attempt to analyse the factors that transformed privatization from an instrument of electoral politics, to a means of raising government revenue, to a pragmatic instrument of economic policy and finally to a strategy of crisis management.

## Making privatization an issue in the 1980s[2]

In the 1970s and early 1980s, the size of the state-owned sector was generally accepted by the two major parties, both of which regarded the nationalized industries as a basic element of the socio-economic consensus. The SPÖ, for its part, had abandoned ownership changes as the basis of its economic policy; the state-owned sector was seen rather as a stabilizing factor in the economy (Meth-Cohn, 1988: 251). The ÖVP had also abandoned privatization in its party programmes. Indeed, in 1982, Wolfgang Schüssel (1982: 146), who was soon to become the most active promoter of privatization, stated that despite some qualifications his party accepted the nationalized industries and recognized their necessity for the Austrian economy. Although it would be too strong to talk of an ideological consensus on this issue, neither party had ideological objections to retaining the status quo.

The political debate over privatization began to re-emerge in 1982 in the context of the ÖVP's adoption of the neo-liberal economic policy that had proven to be so electorally successful for its sister parties in Britain, the USA and Germany. The background to this change was less a fundamental rethinking of economic policy on the part of the ÖVP, than an attempt to articulate a constructive alternative to the SPÖ's Austro-Keynesian policy, which was beginning to lose popularity. During the 1970s the ÖVP had not presented fundamental policy alternatives to the SPÖ's economic policy, but promised to implement a similar economic policy with greater skill. This strategy did not result in electoral success, and the SPÖ was able to retain its absolute majority of 1971 in both 1975 and 1979. At the beginning of the 1980s, macro-economic performance deteriorated and the previously hidden costs of Austro-Keynesianism (in particular public debt, taxation and structural problems) became visible (Gerlich and Müller, 1989). The neo-liberal alternative, consisting of budgetary cuts and shifts in priorities, a comprehensive tax reform including substantial tax relief, flexibility, deregulation and privatization, was able directly to address the problems caused by the SPÖ's policy and thus had considerable potential for electoral success. In addition, privatization was particularly important in promising to deal with the question of the nationalized industries, which were beginning to show huge losses (Itzlinger et al., 1989). In the context of increasing constraints on budgetary expenditure, it was important to find a way of financing the nationalized enterprises outside of the budget.

The scope of the ÖVP's privatization goals, developed in more detail in a proposal published in 1985,[3] was very moderate. The majority of shares in the major nationalized firms, including the ÖIAG, the two banks and the electric power industry, were to remain in state hands, and only non-strategic firms were to be privatized totally or in large part. Nevertheless, the ÖVP had very high expectations as to the consequences of such a minimal privatization. It would enlarge the financial room for the state to engage in new activities, such as promoting new technologies and environmental policy; it would intensify competition and improve the performance of the economy; the productivity and efficiency of the nationalized firms would improve; and privatization would lead to a broad expansion of ownership.

The lack of balance between concrete policy proposals and expectations pointed to the fact that the demand for privatization was not so much a well worked-out policy based on fundamental rethinking as an attempt to articulate a clear alternative to the SPÖ, in the context of growing dissatisfaction with the rising costs of the nationalized industries. The ÖVP has always comprised a broad spectrum of different ideologies and consequently displays a very pragmatic attitude to ideological issues (Müller, 1991). As a conservative party, the ÖVP had always been sceptical about state ownership, and the social reform wing supported worker ownership rather than public ownership. It was, then, not difficult in terms of intra-party politics for the ÖVP to adopt privatization as part of the party programme but, as its past attitude demonstrates, neither was it an inevitable development. Indeed, the most important argument for adopting a privatization policy was electoral: as shown in Tables 8.1 and 8.2, Austrians were becoming increasingly unwilling to pay for the nationalized industries and the attitude towards privatization was becoming increasingly favourable.

Privatization was not only in itself a potential vote-getter, the failure of the nationalized industries was the example which could best demonstrate the superiority of the ÖVP's new economic policy over that of the SPÖ: state intervention in the economy is economically disadvanta-

**Table 8.1**  Austria: attitudes towards financial help for the nationalized industries out of the federal budget (1981–6)

| % of population | 1981 | 1982 | 1983–7 | 1983/10 | 1986 |
| --- | --- | --- | --- | --- | --- |
| In favour of financial aid | 75 | 69 | 60 | 44 | 40 |
| Against financial aid | 17 | 31 | 34 | 52 | 56 |

*Source:* W.C. Müller (1986).

**Table 8.2**   Austria: attitudes towards privatization (1979–86)

| % of population | 1979 | 1986 |
|---|---|---|
| Some nationalized firms should be privatized | 17 | 63 |
| Number of nationalized firms should remain the same | 67 | 29 |
| New firms should be nationalized | 11 | 3 |

*Source*: P.A. Ulram (1990).

geous, nationalized firms produce losses, jobs are lost and tax money wasted. In short, the ÖVP's sudden conversion to privatization was primarily an attempt to exploit a new electoral potential and thus, after more than a decade in opposition, defeat the SPÖ.

The SPÖ was initially opposed to the ÖVP's privatization proposals, claiming that the problem of the nationalized industries could not be solved by ideologically motivated attacks on state ownership. That the nationalized industries were state-owned, the SPÖ insisted, was not the problem; consequently, privatization could not be the solution (Ostleitner, 1987: 600). The SPÖ effectively dismissed the entire question, leaving it to the SPÖ-dominated Working Group for the Public Economy (Arbeitsgemeinschaft der Gemeinwirtschaft) to defend the nationalized industries. In *Privatisation – The Wrong Alternative*, Tieber and Swoboda claimed, 'Those who want to forget or suppress the historically based and proven system of Austria's mixed economy . . . are clearly just trying to remove state influence on the Austrian economy for ideological reasons'. (Tieber and Swoboda 1984: 3).

The SPÖ's unwillingness to address the issue of privatization in substance changed at the end of 1985 and the beginning of 1986. In November 1985 the largest nationalized enterprise, the VOEST steel firm, reported enormous losses following speculation on the oil market, which amounted to a financial breakdown. The management of Chemie Linz had been involved in similar speculation. In both cases, this had been designed to cover up losses resulting from the firms' terrible economic performance. The ÖVP claimed that these events confirmed the party's strategy, and 'radicalized' its policy to include majority privatization. The SPÖ-led government, in particular the Minister for Public Economy, Ferdinand Lacina, took immediate measures to deal with the situation, sacking the entire management of the VOEST, and pushing through a depoliticization of the nationalized sector. The nationalized industries were in future to follow only market-oriented goals.

Opponents of this course within the SPÖ were quick to point out that depoliticization and market-oriented goals meant a fundamental acceptance of the validity of the ÖVP's neo-liberal principles, including privatisation.[4]

The party leadership, and in particular Franz Vranitzky, Finance Minister and from mid-1986 Chancellor, accepted this logic, realizing not only that the SPÖ's previous economic policy was no longer valid, but that support for privatization would play a vital role in the September general elections. By mid-1986, the SPÖ had begun to argue that privatization was not an ideological issue but a pragmatic one. Partial privatization could be a way of solving some of the problems of the state sector, especially insofar as the budget was concerned; at present, however, it would be more or less impossible to find buyers for many of the nationalized firms, so the immediate necessity was to ensure that these firms were brought back into the black through strictly market-oriented behaviour. Although in the 1986 electoral platform itself the SPÖ included only the vaguest outlines of a privatization policy, in statements and interviews Vranitzky accepted the possibility of partially privatizing some of the more profitable nationalized companies, a strategy which was primarily designed to attract voters.

## Developing a privatization policy – 1986

The elections of 1986 resulted in a virtual tie for the SPÖ (80 seats) and ÖVP (77 seats), despite losses for both parties. One reason for the SPÖ once again being strongest party was that it had more or less adopted the ÖVP's economic policy, thus taking the wind out of the latter's sails. The two parties decided to form a grand coalition government, with the declared intention of implementing structural reforms to deal with the deep-seated economic problems that had become evident in the first half of the 1980s. The coalition negotiations, which lasted until January 1987, resulted in the adoption of a neo-liberal policy based on the twin poles of budget deficit reduction and restructuring. Privatization was to play a role in both of these areas. For the former, it would immediately bring additional income into the budget; in the longer run, it would mean an end to budgetary financing for the nationalized industries. The role of privatization in restructuring was, at this point, less well-defined. In general, privatization was regarded as a way of raising money to make restructuring possible; beyond this, the reorganization of the ÖIAG, in particular, would define core areas, allowing for the sale of non-core parts.

Despite the general policy convergence, privatization was a controversial issue in the coalition negotiations between the SPÖ and ÖVP. The two parties eventually agreed on a final financial contribution to the nationalized industries, but the amount was small enough that privatization would be required to provide additional financing. All firms would be examined to see whether their shares could be introduced on the capital market, but the SPÖ negotiators (under considerable pressure from the unions) insisted on the compromise that only minority shares would be privatized. This was acceptable to the ÖVP, which regarded the very introduction of a privatization policy as a significant breakthrough.

Given Vranitzky's quantum leap into supply-side economic policies, criticism within the party was relatively moderate. This can partly be explained by the political situation. First, this shift had been responsible for the party's relative electoral success. Second, an ÖVP-FPÖ coalition would not have been favourable and within the grand coalition the SPÖ needed the ÖVP's support for the financial aid package for the nationalized industries. But at least on the part of SPÖ economic policymakers, it was also a move away from what had clearly become an unworkable nationalized industry policy. The SPÖ leadership acknowledged that the previous policy had failed in several respects. First, they accepted the need for nationalized enterprises to follow purely market-oriented goals. The state industrial sector cannot be used as an instrument to secure macroeconomic goals (for example, full employment or a specific price policy) because this not only puts the firms at a disadvantage *vis-à-vis* their competitors resulting in poor economic performance, but it also makes it difficult to analyse actual performance – are the losses a result of the additional goals, or are these an excuse for fundamentally poor results? Second, the SPÖ accepted that the state is not an optimal owner. A minister cannot run a firm in the same way as a private owner; under such a situation the enterprise belongs *de facto* to the management and the workers' council, and beyond that to local and regional politicians and the unions. Until 1986 in Austria, political influence on the nationalized industries had been institutionalized by distributing management and board of director positions between the two parties in a system known as *Proporz*. Before meetings of the board of directors (*Aufsichtsrat*), the SPÖ managers would brief 'their' directors, and the ÖVP managers 'theirs', thus virtually abolishing the body's control function. In addition, local politicians would intervene for various reasons by going straight to the minister or chancellor, over the heads of management. On the other side, the individual firms were often reluctant to keep the ÖIAG (the instrument of the minister) correctly and fully informed of their activities. Indeed, the former general manager of the VOEST used to describe the ÖIAG as a 'Russian bureaucracy'.

Exactly what role privatization was to play in the new economic policy was still, however, unclear. The SPÖ saw privatization as politically unavoidable, but not as a solution to the problems of the nationalized industries. Many leading members in the SPÖ were worried that, with the present state of this sector, privatization would mean 'privatizing the profits, and socializing the losses'. They were prepared to accept privatization to a limited degree, using the proceeds to restructure the nationalized enterprises which could then be competitive on the world market. In terms of the nationalized industries themselves, the new approach required clear market-oriented goals, personnel decisions made on the basis of qualifications rather than party membership, clear delineation of worker and ministerial participation in management decision-making. Even if, as Lacina expressed it, 'some of us (i.e. the SPÖ) "no longer understand the world" ', these changes were necessary, given the high export quotas of the major firms.[5]

## Privatization in practice 1987–91: from electoral strategy to industrial policy

By late 1987 the two parties had worked out a detailed privatization programme on the basis of the outlines of the coalition agreement. These measures included the reduction of the state's share in the profitable ÖMV to 51 per cent, a further reduction in the state's minority share in Siemens Austria, the partial privatization of Austrian Airlines and the two banks, leaving the state a 51 per cent share, the sale of 49 per cent of the electric power industry, and the sale of smaller firms. There were basically two motives behind the choice and structure of these privatizations. The first was political, and particularly important for the ÖVP. The flotation of shares in profitable firms such as ÖMV and Austrian Airlines would involve the electorate in the process and would demonstrate that the government was serious about reducing the state sector and its burden on the tax payer. The second motive was crisis management; the government needed to raise money to finance restructuring and to ease budget consolidation. All money from the sale of ÖIAG assets was to remain in the concern and be used for financial reconstruction of the remaining companies; profits from the privatization of the banks and the airline would go directly to the budget; the sum raised by privatization within the electric power industry would constitute funds for the promotion of technology and innovation. At this stage, then, privatization was only indirectly part of the restructuring strategy which involved depoliticization and reorganization rather than privatization *per se.*

Between 1987 and 1990, steps were taken to fulfil this programme. Within the ÖIAG, 30 per cent of shares in the ÖMV were floated in two tranches; the ÖIAG share in Siemens Austria was reduced to 25 per cent, and around 60 smaller firms, with some 13,000 employees were sold in whole or in part. Up to 1990 the revenue from these sales amounted to some AS14 billion. By 1989, the state share in the Länderbank and Creditanstalt was reduced to 51 per cent, (although its stake in voting shares remained higher), bringing in total revenue to the budget of AS1,826 million. The banks were free to privatize their industrial assets as they wanted. Between 1988–90, following a concentration of shares in the main electric power company, the Verbundgesellschaft, the state share was reduced to 53.8 per cent,[6] raising revenue of AS5,194 million. The state share in Austrian Airlines was reduced from 99.1 per cent, to 51.9 per cent, bringing in AS1,150 million. A number of smaller companies (in porcelain, tourism, transport, film and explosives) that had ended up in state ownership for a variety of reasons, were sold bringing in around AS720 million. In addition, the Hauptmünzamt (responsible for minting coins) was sold to the Austrian National Bank in 1989, bringing AS8 billion into the budget. This was a transfer within the public sector rather than a genuine privatization, but it served the same purpose of raising money for the budget. In this way privatization also played an important role in overcoming problems within the coalition. Since the government had announced a definite schedule for reducing the budget deficit, the additional income from privatization made the annual budget negotiations considerably easier than they might have been. Thus, to some extent this can be seen as selling-off the family silver in order to keep the family (i.e. the coalition) together.

The main actors involved in the development of privatization policy were the parties' teams in government. Austria's private industry, though generally in favour of privatization, is dominated by small and medium-sized firms that have little direct economic interest in privatization. The managers of the nationalized industries – selected for their positive attitudes towards privatization and their restructuring experience – had an indirect influence on the process, encouraging the politicians that their policies would work and at times setting more ambitious goals.

Once the privatization programme had begun, the SPÖ economic policymakers in the government, especially Chancellor Franz Vranitzky, Finance Minister Ferdinand Lacina, and Minister for Public Economy,

Rudolf Streicher, began to develop their position substantially on the role of privatization. Instead of seeing it as potentially disadvantageous for the economy ('privatizing the profits and socializing the losses'), they began to regard privatization as an integral part of the policy designed to restructure and modernize the Austrian economy in preparation for EC membership. In the course of this shift, the SPÖ abandoned its reservations about retaining a majority in the state sector in favour of looking at the strategic requirements of the economy as a whole.

What the SPÖ economic policymakers added to the privatization policy can be seen most clearly in the two core parts of the state sector: the ÖIAG and the banks. As far as the ÖIAG is concerned, the SPÖ argued for a halt to privatizing profitable branches in favour of keeping the concern as a strategic unit which could itself be privatized. The argument behind this is that Austria is characterized by small and medium-sized companies and requires a large conglomerate to further the internationalization of the economy and to make use of economies of scale in technological development. What made it possible to start thinking in these terms was the spectacular recovery of the ÖIAG due both to the structural reforms that had taken place and to the improvement in the world economy (especially in the steel sector). From an operating loss of AS8.3 billion in 1987, the ÖIAG managed to break even in 1988 and produced profits of AS8 billion between 1989 and 1991. As parts of the earlier restructuring, the ÖIAG had been divided into seven autonomous branch holding companies. Under the new strategy, six of these were placed under the strategic direction of a new holding company, Austrian Industries (AI), with a board of directors comprising each of the sectoral managing directors and two central directors. The ÖIAG itself became a financial holding company for AI, with the additional responsibilities of managing the nationalized industry debts and the mining holding company, which has little hope of becoming profitable in the short term. Privatization would be implemented by floating shares in AI at a time that was appropriate both in terms of the companies' financial status and of the stock market. The first step was taken in 1990, with the issue of a five-year 'Going Public' bond convertible into shares on preferable terms.[7] The original plan, negotiated with the ÖVP following the 1990 elections and laid down in the coalition agreement,[8] was to raise the capital of AI by issuing new shares by the end of 1993 at the latest. If it proved impossible to issue shares before this time – either because of problems in the steel industry or due to unfavourable stock market conditions – capital requirements would be covered by selling off further shares at the sectoral level (for example, by floating a further tranche of ÖMV shares). From 1994 the old shares of AI were to be floated at a ratio of three new shares for every old one. Two thirds of the income from the sale of the old shares would remain within the ÖIAG and be used for paying off old debts. The other third would go to the budget, which would receive some AS4.5 billion from the privatization of AI by 1994. Once new shares made up 30 per cent of the AI's equity, the process would be speeded up, and two thirds of the proceeds from the privatization of the old shares would flow to the budget.

In the banking sector, the SPÖ, under the direction of Finance Minister Ferdinand Lacina, has also abandoned its insistence on retaining a majority state share in favour of strategic restructuring. Before the 1990 elections, and despite opposition from the unions, Lacina made it clear that he was not opposed to full privatization of the Creditanstalt and Länderbank.[9] Privatization, however, could only take place under two conditions. The first was that the banks must remain primarily in Austrian hands. As with the privatization of AI, the SPÖ was concerned to ensure the maintenance of the few nationally owned strategically important enterprises, given the very high level of foreign ownership in the Austrian economy (see Ederer *et al.*, 1985; Beer *et al.*, 1991). The second condition was that the sale of the state share be part of a package involving a resolution of the structural problems of the banking sector. In particular, this meant the creation of larger banks that could compete on the international market. The coalition negotiations of 1990 substantiated this position. The two parties agreed that the legal restraint on privatizing more than 49 per cent would be dropped, that new shares would be issued, thus automatically reducing the state share, and that 'further substantial steps towards privatization' would take place 'while defending national interests in the context of structural reforms' in the banking sector.[10]

The ÖVP negotiators originally wanted a clearer definition of what steps would be taken to privatize the banks. The SPÖ ultimately managed to persuade them that the open timetable was not intended as a delay tactic by arguing that, given the uncertainties of the stock exchange and the banks' financial results, it is disadvantageous for the seller to be forced to sell at a date specified in advance. The ÖVP was also worried about linking privatization to structural reform, but finally accepted that the SPÖ, and the Finance Minister in particular, were serious about implementing privatization.

Under this agreement, the management of Creditanstalt and Länderbank were free to look for partners within the conditions outlined above. In 1991 the first steps were taken to restructure the banking sector. Länderbank merged with the much larger Zentralsparkasse der Gemeinde Wien creating the new Bank Austria. The state has only a minority stake in this bank; Bank Austria is free to look for strategically interesting partners, including foreign banks, to which the state would sell its shares. Creditanstalt is large enough not to require such a radical step; instead its reform strategy is to expand by attracting institutional investors and by issuing shares to the general public. In 1991, the state reduced its share in Creditanstalt to 49.95 per cent (although it still has a majority of voting shares), raising revenue of AS354 million.

The shift that had taken place at governmental level was reflected in a somewhat diluted form in the new SPÖ party programme, *Sozialdemokratie 2000* (1989). Here it was accepted that the nationalized sector was not a goal in itself; the central question was what contribution it could make to achieving the SPÖ's goals. According to the programme, 'the question of whether public ownership in the economy makes sense, can only be answered by looking at the specific requirements of the economy and society'. This means that a 'healthy, economically self-sufficient existence for the enterprises' has priority over the question of ownership.[11] External macroeconomic policies cannot be implemented through the state-owned sector without endangering its competitiveness on the world market and thus turning it into a burden on the budget. The existing industries can, however, be maintained as a nationally owned large concern to the benefit of the entire economy. On the surface, this rethinking of the issue hardly seems to amount to an embracing of privatization. The ÖIAG, for example, could fulfil these conditions in principle without being privatized at all. The need for privatization, however, becomes evident in the question of financing. Politically, it would be unacceptable for the nationalized industries to burden the budget. More importantly, if the enterprises are to be run without any state intervention, financing cannot be based on political acceptability; they must have access to the capital market for equity financing, which automatically reduces the state share

Since 1987 the ÖVP has tended to regard privatization as a goal in itself, advertising it as one of its main contributions to the coalition's work, and promising to push ahead with full privatization. In the 1990 election campaign, the ÖVP presented a proposal that would bring in AS175 billion over the next 10 years. Given the small size of the Vienna stock exchange, which even at its high point in 1989–90 could only have absorbed new issues of approximately AS20 billion per year, this policy was unrealistic. It would moreover have exhausted the financial market's potential to finance the expansion of medium-sized companies, one of the ÖVP's main economic goals. As a result, the new SPÖ-initiated strategy was eventually supported by most of the economic policymakers within the ÖVP. It was generally accepted that the SPÖ's unwillingness to present a concrete timetable for privatization was not a way of delaying it. Ironically, as a consequence, although the ÖVP was responsible for the introduction of privatization (and for the new direction in economic policy), it was unable to reap the electoral benefits of the change. Given the policy convergence between the two parties, the issue of privatization was removed from the electoral agenda. A poll taken in 1988 showed that 82 per cent of the population favoured at least some privatization with only 11 per cent against. The difference between supporters of the two major parties was slight. Polls conducted in 1989 and 1991 also showed majorities for privatization of 69 per cent and 72 per cent respectively.[12] Moreover, with the SPÖ responsible for implementing privatization through its control of the relevant ministries, the improvement in the state sector was not attributed to the ÖVP, but to the government or even the SPÖ.

## Privatization in practice 1992–3: from industrial policy to crisis management

Many observers were sceptical about the economic viability of AI's ambitious plans. Indeed, during 1992 several problems emerged that forced decision-makers to rethink their strategy. The first was the general slow-down in economic growth, exacerbated by increasing competition in the raw material sectors from Eastern Europe. This slowdown revealed the continued existence of unsolved structural problems that had been hidden by the brief boom. In addition, AI's problems were exacerbated by bad decision-making in the non-ferrous metal sector, AMAG. The company had followed an ambitious strategy of internationalization, expansion and diversification during the boom period of the second half of the 1980s. It is now clear that the strategy was neither planned carefully enough nor executed with sufficient skill to cope with the new environment. These factors resulted in drastic losses for AMAG in 1992 of around AS5 billion. The new management calculates that AMAG will require at least AS13 billion for financial restructuring.

The slowdown in economic growth had also affected the other sectors, in particular the ÖMV, formerly the natural candidate for privatization. In 1992 it was able to contain its losses at AS270 million only by releasing reserves. In addition, the share price dropped dramatically following poorer than expected results and claims of insider trading. In

1993 the situation worsened, and losses are estimated at up to AS4.7 billion.

As a consequence of these factors, AI went into the red again with total losses of AS4.8 billion in 1992. The losses would have been around AS7.3 billion if the nationalized industries had not resorted to the trick of AI selling the ÖMV to its mother company, the ÖIAG, thereby activating silent reserves.

In autumn 1992 AI developed a new plan by which profitable companies within the branch holding companies were to be floated on the exchange as soon as possible. AI's share of ÖMV was to be reduced from 72 per cent to around 26 per cent, by bringing in a strategic partner. The capital would then be used by AI for restructuring, allowing for a flotation of AI shares in 1994–5. But in 1993 it became clear that the problems were much more severe than previously thought. Selling off ÖMV shares and other assets would not bring in enough money to restructure the other companies, in particular the AMAG. Management insisted that they would require further help from the state, but political decision-makers were determined not go back on earlier promises by providing additional funds. The ÖVP was clear on this from the beginning, but even top SPÖ politicians (and also lower ranks) made no attempt to raise the issue, demanding instead that the state should not insist on receiving the 'dividend' of AS3.4 billion agreed to for the period up to 1994 in both the 1990 coalition agreement and in a 1991 law. Furthermore, the SPÖ suggested that the state should guarantee bank credits to the AI amounting to AS14 billion.

The alternative to this solution would have been to allow AMAG to go into bankruptcy, an option which was not regarded as viable. Not only would it have had social and political ramifications, but it would have been costly in economic terms. Apart from the direct costs, decision-makers believed that if AI were to default on its loan payments it might undermine Austria's position as a sovereign borrower. If it were to lose its triple A status, this would be more costly – both directly and indirectly – than paying for AMAG. Consequently, the ÖVP was willing to support a state guarantee as long as the guaranteed amount was kept low and it was ensured that the guarantee would not have to be used. In implicit exchange, the ÖVP was given considerable influence over the reorganization of the nationalized industries.

The SPÖ's reorganization plan was based on a study by the British investment bank Warburg and focused on trying to preserve as much as possible from its previous concept of maintaining an industrial concern which would be privatized as a whole. The concern would be considerably reduced in size because of the need to sell profitable firms in order to raise the money needed for the financial reconstruction of the remaining nationalized sector. AMAG would become part of the ÖIAG to prevent it from being a millstone around the neck of AI. The firms remaining in the new AI would be in the steel and engineering sectors (basically what had been the VOEST, the SGP and Elin before the last reorganization). According to Warburg, it would be possible to sell a majority of the shares of this concern via the stock exchange by mid-1994.

This programme was attractive to the SPÖ not only because it upheld the original idea of a large industrial concern that would have positive spill-over effects for the economy at large, but also because it would ensure that the steel sector would be privatized. On its own, it would be unable to find a buyer and would remain state-owned with all the financial and political risks that that entails.

The ÖVP was not, however, willing to accept this scaled-down version of a concept that had just failed. It insisted on providing state guarantees for a limited period only, and only step-by-step in exchange for the privatization of AI firms. Knowing that the SPÖ would neither allow AI to go bankrupt nor risk the collapse of the grand coalition government on the grounds of providing funds for the nationalized industries, the ÖVP remained firm and eventually succeeded in pushing through its ideas.

In November 1993 the coalition parties signed a new agreement on the nationalized sector which means nothing less than the abolition of what was once relatively the most important state-owned industrial sector in Western Europe. All that will remain in state hands is minority shares and industrial liabilities. Although the SPÖ minister for public economy, Viktor Klima, made a point of saying that he had also found the Warburg plan a little hazardous, it is clear that this was a major victory for the ÖVP. The SPÖ was able to secure concessions that relieve the nationalized industries from paying the AS3.4 billion dividend and provide the ÖIAG with credit of up to AS5 billion (which has to be paid back from privatization revenue). Otherwise the agreement bears the ÖVP's imprint. AI will be abolished, reinstating the ÖIAG as the sole holding company. Entrepreneurial decisions will be made at the firm level rather than by the ÖIAG, which will be slimmed down accordingly. The parties agreed to sell off quickly a number of firms that are attractive to foreign investors, and to look for further candidates for immediate privatization.

The core companies of AI will be treated as follows. The steel sector and the engineering sector will be concentrated in two firms: the VOEST-Alpine Stahl AG and the VOEST-Alpine Technologie AG.

Fifty-one per cent of the latter, which is profitable, will be privatized on the stock exchange by mid-1994. To ensure the co-operation of the steel and engineering companies, they will hold a 25 per cent stake in each other. The remaining 24 per cent and 75 per cent stake respectively will remain in the hands of the ÖIAG.

According to Viktor Klima, the ÖIAG and the steel company remain free to sell their shares in the engineering company if it seems appropriate or financially necessary. A majority of the ÖMV will be privatized by 1995, and the remainder thereafter. The refined metals group Böhler-Uddeholm and the AMAG will be financially restructured and shares will start to be issued in 1996. A majority of both firms will be privatized, although 'Austrian interests will be secured' according to the vague formulation of the agreement.

The privatization programme will be implemented by the ÖIAG and supervised by a sub-committee of the board of directors responsible for optimizing and speeding up privatization. The AS5 billion credit will be provided gradually by the government on the basis of a joint proposal of the minister for public economy (SPÖ) and the secretary of state in the finance ministry (ÖVP).

In contrast to the AI/ÖIAG sector, there has been considerable continuity in the privatization strategy towards the banks and other state-owned companies. Further privatization of Creditanstalt in 1992–3 raised AS298.6 million and reduced the state share to 48.7 per cent (albeit with around 70 per cent voting rights). Creditanstalt management has preferred a strategy of dispersing ownership by selling bank shares rather than by bringing in strategic partners. In 1993 the government managed to sell one third of Casino Austria AG – the largest gambling company in the world and a very profitable enterprise – to Münze Österreich, the company which mints coins for the Austrian central bank. This transfer within the public sector, designed to avoid the risk of selling to organized crime, raised AS600 million for the budget. Nevertheless this performance was far below the budget plan for 1993, which included AS7.6 billion in privatization revenue. As of November 1993 only AS800 million had been raised, a shortfall due to the economic downturn that meant a deterioration in the performance of both the stockmarket and the companies.

## Conclusion

Privatization began in Austria as a political programme, designed to take advantage of the electorate's increasing dissatisfaction with the nationalized industries. In the 1986 elections, both parties referred to privatization as a way of increasing their electoral fortunes, but neither had developed a clear idea of what role privatization would realistically play in future economic strategy. For the ÖVP, privatization was based largely on the ideological conviction that private firms are more successful than state-owned firms. Although this was argued quite plausibly in the face of the huge losses of the nationalized sector, the party's view as to how privatization would alter the existing situation was not well worked out. Indeed, the ÖVP's claims for the impact of privatization went well beyond its very moderate proposals in practice. For the SPÖ, initially, the acceptance of privatization as a possible policy instrument was almost entirely the result of the failure of its previous policy. Before the exposure of the ÖIAG's losses at the end of 1985, the SPÖ had tended to reject privatization on pragmatic grounds; in the elections, the party shifted its position towards accepting it where necessary on pragmatic grounds.

During the coalition negotiations of 1986–7, the two parties agreed upon a limited privatization programme, but, as has been common in privatization policies in other West European countries, neither had a clear idea of what concrete goals were to be achieved by each individual privatization (Vickers and Wright, 1988: 5). At this point, the implementation of privatization was intended partly to satisfy electoral claims, but had the additional role of aiding the budget consolidation process. For these reasons, partial privatization of the most profitable companies was begun with little sense of how this fitted into the overall restructuring programme. Privatization would fill the state coffers and reduce the demand for budgetary financing from the nationalized industries.[13] These two goals – electoral and budgetary – were to some extent complementary, in that much of the public opposition to the nationalized industries was based on the extent of financial aid they required, on the other hand, the two goals are also to some degree at odds, in that shares prices have to be kept low enough to ensure a politically successful privatization, thus potentially reducing the proceeds. Consequently, unlike in Britain, where support for privatization (and votes) were 'bought' by pricing shares lower than the market value, the Austrian government tried to reach an 'optimal' price, at which the proceeds would be as high as possible to raise revenue for the budget and ÖIAG restructuring, without risking undersubscription or destroying the market for future issues.

Once privatization began, however, economic policymakers in the SPÖ developed a more integrated role for it in the restructuring process. Accepting the ÖVP's initial argument that the state is not a suitable owner, and thus more or less taking the issue of privatization out of the electoral arena, they developed a strategy for decreasing state influence in the economy, linked to a restructuring programme that would ensure that Austria retained some large nationally owned enterprises that could compete on the world market. Despite retaining a stronger rhetoric on the need for privatization *per se*, the ÖVP largely accepted the SPÖ's interpretation of the role of privatization within the government's economic policy. This strategic interpretation of privatization was particularly evident in policy towards the ÖIAG and the banking sector, where privatization was aimed at providing additional capital that would allow the enterprises to expand. It is also evident, however, in the smaller privatizations: Austrian Airlines and the Austrian travel agency, for example, are now looking for partners to buy into the enterprise, thus allowing for strategic expansion. Unlike the above sectors, the partial privatization of the electric power industry was to a large degree sub-optimal in terms of restructuring, having left a monopoly without sufficient regulation.

In the ÖIAG, the strategy of privatization as industrial policy did not work. The temporary recovery ended in 1992–3 in a financial débâcle that could only be solved by giving up almost all of the strategic ambitions. The idea now seems to be to sell now what can be sold off and to sell the remaining assets as soon as possible. This means that only those industrial companies that are not viable will remain in state ownership. These will either be privatized cheaply or gradually closed down.

The remainder of the public sector – in particular utilities and municipal services – is unlikely to be privatized. Although it would bring revenue into the budget, polls indicate that this would be an electorally unpopular policy, and Austria's pragmatic route to privatization has meant an absence of conviction in politicians in the Margaret Thatcher mould to push through the policy against public opposition. Nevertheless, the principles that underlie the privatization strategy – the superiority of the market and the unsuitability of the state as owner – will be of importance in reforming this sector. In this sense, the politics of privatization will go on even after the last industrial share is sold.

## NOTES

1. See *Die österreichische Gemeinwirtschaft* (1982).
2. For a more detailed account of this debate until the beginning of 1988 see Müller (1988: 103–11).

3. ÖVP (1985), *Mehr Privat – weniger Staat*, November.
4. See, for example, H. Tieber (1986), 'Verstaatlichte: War alles falsch?', *Die Zukunft*, **2**: 7–10, here p. 9.
5. Lacina, F. (1986), 'Verstaatlichte: Auf neuem Kurs', *Die Zukunft* **4**: 13–15
6. This share could be reduced to 51 per cent if all those who purchased shares take advantage of additional bonus shares.
7. The preferential terms for the convertible bond allow subscribers to purchase Austrian Industries shares at the issue price minus 5 per cent for a period of 13 months, regardless of the market price.
8. *Coalition Agreement 1990*, Vienna, Bundespressedienst: 36–7.
9. See *Wochenpresse*, **35**, 30 August 1990: 30–2; and *Profil*, **41**, 9 October 1990: 58–9.
10. *Coalition Agreement 1990*, Vienna, Bundespressedienst: 37–41.
11. SPÖ (1989), *Sozialdemokratie 2000*: 50, 61.
12. Dr Fessel and GfK Institut, representative surveys.
13. The proceeds from privatization between 1987 and 1992 have been estimated at AS33 billion. See 'Editorial' (1991), *Wirtschaft und Gesellshaft*, **17**(4): 431.

## References

Beer, E. *et al.* (1991), *Wem gehört österreichs Wirtschaft wirklich?*, Vienna, Orac.
*Die österreichische Gemeinwirtschaft* (1982), Vienna, Jugend & Volk.
Ederer, B. *et al.* (1985), 'Eigentumsverhältnisse in der osterreichischenWirtschaft', Sondernummer, *Wirtschaft und Gesellschaft*, 11.
Gerlich, P. and Müller, W.C. (1989), 'Austria: a crisis resolved or a crisis postponed?', in E. Damgaard, P. Gerlich and J.J. Richardson (eds), *Western Europe in Crisis: Political and Policy Responses*, Aldershot, Gower: 146–62.
Itzlinger, A., Kerschbamer, R. and Van der Bellen, A. (1989), 'Verstaatlichte Industrie (ÖIAG-Konzern)', in H. Abele, E. Nowotay, S. Schleicher and G. Winckler (eds), *Handbuch der österreichischen Wirtschaftspolitik*, 3rd ed., Vienna, Manz: 421–42.
Langer, E. (1966), *Die Verstaatlichung in Österreich*, Vienna, Verlag der Wiener Volksbuchhandlung.
Lauber, V. (1992), 'Changing priorities in Austrian economic policy', *West European Politics*, **15**(1), 147–72.
Meth-Cohn, D. (1988), 'Der Abbau der Verstaatlichungsidee in der SPÖ und der Labour Party', *Österreichische Zeitschrift für Politikwissenschaft*, **17**(3), 249–62.
Müller, W.C. (1986), 'Mikrookonomische Steuerung und Parteien-Konkurrenz in Österreich', in H. Abromeit, G. Himmelmann and U. Jurgens (eds), *Steuerungsinstrument öffentliche Wirtschaft?*, IIVG/discussion paper 86–214, Berlin, Wissenschaftszentrum: 181.
Muller, W.C. (1988), 'Privatising in a corporatist economy: the politics of privatisation in Austria', *West European Politics*, **11**(4), 101–16.
Muller, W.C. (1991), 'Die Österreichische Volkspartei', in H. Dachs *et al.* (eds), *Handbuch des politischen Systems Österreichs*, Vienna, Manz: 227–46.

*Öffentliche Wirtschaft und Gemeinwirtschaft in Österreich* (1992), Vienna, Manz.

Ostleitner, H. (1987), 'Die österreichische Sozialdemokratie und die "Privatisierung" ', *Wirtschaftspolitische Blätter*, **34**(5/6): 600–609.

Parris, H., Pestieau, P. and Saynor, P. (eds) (1987), *Public Enterprise in Western Europe*, London, Croom Helm.

Schüssel, W. (1982), 'Zuden wirtschaftspolitischen Positionen der Österreichischen Volkspartei', in H. Abele, E. Nowotny, S. Schleicher and G. Winckler (eds), *Handbuch der österreichischen Wirtschaftspolitik*, Vienna, Manz: 143–50.

SPÖ (1989), *Sozialdemokratie 2000.* 50, 61.

Tieber, H. and Swoboda, H. (eds) (1984), *Privatisierung – die falsche Alternative*, Vienna, Arbeitsgemeinschaft der österreichischen Gemeinwirtschaft.

Ulram, P.A. (1990), *Hegemonie und Erosion. Politische Kultur und politischer Wandel* in Österreich, Vienna, Böhlau: 128.

Vickers, J. and Wright, V. (1988), 'The politics of industrial privatization in Western Europe. an overview', *West European Politics*, **11**,(4), 1–30.

Winckler, G. (1988), 'Der Austrokeynesianismus und sein Ende', *Österreichische Zeitschrift für Politikwissenschaft*, **17**(3), 221–30.

# CHAPTER 9

## SWEDEN:
## PRIVATIZATION AND DEREGULATION

### Jan-Erik Lane

## Introduction

Sweden used to be a private society, but the strong emergence of its welfare state after World War II has turned the country into a public society with about two thirds of the GDP passing through its public sector. In 1950 25 per cent of total resources were allocated by the public sector with 12 per cent going to the state, 10 per cent to the local governments and 1 per cent to the social insurance institutions. In 1990 the corresponding figures were 61 per cent of the GNP going to the overall public sector, 24 per cent to the state, 27 per cent to the local governments and 10 per cent to the social insurance institutions.

The Swedish welfare state has been based on the concept of the bureau as the suitable organizational format for the provision of welfare services. This model combined taxes on the revenue side with budget allocation on the expenditure side. It was argued that taxes should be preferred to charges on the demand side whereas public bureaucracies should be employed on the supply side. Not until the mid-1980s was there a reorientation towards choice and competition (Table 9.1).

**Table 9.1** Sweden: models of provision

|  |  | Supply side | |
|---|---|---|---|
|  |  | Bureaux | Enterprises |
|  | Taxes |  |  |
| Demand side |  | I | II |
|  | Charges | III | IV |

In a most general sense, the new policy reorientation towards privatization has meant that instead of an ideologically constrained focusing on the combination of taxes with bureau provision (I), there is now open talk of various organizational alternatives combining charges with enterprises, private or public (IV). Thus, choice on the demand side is sought together with competition in supply replacing obligation in the form of taxes and hierarchy in the guise of budget allocation by means of bureaus.

Today 'privatization' is a key word in the political debate in Sweden, but it is by no means an unambiguous concept. We shall see that a variety of strategies, all aiming at public sector reform, is covered by the term 'privatization'. At the same time one may note that it is somewhat of a policy paradox that once the strong preference for public provision of welfare goods and services inherent in the so-called Swedish model had mellowed (Lane, 1991), then the presently weak condition of the Swedish economy is such that any programme of privatization in the sense of sell-out will take years to be implemented. This is in particular true of the new attempts to privatize state enterprises, initiated by the non-socialist government which came to power in 1991.

## The Swedish model

It should be emphasized that the public sector bias in Swedish society never included a strong dose of socialism in the sense of ownership of the means of production. The Social Democrats took an early pragmatic stand-point to this basic problem in Marxist ideology, which the party had transplanted from Germany to Sweden. More important than the highly sensitive issue of turning private companies into public corporations was the build-up of the welfare state, or the so-called Folkhemmet where the standards of living could be raised by public policy-making by means of a high tax state – a policy which was also supported by non-socialist parties, in particular the centre-placed ones (Lewin, 1988).

The institutional framework for the structuring of the relationship between the public and private sectors in Sweden was outlined in the so-called Swedish or Scandinavian model (Esping-Andersen, 1985). It developed out of the great depression in the 1930s as a compromise between capitalism and socialism. Market institutions should be combined with a welfare state, where efficiency was the main goal of the former and equality as social justice the end of the latter (Lane, 1991). The success of the Swedish model is the result of a pragmatic course with regard to private and public enterprise (Pontusson, 1988).

Until the mid-1970s there was wide agreement between the political parties that public enterprises would only play a minor role in the economy, taking care of functions in which private enterprises would not be interested or where state ownership was to be preferred for national reasons. The strong dose of corporatism in the Swedish political system as well as the rapid public sector expansion opened up new opportunities for exercising influence over the private sector. It was believed that an advanced economy in rapid growth on the basis of full employment and low inflation was feasible, if there were institutions for interest-concertation and interest-intermediation involving strong trades unions and employers' association in the major organizations.

Since the Social Democratic party had long ago done away with any doctrinaire socialist plans it was a big surprise that the question of the ownership of the means of production again became politically relevant in the mid-1970s. *Löntagarfonder* (wage-earners' funds) were introduced in the early 1980s by the socialist government in an attempt to change the structure of ownership within the private sector. The system consisted of five huge state regional funds of shares in private joint-stock companies built up by means of obligatory charges levelled on the profits of these private corporations.

The introduction of the wage-earners' funds caused a bitter political conflict between the socialist and non-socialist parties, which ended with the decision of the new non-socialist government in 1992 to dismantle them. To the non-socialists it was apparent that if all state-owned equity funds were combined in a common strategy – the wage-earners' funds, the pension funds in the ATP-system (supplementary pension funds) and the state bank (Nordbanken) – then government could exercise considerable influence on private enterprises by acquiring large key stock assets and co-ordinating their vote strategies on board meetings. Actually, the state is heavily involved in several corporations by means if its equities holding: Volvo, Astra and Svenska Handelsbanken, as well as AGA, whereas a few local governments control major energy corporations like Sydkraft AB and Gullspong AB.

The policy of the non-socialist government was not only to undo whatever traditional socialist ambitions the Social Democrats may have had in the 1980s, but also to implement a bold plan to privatize some of the large state enterprises.

## Public enterprises

The public enterprise sector was not large compared to other Western European countries. It involved three layers: (i) commercial state agencies; (ii) state-owned joint-stock companies; (iii) local government corporations. In 1990 there were seven commercial state agencies active within the following areas: postal services, telecommunications, state railways, civil aviation administration, hydro-electric power, forest service and navigation administration. The legal status of a commercial state agency or *affärsverk* is a hybrid between a public bureau and a private company. In the same year the number of significant state-owned joint-stock companies was about 70, with 6 being financial corporations (Appendix 9.1, p. 196). Finally, in 1990 there were 1370 local government enterprises, several of which were joint-stock corporations within infrastructure, owned more or less completely by these local governments.

The orientation of the public enterprises is in accordance with the public finance tradition. Thus, several of the commercial state agencies may be looked upon either as natural monopolies (Vattenfall, Televerket) or public regulation boards (Luftfartsverket, Sjøfartsverket). The local government enterprises tend to be public utilities. In addition, several state joint-stock companies developed out of a perception about market failure, meaning that they would concentrate upon functions to which private enterprises could not or would not give a high priority.

A few of the most well-known public corporations, such as the SSAB Steel Company, the LKAB Mining Company and the ASSI Timber Company, originated from regional policy considerations in an attempt to create employment in sparsely populated areas. Other corporations, like Celsius AB, Zenit AB and NCB AB, became state joint-stock companies because they and their numerous employees had to be rescued from private company bankruptcy. Finally, the liquor monopoly Vin & Sprit AB, the lottery monopoly Penninglotteriet and AB Tipstjänst had their roots in external considerations as well as in state revenue interests.

The strong trust in public institutions that exists in Sweden explains why the country became the largest welfare state, which never really involved the traditionally socialist creed of a state-orchestrated economy. It is telling that between 1976 and 1982 the non-socialist government nationalized more corporations than the Social Democrats had done in their entire period of rule since 1932. In a series of rescue operations it took over a number of enterprises that were important for employment reasons but had failed in the economic depression of the late 1970s. The nationalization of enterprises has been looked as an important instrument for the achievement of the goal of full employment. It has been used in this pragmatic way by all the major political parties (Olsen, 1992), but the ideas of a planned economy or economic statism had few supporters. The virtues of a capitalist economy should be safeguarded, but its vices should be counteracted by the government (Pontusson, 1992).

However, at the same time the importance of the public enterprises should not be underestimated. Among 4.1 million employees in Sweden, 2.43 million work in the private sector and 1.67 million in the public sector. Out of the 1.67 million in the public sector, 1.3 million are employed by the regional and local governments, which allocate almost 30 per cent of the Swedish GDP. Among some 400,000 state employees, roughly 140,000 are employed by the large state commercial agencies as follows:

- Swedish Post: 57,400 employees;
- Swedish Telecom: 43,700 employees;
- State railways: 35,000 employees;
- Vattenfall: 10,200 employees;
- National Forest Enterprise of Sweden: 5,200 employees;
- Swedish Civil Aviation Administration: 3,200 employees;
- National Maritime Administration: 1,200 employees;
- Swedish National Grid: 400 employees.

The current legal status of these enterprises is undergoing change. First the huge Swedish State Power Board was transformed into Vattenfall Limited from the 1 January 1993, leaving the large transmission net with a small commercial agency. The National Forest Enterprise became a joint-stock company on 1 July 1992. It is now a joint-stock company, also consisting of the ASSI, a state joint-stock company and the NCB, a private company taken over by the state when going bankrupt. Second, there are investigations into the possibility of transforming some of the other commercial agencies, in particular Swedish Telecom (1993), and the Civil Aviation Administration with its running of the airports (1994) into joint-stock companies with either state or private owners.

The joint-stock companies owned by the state have about 160,000 employees, but they are regarded as private sector employees, even though some of these companies are owned by the state commercial agencies. Samhall, a non-profit organization for producing products by people with handicaps, employs 30,000 people. This means that the total number of employees in state enterprises is some 300,000, which is actually somewhat higher than the total number of employees in the public sector comprising the civil servants proper (250,000). If one adds the number of local government employees that handle public utilities of various kinds when organized as joint-stock companies (water, sewage and electricity distribution), then one may conclude that some 10 per cent of the work force belongs to public enterprises of one sort or the other.

## Industrial policy

In the late 1960s the Social Democrats launched the idea of a Swedish industrial policy. It was argued that sustained economic growth and regional employment balance required an active industrial policy on the part of the state and a Ministry of Industry was introduced in addition to the Ministry of Finance. The type of industrial policy favoured by the Social Democrats clearly implied that state influence in the private sector would increase along different routes. It is actually interesting to see that the new industrial policy comprised a variety of goals that proved to be difficult to accomplish simultaneously.

First, the state joint-stock companies were to be organized in such a manner that they would become competitive and profitable. Thus, in 1970 the State Enterprise Corporation, Statsforetag ABl, with a work force of some 34,000 employees, was created, bringing together a number of promising corporations while at the same leaving out weaker companies such as Swedyard due to its heavy losses. However, the State Enterprise Corporation was also to take so-called societal considerations into account in its decision-making, which has resulted goal conflicts and ambiguities, as the requirement of profitability does not always harmonize with regional policy or employment ambitions.

In 1984 the Statsforetag AB changed its name to 'Procordia', as the outcome of a basic restructuring where simple profitability became the main objective. The loss-making corporations – LKAB (iron mining), ASSI (forest products) and SSAB (steel production) – were left out of the new company, resulting in a reduction in size from 46,000 to 26,000 employees between 1981 and 1983. Instead it acquired key companies in medical drug production, biosystems and food products, which have turned Procordia into a very profitable and well-managed enterprise, listed on the Stockholm Stock Exchange from 1987 by means of a 19 per cent equity flotation. It now has 41,000 employees and is owned jointly by the state and Volvo AB. From 1994 it will be divided into two separate companies, one producing pharmaceutical products, and the other producing food products.

Second, the new industrial policy did involve some elements of state *dirigiste* ambitions. By means of a new investment bank, a new large postal and credit bank (PK-Banken, later Nordbanken) and more autonomy for the state pension funds to buy stocks in Swedish companies, the conduct of business in the private sector was opened up to government influence. Here we have a somewhat belated socialist ambition, which when combined with the strategy of a system of wage-earners' funds provokes heated political conflict.

However, in the late 1980s the socialist ambition behind the new industrial policy faded under heavy attack from the private business community (the Swedish Employers' Association, SAF.) It was partly reinterpreted to emphasize a financial strategy that was basically capitalist in spirit. Thus, the government-owned enterprises began to be looked upon as sources of revenue at the same time as dissatisfaction with the Swedish tax state became visible. Both state and local government companies were given more strict financial objectives defined by means of profitability criteria derived from the private sector. This strategy implied a clear and definitive break with the first goals of the industrial policy laid down in 1967–8. At the end of the 1980s it was broadened to cover all kinds of state and local government enterprises (i.e. also the state commercial agencies and the public utilities at local government level).

The large state commercial agencies as well as the public utilities owned by local government had been administered by traditional public administration principles up until the 1980s. Several public enterprises were governed by means of budgetary principles used in the yearly state budget process, but their basic orientation towards economic tasks and financial procedures had been acknowledged in a formal way. They were dependent upon the yearly interaction of budgetary requests versus government appropriations, especially with regard to investments and price setting. However, more and more special strategies and procedures had been developed to handle problems in relation to the value of their assets and investments. The philosophy for managing state commercial agencies and local government public utilities was derived from ideas about non-profit firms with break-even price setting. They were to provide their services at the lowest cost possible without a profit motive.

However, this philosophy for the public management of infrastructure facilities was abandoned formally by the state in 1987, when private management principles were introduced by the state government, first in relation to the huge electric power board and then extended to cover all state commercial agencies. Public capital should be managed in accordance with the same rules as applied to private capital in the economy at large. The implication that local government public utilities are also to be managed by principles relating to asset profitability and economic returns for the owners remains a controversial issue, calling for changes in the state laws and guidelines concerning local governments. Yet it still remains the case that local government public utilities, for example, water supply, are not allowed to raise a profit.

To sum up, over the years there emerged more by accident than by fiat a state company sector that included a mixture of enterprises in terms of organizational structure and covered a wide variety of products. Thus, the state enterprise sector included *inter alia* steel-plants, timber enterprises, mining companies, communication businesses, liquor stores and a bank, as well as other financial institutions, infrastructural corporations, pharmaceutical and food companies and a number of non-profit organizations (Dramaten, Operan). (See Appendix 9.1.) Yet this sector has never been allowed to grow enough to challenge the power positions of major private constellations such as the Wallenberg group, the Volvo group or the two main private banks, Skandinaviska Enskilda Banken and Svenska Handelsbanken.

## Privatization

The turn towards private management principles by the Social Democrats was not combined with stronger privatization ambitions, because the state should retain ownership over the commercial state agencies as well as the joint-stock companies, according to social democratic ideology. These enterprises were not to be run differently from private ones, but they could not be sold off to private interests. Similarly, the local governments would retain control as they transformed their public utilities from bureaux on the public budget to joint-stock companies in the private sector. The background to this is that in Sweden during the 1980s there was a general drift away from state-planning ideas towards a reconsideration of market values. Actually, a number of different organizational reforms were embarked upon, all denoted by privatization.

In 1991 a major investigation into the extent of competition in the Swedish economy concluded that numerous measures could be taken by the state to enhance competition within domestic markets. Instead of public-sector control, market forces could be used for the enhancement of consumer interests, even if this meant a collision with monopolies, both private and public. Thus, deregulation became a key word, resulting in regulatory reforms of, for example, the airlines, taxi-cab operations and the entire bank and financial sector.

Yet the first real decisive break with the industrial policy already embarked upon in the late 1960s came with the defeat of the Social Democrats in 1991. Now for the first time privatization as a fundamental policy alternative was launched in the sense of sell-off. The non-socialist government stated that as much as possible of the state enterprises should be sold off during the 1990s. A privatization committee was set up in order to identify a comprehensive strategy for privatization that would give the state as much as revenue as possible, given the shape of the economy and the interest from domestic and international investors.

When the socialist government returned to office in 1982, after its defeat in 1976, it pursued a basically non-socialist policy – halting public sector expansion and underlining the crucial importance of a strong private sector with profitable multi-national companies such like Asea, Volvo, Saab, Ericsson, Astra, Electrolux, Aga, Atlas Copco and Trelleborg. Not only did the government, under the auspices of Finance Minister Kjell Olof Feldt, depreciate the currency by some 16 per cent, producing sharp increases in private company profits, but it also initiated a policy of inserting financial instruments into the public sector in order to improve internal governance – replacing the traditional system of detailed legal control with productivity and efficiency norms. Thus, large companies such as the railway corporation SJ were transformed from a state agency into more of a private enterprise. Moreover, subsidies to ailing state enterprises were cut back.

The non-socialist government replacing the Carlsson regime took up where Feldt had ended partly due to resistance from the trade unions. The non-socialist government rapidly embarked on an aggressive policy of deregulation and privatization. Thus, the air transportation system was deregulated from 1 July 1992, with clear implications for the Scandinavian Airlines System, owned by the Scandinavian governments. Vattenfall's market power was shrunk by placing the main transmission network for electricity that Vattenfall controlled into a separate state agency meaning that all electricity producers and distributors may use the national transmission system. Similarly, the railway tracks no longer belong to SJ and other railway companies have entered into competition with SJ for services on various lines. The advantages of public regulation were questioned, in particular concentrating on the so-called economic regulation or entry regulation (i.e. the translation of natural monopolies into legal monopolies by means of state consessions).

As a matter of fact, when the privatization wave finally reached the Swedish welfare state it took on several modes. The following processes have been referred to as privatization: (i) deregulation; (ii) sell out; (iii) hiving off to government-owned joint-stock companies; (iv) contracting and franchising; (v) bidding and tender; (vi) charges instead of taxes; (vii) insertion of private management methods of governance into the private sector.

Privatization in all its forms depends upon the mood of the time. When state regulation started to be looked upon as resulting in inefficiency costs, several kinds of regulatory regimes were dismantled, including, for example, the taxi-cab system. But it must be pointed out that one major deregulation reform in Sweden failed completely, the deregulation of the financial markets in the second half of the 1980s. This resulted in an excessive expansion of the credit volume in the banking system, which proved fatal when the high levels of activity in the national and international economies faded in the late 1980s, worsening the economic depression of the early 1990s.

The losses by the small number of banks and other financial institutions were enormous, which will have consequences for the possibility of privatization proper or sell-out. Without major support from the Ministry of Finance the large state bank Nordbanken would have gone into bankruptcy in 1991. Had it not been for the collapse of the financial boom the privatization of the major state enterprises would have been pursued at greater speed than is now feasible.

Paradoxically, the ideology of privatization is at its peak in traditionally socialist Sweden when the economic problems appear to be more difficult than ever before experienced in modern times. When the new non-socialist government took office after the election in 1991 one of its chief objectives was to strengthen the private sector in Sweden. Well aware of the disappointment with the achievements of the non-socialist governments between 1976 and 1982, when the public sector actually grew more rapidly than before during the long socialist rule from 1933, including the fast enlargement of the state debt Premier Carl Bildt announced a market-orientated policy, including the deregulation of several sectors of the economy, entrance into the EEC and the sell-out of several state companies.

The decision on the part of the Riksdag to ask for Swedish membership of the European Community is part of the general drive towards market values. Thus, a new bureau for the supervision of conditions of competition was introduced in 1992, faced with the task of implementing harsher rules against price collusion and competition constraints and combining the previous state agency for price control and competition (SPK) with the ombudsman for industry (NO). It remains to be seen, however, how the policy of privatization is to be related to the policy of deregulation when it comes to firms that have enjoyed a legal monopoly like Swedish Telecom. Sell-out of public enterprises may require new regulatory schemes in order to counteract monopolistic behaviour (Vickers and Yarrow, 1989), which fact has been given scant attention in the Swedish policies.

The most visible signs of the crisis in the Swedish economy consist of the central government budgetary deficit that now stands at about 15–20 per cent of the GDP and the accumulated state debt which is almost 100 per cent of the GDP. The Swedish difficulties not only involve a severe economic depression but also a profound public sector financing problem. The retrenchment of the private sector in Sweden has resulted in a relative growth of the overall public sector to roughly 73 per cent of the GDP.

## Approach to narrow privatization

A special committee, the Privatiseringskommisionen, was set up early in 1992 to handle the privatization of 34 state companies, including well-known state enterprises such as Nordbanken, Vattenfall, Televerket and Linjeflyg in the airline sector, ASSI and Doman AB in forestry, Procordia in biomedicine and food products, and Celsius in shipping. The committee is headed by one of the leading spokesmen for the country's largest financial trust, Curt Nicolin from the Wallenberg group – a choice that perhaps has made a difficult task also somewhat a delicate one. The state equity holdings are to be sold to the employees in those companies, to the broad public and to institutional investors, both national and international.

So far the privatization efforts of the special committee have met with limited success. This is partly due to the severe crisis in the Swedish economy and partly as a result of the sustained international economic recession. The government has laid down that the sell-off of each company has to be conducted on terms which strongly consider a proper profitability rate of the state capital invested in these 34 companies. Since some of these state enterprises, like Televerket and Vattenfall, have huge capital assets it may not be easy to find interested investors inside or outside the country. However, the recent improvement of the world's financial markets could provide opportunities for the non-socialist government in Sweden to step up the tempo of the privatization process, knowing that there is an election in 1994, which may bring back to power the Social Democrats, who have a different attitude towards selling off the state jewels.

The privatization process began in somewhat dramatic fashion, when the leader of the Volvo-Skanska group, Pehr Gyllenhammar, announced that Volvo would like to buy Procordia, in which it already had a 40 per cent stake. The Privatiseringskommissionen, with Curt Nicolin, categorically refused. The price offered by Volvo did not meet with the ambitious standard for selling off state companies, but it was argued in addition that the new trust Volvo-Procordia was based on an inadequate industrial conception. Although Swedish privatization is not going to be an easy task and will require a lot of time and the implementation of international capital, some progress had been made by 1993.

The SSAB and the Celsius industries were sold off. Procordia is next in line, after it has been split into two companies, with Volvo retaining a major interest in its food production industries. The new pharmaceutical enterprise, Pharmacia, will be amalgamated with an Italian company, Farmitalia Carlo Erba. Several of the commercial state agencies have been transformed into joint-stock companies with the state as the owner, but privatization proper is planned at a later date. Linjeflyg has been sold to SAS. Nordbanken is in line for privatization at the same time as Gotabanken, which the state had to take over as it was basically insolvent. They will be sold either to the SEB or the SHB. Svensk bilprovning, which checks car parks annually, is to be privatized.

The non-socialist government has so far favoured large and financially strong investors when selling off state enterprises. Only a smaller share has been reserved for the general population. It has been argued that the government could offer a larger portion of the shares to small private investors in the domestic market.

## Privatization in a wide sense

In the meantime a lot of semi-privatization is taking place that had already been initiated in the 1980s when private market mechanisms began to be imported into the public sector in order to enhance flexibility, adaptation and efficiency. Private alternatives to public-sector provision of goods and services became relevant in Sweden during the 1980s to an extent that one may talk about a break-through in market philosophy in the early 1990s. The attractiveness of the private sector, its decision-making mechanisms and incentives, increased during the 1980s. This partly reflected an ideological reorientation not only within the Social Democrats but also among broad population groups with regard to the heavy tax burden. Research conducted within various state agencies, including the famous independent Expert Group on Public Finance within the Ministry of Finance, indicated that the public sector in Sweden had run into severe problems concerning both productivity and effectiveness (ESO, 1982–1992). In the early 1990s there have been signs of a policy reversal among all the political parties, underlining private choice and competition in supply, the market substituting for the public sector in the provision of basic welfare services such as health care and children's day care.

Growth in the public sector had hardly come to a standstill when the quest for privatization began. The search for new ways of allocating resources as a reaction to the rapid build-up of huge public budgets and bureaucracies has been channelled along two lines of development. On the one hand, we have the attempts to privatize in the proper sense, replacing public with private ownership. On the other, there are sweeping reforms of the public sector in attempts to insert more market-decision mechanisms into systems of public provision, while at the same maintaining the public principle.

The first attempts at privatization in the broad sense came in the infrastructural state where the goods and services to be delivered are marketable, such as water and electricity. It was then argued that the welfare state could also stand some competition from the private sector in relation to services such as health care and education. However, it was not until the early 1990s that these attempts at privatization met with some understanding as well as direct support from the political authorities who used to argue that welfare services should be allocated equally to all citizens by one supplier. The second wave of privatization involved the turn to semi-market allocation techniques. Various new methods for the delivery of welfare-state services have been tried, even when the zest for reform of traditional methods of public administration has not been matched by the available technology. Market values seem to have hit Sweden with a vengeance.

In Sweden until 1985 the budget was considered by many policymakers and planners to be a superior mechanism for the allocation of resources and the promotion of social justice by means of income redistribution compared with market mechanism, at least insofar as goods and services displayed positive or negative externalities or economies of scale in production or consumption. This budget preference resulted in the fastest public-sector growth process of all the OECD countries. However, the severe state debt crisis between 1976 and 1985 opened the debate concerning the pros and cons of budget versus market allocation. At the same time as public-sector growth was temporarily halted at roughly 67 per cent of the GNP in 1982, a search for the implementation of market incentives within public administration was initiated. The transformation of the established principles for governing the state and the local governments involved a *smorgåsbord* of different measures described below.

## Hiving off

The local government regulatory system used to prescribe in detail how they should run their operations, mandatory as well as voluntary. The public sector expansion has, however, led to the development of large local governments with substantial budgets. In order to innovate local government administration, in the 1980s local governments started to move activities from the public budget structures to joint-stock companies in the private sector, where the municipality would own all the stocks, or to private foundations, whose boards they would appoint. There is now a huge system of some 1300 local government companies, and their assets are as large as those of the municipalities. The placement of activities outside normal local government budgets means more flexibility, as their status is that of a private company, and less control, as they do not have to adhere to traditional norms of public scrutiny.

The same process has taken place within the national government. The state has attempted to make its own enterprises more effective and competitive, hiving them off from the national budget into the private sector by turning them into joint-stock companies where the state owns most of the shares. Thus, market-style decision mechanisms and private sector incentives have been spread around the state during the 1980s. One such phenomenon is the emphasis on decentralization and another form is the deregulation of both the private and public sectors.

## Decentralization, framework legislation and budgeting

It is generally believed that efficiency and productivity will be enhanced if decisions are moved downwards in the hierarchy of the public sector. Flexibility and adaptation are emphasized more than co-ordination and control. Thus, decentralization has taken place both within the state and the local governments as well as from the state to the local governments. Typical elements in the decentralization policy have been the employment of framework legislation and programme budgeting. These policies have partly been influenced by the ambition to replace *ex ante* methods of public administration such as planning with *ex post* techniques such as evaluation.

*Internal markets*

The search for strategies away from the prevailing bureau model in the public sector has led to attempts at entirely new forms for the allocation of resources in state and local governments. Instead of the standard public administration model, local governments have begun using so-called 'internal markets'. Thus, some county councils have made the various medical clinics or the local units in the primary health care system the foundation of health care, meaning that the clinics sell the services they produce to buyers (the politicians). Similarly, the municipalities have been reorganized in such a way that buyers interact with sellers on product or services markets.

In addition, there are now ongoing reforms in the municipalities of the budgetary system in order to calculate more exactly each and every cost, as well as the revenues which single units attract. All over the public sector there are attempts to employ charges as the mechanism for raising revenues. Considerable work has been devoted to the calculation of market-correct user charges for the payment of the services of state commercial agencies and local government.

*Individual wages*

To insert more market-like incentives into the established structures of the public sectors it has become accepted that wages may be determined on an individual basis. The employer may decide to differentiate the salary as a function of individual work effort. Some private-sector hiring practices are now employed throughout the public administration to create productivity-enhancing mechanisms.

**Conclusion**

The Swedish or (as it is sometimes called) Scandinavian model of a welfare state has received international attention, designated as a model to be imitated elsewhere. Essentially it revolved around a preference for public budget making, or budgeting as superior to markets for the allocation of resources and the redistribution of income. This budget preference was manifested in public-sector growth from around 25 per cent of GNP in 1945 to a staggering 67 per cent in 1982. The Social Democratic governments managed to halt public-sector expansion, reducing it down to 60 per cent in 1990. However, the severe economic crisis in the country has resulted in the public sector now standing at a staggering 73 per cent, due to the sharp reduction in employment in the private sector.

The choice between market- and public-sector provision arose in the 1980s when the seminal process of public-sector growth was halted in 1982. Various kinds of privatization strategies were tried: contracting, substitution of taxes by charges, replacement of public bureau provision by public joint-stock companies, contracting, sales-lease-back strategies, deregulation and the insertion of private incentive mechanisms into the public sector. It was, however, not until the new non-socialist government initiated a policy for an extensive sell-off of public enterprises in 1991 that privatization was embarked upon in a real sense.

However, the Swedish model had hardly been recognised by the OECD when things began to fall apart. During the 1980s market solutions were been given much more attention, although attempts at real privatizations were few. The public sector expansion has been halted and there is a constant search for market-like mechanisms that may improve the functioning of the public administration system. Thus, we find various types of semi-privatization: commercialization, corporatization, contracting, sales-lease-back and extensive decentralization, as well as deregulation. Although Swedish society is still a public one, there is more hesitance, even among Social Democrats towards the traditional principles of public administration and a strong desire for more experiments in various forms of privatization.

However, true privatization on a large scale has not yet occurred. But the non-socialist government has embarked on a major new policy initiative to sell off several large state enterprises. There are two major constraints on the search for true privatization in Sweden. On the one hand, there is a lack of capital available in the private sector, since some of these state companies have huge capital assets; it may be the case that international investors could get the programme going. On the other hand, some problems of regulation have to be addressed when privatizing the state commercial agencies due to their status as monopolies. How the policy of privatization is to be combined with a new regulatory policy remains to be debated thoroughly in Sweden.

**Appendix 1: Structure of state enterprises 1990**

*Enterprises with profitability targets*

*Joint-stock companies:* AB Aerotransporter, ASSI, Celsius Industrier, ESKA Statskonsult, LKAB, Procordia, SSAB, SSPA Maritime Consulting, SGAB, Svaløf AB, Swedair, Tumba Bruk

*State commercial agencies:* Domaenverket, Førsvarets Fabriksverk, SJ

*Financial Institutes:* Føretagskapital, Industrikredit, Investeringsbanken, PK-Banken

*Enterprises with mixed objectives*

Graengesberg Gruvor, Posten, Studsvik Energiteknik, Televerket, Vattenfall, Rymdbolaget

*Social monopolies*

Apoteksbolaget, Kurortsverksamhet, Samhall, Systembolaget, Vin- och Spritbolaget. Penninglotteriet, Tipstjaenst, Svenska Bostadfinansierings AB, Svensk Exportkredit, TEMU Interactor, Operan, Dramaten

*Regulating boards*

Luftsfartverket, Sjøfartsverket, Statens Anlaeggningsprovning, SEMKO, Svensk Bilprovning

*Source:* Olson (1989).

# References

Esping-Andersen, G. (1985), *Politics against Markets. The Social Democratic Road to Power*, Princeton, Princeton University Press.

Expert Group on Public Finance (ESO), Publications 1982–1992, Stockholm, Ministry of Finance.

Lane, J.-E. (ed.) (1991), 'The Swedish Model', *West European Politics*, special issue.

Lewin, L. (1988), *Ideology and Strategy*, Cambridge, Cambridge University Press.

Olson, J. (1989), *Vad Ska Staten Äga? De statliga företagen inför 90-talet*, Stockholm, Ministry of Finance.

Olsen, G.M. (1992), *The Struggle for Economic Democracy in Sweden*. Aldershot, Avesbury.

Pontusson, J. (1988), 'The Triumph of pragmatism: nationalization and privatization in Sweden,' in J. Vickers, and V. Wright (eds), 'The Politics of Privatization in Western Europe', *West European Politics*, **11**(4): 129–40.

Pontusson, J. (1992), *The Limits of Social Democracy. Investment Policies in Sweden*, Ithaca, Cornell University Press.

Rernaghan, K. (1990) (ed.) 'Symposium on the progress, benefits and costs of privatisation', *International Review of Administrative Sciences*, **56**(1).

Vickers, J. and Yarrow, G. (1989) *Privatization: An economic analysis*, Cambridge, MA, MIT Press.

# CHAPTER 10

## PRIVATIZATION IN THE NETHERLANDS: THE RESULTS OF A DECADE

## Rudy B. Andeweg

### Dutch privatization 1982–93

*The ambitions*

In 1982 a coalition of Christian-Democrats (CDA) and Conservative Liberals (VVD), Prime Minister Lubbers' first Cabinet, took office as a self-proclaimed 'no-nonsense' government, committed to fight the economic and fiscal crisis by reducing the role of the state in socio-economic affairs. The Cabinet's most important policy document, the coalition agreement, outlined five 'major operations' for this purpose: reorganization (of the bureaucracy), reconsideration (of specific programmes), decentralization, deregulation, and privatization. Although the privatization programme was officially launched in 1982, it was based on a number of earlier proposals. In 1980 a Royal Commission on Administrative Reform (the Vonhoff Commission) recommended 'decentralization to the private sector' (the term privatization was not yet in. vogue then) as a means of reducing overload and increasing administrative efficiency. In 1981 an interdepartmental committee of civil servants, set up to reconsider a number of government programmes, advocated privatization as a means of reducing government spending. Meanwhile, the Wagner Commission (a tripartite commission advising the government on economic recovery, led by the former chairman of Royal Dutch Shell) proposed privatization as a means of strengthening the market economy. These three recommendations found their way into numerous government documents as the official motives for the privatization programme: increase administrative efficiency, reduce the government's budget deficit, and reinvigorate the market. An interdepartmental committee was created to locate those government services that could be privatized.

It is important to note that the roots of Dutch privatization are neo-corporatist/bureaucratic, not party-political, and that, other than in the UK, privatization never became an ideological quest: the trumpets of 'popular capitalism' have never been sounded in the Netherlands, and privatization was merely regarded as a pragmatic solution to specific administrative and economic problems.

## The results

A comparison of the results of the Dutch privatization programme with the situation in other countries is confounded by the fact that official documents in the Netherlands define privatization as the legal transfer of a task or a government agency from the scope of public law to the scope of private law. The question of ownership or control over a particular activity does not enter into the definition, and divestment of shares by the state is not even recognized as part of the privatization programme. Much of what the Dutch government claims as results of its policy of privatization would not be regarded as privatization in most other countries: the 'contracting out' of tasks hitherto performed by one of the departments of state; the transformation of government agencies into tripartite bodies (employers, trades unions, and state), semi-autonomous agencies, or foundations (with the executive board consisting of government officials).

'*Privatisation á la Hollandaise*' even includes the conversion of state enterprises into state-owned companies. Of such 'privatizations', those of the Post Bank and the PTT are by far the most important ones in terms of the number of employees involved (10,000 and 90,000 respectively). In 1986, after ten years of deliberation, a Post Bank was created as a limited liability company, with the government as sole share-holder. This was an initiative of the Social-Democratic Minister of Finance Duisenberg (currently President of the Dutch Bank) and intended to introduce some healthy competition into an oligopolistic banking world. It was therefore more a form of state intervention than of privatization, and perceived as such by the commercial banks. The PTT was transformed from a state enterprise into a company owned by the government in 1989. A state enterprise is a company run by the government, set up by a special act of parliament, under full ministerial responsibility, and governed by administrative law. There used to be four state enterprises: PTT, IJmuiden Fishing Port Authority, the Royal Mint, and the Government Printing Office, which are all now privatized. PTT was transformed into a company with limited liability,

thereby freeing it from a number of financial and accountancy constraints. This was thought necessary to protect PTT from increasing
international and national competition. With a few exceptions PTT's
monopoly was left intact. It has therefore been perceived by some com-
mentators as a form of state protection, rather than as privatization.

The 'pseudo-privatization' of Post Bank, PTT and a number of smaller
state enterprises and government agencies have moved a total of about
125,000 civil servants into the private sector. However, only ten of these
'privatizations' have surrendered complete control over a given agency
to a privately owned company; these, involved a mere 900 employees.

Relinquishing state control over economic activity by giving up
ownership is not considered part of the official privatization programme,
but this does not mean that it has not taken place. It has long been
standard policy to dispose of the government's shareholdings whenever
profitable to do so, in a pragmatic case-by-case way. The most important sales involve the airline KLM, the chemical giant DSM, and the
Post Bank. At the start of the privatization decade, the government
owned 78 per cent of KLM Royal Dutch Airlines. In 1984 the government sold some of its shares in KLM, at the same time as new
shares were issued. Both the real and the 'silent' privatization lowered
the government's proportion of shares in the airline from 78 to 55.4 per
cent. A second share issue in 1986 led to a further decrease to under
50 per cent. At the time of writing, the government's holding of KLM
shares is 38.2 per cent.

When the Dutch collieries were closed down in the 1960s, the mostly
state-run coalmines were transformed into a successful chemical industry, DSM. As early as 1966 DSM was 'corporatized' from a state enterprise into a company owned wholly by the government. In 1989 the
government sold two thirds of its shares in two tranches (one in January,
the other in September) for about $1.5 billion. The DSM case is inter-
esting in two respects. First, the sale of the government's shares resem-
bled similar privatizations in France and the UK: lots of publicity, the
razzmatazz of the unveiling of the price per share, rules to give preference to small investors and the company's own personnel. Second, in
the case of DSM, the pseudo-privatization of a state enterprise into a
state-owned company has been an intermediate stage on. the road to
'real' privatization. For DSM this intermediate stage lasted for more than
two decades, and was almost certainly not intended as such. There are
indications, however, that this has now become something of a policy:
still owned by the state, the company can get used to market conditions
before it is sold; in this way the company's market value is 'fattened
up'.[1]

The Post Bank is an example of this strategy. It has merged with a commercial bank (NMB) and with an insurance company (Nationale Nederlanden). In December 1989 the government sold part of its shares for $725 million, and its holding in the new company is now a mere 6.6 per cent. Although the state plans to retain a larger part of its holding in PTT, a sale of PTT shares is planned for 1994. Currently, the government is actually increasing its investments in Dutch Rail: together with plans to split Dutch Rail into separate companies for operations and for infrastructure, this is seen by many commentators as a move to prepare Dutch Rail for privatization.

The sales of DSM and Post Bank were very successful, being several times over-subscribed. In addition to these big sales there have been a number of smaller divestments: the state's holdings in the aircraft company Fokker have been sold, its shares in Volvo car were exchanged for a smaller holding in the new Nedcar company. These smaller holdings were mostly traded privately (such as to DASA in its take-over of Fokker) or sold on the stock market.

All this goes to show that 'real' privatization has taken place in the Netherlands, even though is not recognized as such by Dutch policymakers. On the other hand it also becomes clear that the results are very meagre: the total revenues of all the privatizations in the 1982–92 decade only add up to about $2.75 billion. Our description so far has only taken in privatization by the central government. Privatization has also taken place at the level of provincial and municipal government. It is estimated that 20,000 jobs have been affected by local privatization. Again, most of it is in the form of contracting out (waste removal, maintenance). The big projects involve the utilities: all the major energy and water industries have been converted into companies with limited liability, but without exception they are still owned by the provincial governments. Subnational authorities own little besides these utilities: the Netherlands is probably the most centralized state in Western Europe.

Even if we include subnational privatizations, the results of the privatization programme are not very impressive. One Dutch study agreed: 'The political momentum that is given to the issue of privatization is not very great. The chance that privatisation will result in a fundamental change of the balance between the private and public sector has become very small indeed' (Snellen, 1985). A recent Dutch analysis of all 'major operations' (appropriately subtitled 'reality or rhetoric?') concludes that the process of privatization is faltering. The lack of success was also noted in comparative studies: 'Overall, concrete results of privatization of government services in the first round have been especially meagre, certainly in comparison with developments abroad' (Kent, 1987). Vickers and Wright put the Netherlands in the category of countries where the privatization programmes may have tampered with the public private boundary, but where they have not shifted it as in France and the UK (Vickers and Wright, 1989).

## The privatization paradox

The results of Dutch privatization efforts are even more insignificant when compared to the size of the public sector in the Netherlands. The share of the national income claimed by the public sector increased rapidly from about 35 per cent in 1969, to just over 70 per cent in 1983. Since 1983 the relative size of the public sector has started to decrease to about 60 per cent in 1993.

Despite this decline in recent years, the Dutch public sector is one of the largest in Western Europe: in percentages of the national income it is at least 5 per cent ahead of France, and fifteen per cent ahead of the UK. By 1982, when the privatization programme was started, there was widespread criticism of the omnipotent state in the Netherlands, and privatization was seen as one of the most appropriate instruments to redress the perceived imbalance between private and public sector. Privatization enjoyed sufficient support, at least, for a special Dutch language journal *Privatisering* to be published. So why has privatization not been more successful?

### Constraints

The implementation of privatizations has been delayed by several factors. In many cases, privatization has been accompanied by extensive new regulation, by concessions (most notably in the case of PTT), or contracts. Moreover, whenever the government wants to create a legal entity, legislation by parliament is required. Legislation is a slow process in the Netherlands, and the government has no control over the parliamentary timetable. In some cases parliament has stipulated that the government should retain at least a majority or priority shareholding in a privatized company, because it was perceived as (partially) performing a public task. In those cases even the Conservative-Liberal party, which is closest to a free market ideology, has supported continued government involvement.

The 1986 coalition agreement mentioned taxation as one of the impediments to privatization of a state enterprise or government agency. If real estate is transferred as part of the privatization, the new company has to pay a 6 per cent stamp duty. Furthermore, a state enterprise does not pay corporate tax, and a government agency does not charge VAT on its products or services. Privatized companies have to pay these taxes, which is likely to force them to raise their prices and makes privatization a less attractive option. The government responded to this problem by deciding that if VAT is a prohibitive objection to a privatization then the Minister of Finance is allowed to reduce the burden by a maximum of 10 per cent of cost price, for a maximum of 5 years. In all the major privatizations of state enterprises (Post Bank, PTT, Government Printing Office) special legislation has also exempted the new companies from having to pay stamp duty on their newly acquired real estate.

On the basis of the experiences with these constraints in the first privatizations, the interdepartmental committee on privatization has developed a *Privatization Handbook* to provide a scenario for future privatizations and to indicate ways to circumvent the constraints that have just been mentioned. This should reduce the obstacles, but it should also be emphasized that the legal and fiscal constraints affected only the implementation of decisions to privatize. They contribute but little to an explanation of the paradox of large public sector and few privatizations.

*Resistance*

The explanation cannot be found in the political arena either. As we move from left to right through the political spectrum we expect gradually to find more support for privatization, and we do. However, even on the left only one party, Green Left, is explicitly opposed to privatization. Its 1989 election manifesto advocates 'socialization of the economy' and democratization of major companies and financial institutions. 'In this framework, public enterprises should not be privatized; on the contrary, they should be democratised.' Green Left (a merger of the Communist Party, the Pacifist-Socialist Party, and the Radical Party) has 6 of the 150 seats in the Second Chamber of Parliament and is not regarded as a potential governing party. The Social-Democrats do not specifically mention privatization in their manifesto, but they do not explicitly oppose privatization either. They are in favour of 'functional decentralization', a term sufficiently vague also to include some forms of privatization. It should be noted that the

Dutch Social-Democrats have never been committed to nationalization, with the possible exception of land ownership. Already before they entered a governing coalition for the first time in 1939, they had adopted planning instead of nationalization as their economic policy. This tradition probably explains why they are not more opposed to privatization today. All other parties are explicitly in favour of privatization. The centre-left D66 advocates case-by-case pragmatic decisions on privatization, and claims that about $250 million can be gained during the 1989–94 Parliament by selling shares, land and houses. The Christian-Democratic manifesto speaks of 'a permanent emphasis on socialization and privatization of government tasks' and contains some specific proposals. The Conservative Liberals want to stimulate further privatizations, as do the small orthodox Protestant parties. The gradations in enthusiasm for privatization are not entirely without significance. As we shall discuss, the change in the composition of the governing coalition in 1989, from Christian-Democratic–Conservative Liberal to Christian–Democratic–Social-Democratic has led to change in emphasis within the privatization programme, and also to less emphasis on privatization itself. However, this development can only explain why more has not been privatized in the last three years, whereas it was already clear that Dutch privatization would be rather modest before 1989.

For resistance to privatization we have to look primarily to the trades unions. The largest trade union federation, FNV, follows its civil service union, ABVA/KABO, in its opposition to privatization. Union membership has declined precipitously from over 40 per cent in 1970, to about 24 per cent in 1990, but within the public sector the unions are still relatively strong (over 40 per cent of civil servants are unionized). In typical Dutch fashion, the unions couch their opposition in terms of the general interest (government services being more efficient than they are given credit for, alternative strategies for increasing effectiveness and efficiency being more promising), but trade union opposition seems based primarily on anxiety about loss of jobs, income and pension rights. In most cases, the government has been willing to buy off this opposition. Government memoranda in 1985 and 1988 offered to avoid forced lay-offs by promising positions elsewhere in the public sector to employees made redundant by a privatization. Workers laid off, or dissatisfied with their job, within a year of privatization, were to retain their right to claim civil service unemployment benefits (which are better than ordinary unemployment benefits).

The same strategy has been applied to income. In the private sector lower employees are paid less, and higher employees are paid more, than in the public sector. So the government has guaranteed income levels of the lower paid by making up the difference during the first years after privatization. A Social Charter signed by the government and the new company dealt with such matters. The government has also allowed privatized employees to stay in the Civil Service Pension Fund for a few years, after which the Civil Service Pension Fund pays a compensatory sum to a new pension fund. The government and the trades unions have now jointly set up a Federative Pension Fund for workers in privatized companies. Although the unions continue to oppose privatization verbally, these government measures seem to have preempted more active opposition.

In general, opposition to privatization is isolated and weak. It should be noted, however, that support for privatization is also rather luke-warm. At the beginning of this chapter, we have already emphasized that the privatization programme has never been driven by ideological concerns. It is not even an article of faith among the defenders of the private sector. The largest employers' organization (VNO) is committed to privatization, but in an internal memorandum it is also argued that privatization is economically unnecessary because many public enter-prises already conform to market conditions, that a large-scale sale of government shares could upset the market, and that such a sale is only justified if the revenue raised is not used for government spending, and if there has been prior consultation with the companies involved.

*The size of the public sector revisited*

If neither constraints nor resistance can explain the relative lack of privatization, what can? The answer has to be found in the structure of the public sector. The rapid growth in the public sector has been due largely to income transfers, such as social security. In 1970 income transfers (social security, child allowance, old age pensions, disability benefits), consumed 18.7 per cent of the national income, today it is 33 per cent. Interest payments on government debts increased from 2.9 per cent of the national income to 6.5 per cent. As a percentage of the national income personnel costs and government investments, actually decreased (12 to 11 per cent and 4.4 to 1.7 per cent respectively).

State ownership or state participation in companies have always been very limited. Appendix 10.1, p. 211, lists the state's shareholdings at the end of 1992 (but with the sale of Fokker in 1993 already taken into account). It is a motley collection, each individual holding to be explained by historical accident rather than by any grand design or strategy. In thirteen companies, the state is the sole shareholder. By far the most important of these companies is PTT, followed at a distance by Dutch Rail. The state owns at least 50 per cent of another 17 companies, including most airports and the regional development funds. The state has minority shares in a further 14 companies, including DSM (31.4 per cent), KLM (38.2 per cent), and Hoogovens Steel (12.3 per cent). Compared to ten years ago, before privatization started, the total number of companies has decreased, as has the average percentage of the state's stockholding, but even in 1982 there were less than 50 companies owned wholly or partially by the state. The conclusion that 'there are fewer public enterprises in the Netherlands than in the other countries and their share of the national economy is relatively small' (Parris *et al* (1987), is shared by most studies.

The explanation for the small state share of Dutch business is political as well as economic. We have already mentioned that the Dutch Social-Democrats have not been in favour of nationalization, at least not since they became a potential governing party since the end of the 1930s. A second political explanation may be found in the segmentation or pillarization (*verzuiling*) which characterized Dutch society until the late 1960s. To maintain some form of stable government in such a divided society, great care had to be taken not to overload the centre of political decision-making.[2] As Van Schendelen points out:

In the pillarised society the cleavages between the four main social groupings were such that 'the common government' could handle only a few issues and usually only in a procedural way, leaving as much substantial decision-making as possible to the pillars themselves. These pillars organised their own interference in socio-economic and private life. They created their own welfare organisations (for income, health, housing, education), industrial corporations, trade unions, services, banks and so on (Van Schendelen, 1987).

Thus consociational democracy was one factor in preventing nationalization in the past.

In addition to these political factors, and perhaps of more importance, is the fact that the Dutch economy is an extremely open one. Imports and exports account for approximately 60 per cent and 67 per cent of GNP respectively. As a consequence, Dutch industry is dominated by a small number of very large companies competing on an international market (Royal Dutch Shell, Unilever, Philips). In general, public enterprises tend to represent types of economic activity that are more or less confined to the domestic market; that economic sector is relatively unimportant in the Netherlands. Paradoxically, and as an aside, the open economy may also explain why the Dutch government has not privatized more of the little it owns. The exposure to international competition has made it almost impossible for the Dutch government to use the few existing public enterprises for macro-, rather than micro-economic purposes.[3] Public enterprises have always been run as if they were private companies, with the result that most of them are quite healthy. Thus, the Dutch public sector has avoided most of the odium of inefficiency that fuelled the ideology of privatization elsewhere. Only 15 of the 45 companies in which the state had an interest at the time were operating at a loss in 1992 (KLM being the only important one), whereas 27 companies were profitable. In 1992 the government netted Dfl 4,109,490.000 from its participation in these companies. Given the fact that privatization is not an ideological item in the Netherlands, it may sometimes make budgetary sense for the government to hold on to its stock.

## 'Demand-side' privatization

If we define privatization as 'denationalization', not much has been privatized in the Netherlands, simply because there was not much to privatize. In other countries, however, privatization so defined is the manifestation of a more general process of reducing both the size and the role of the state. Such a retreat of the state can also be observed in the Netherlands, but it manifests itself in different forms. By concentrating on the sale of state-owned stock, we have neglected the 33 official 'privatizations' claimed by the Dutch government. We did mention that they involved 125,000 civil servants; 25,000 of them had been working in one of the central government's ministerial departments. This is 15 per cent of the total departmental workforce, a substantial reduction in the size of the state since the early 1980s.[4]

There has also been a reduction of the role of the state, particularly of its intervention in the economy. The fact that the Dutch state owns so little in so few companies does not mean that it has not intervened in the economy in the past. It only means that the government has always preferred private-law to public-law constructions for its interventions. The 'foundation' is probably the most prominent vehicle for government intervention. The executive of such a foundation often consisted of government representatives, and its income of subventions from the state. Legally the foundation was in the private sector, in reality it was not. Such foundations are widespread, and they provided a way to decentralize policy making to the various *familles spirituelles* that dominated Dutch social and political life until the late 1960s. Sometimes such constructions stand in the way of privatization. Since 1989 the government has wanted to sell the rented houses that have been built with government subsidies, but this policy is frustrated because the houses are owned not by the central government, but by local 'housing corporations'.

Often, however, the fact that many government activities were, legally speaking, already in the private sector, has made it easier for the state to retreat. In the past, the Dutch government has given massive assistance to ailing industries. Occasionally this assistance has been through the acquisition of shares directly by the government, or indirectly by a state-owned company. In general, however, such assistance took the form of loans and guarantees. The government usually appointed a 'government caretaker' to keep an eye on the management of the company concerned, and it attached conditions to the support. Through the caretaker and the conditions, the government sometimes controlled the company, without actually owning it. It could also end its control without having to privatize.

One of these rescue operations, of the Dutch shipbuilding industry, deserves special attention not only because of its notoriety, but also because it became a catalyst for what has been called 'desubsidization', 'demand-side privatization', or 'the hidden privatisation of a pseudo-private sector'. In the 1960s the government decided that the decline of the Dutch shipbuilding industry could only be stopped by rationalization and modernization. The government assumed that such an operation required a concentration of the shipbuilding industry, which was then in the hands of seven independent companies. To stimulate such a concentration, the government made its subsidies conditional on amalgamation. Even the one healthy shipyard among these seven was forced to merge with the others when it needed a government guarantee on a commercial loan to build a new dock. The new conglomerate, RSV, was in fact a shotgun marriage, an artificial creation of the government, but it was never a public enterprise. The company also never became a viable entity, and the government had to step in to rescue the company with ever greater loans and guarantees. With some 30,000 employees, 'seriously considering to let RSV go bankrupt was thinking the unthinkable.'[5] The government caretaker was also the senior civil servant advising the Minister of Economic Affairs on RSV. As the government was drawn in deeper and deeper, 'The Minister and his officials began to meddle in what were basically corporate decisions: the acceptance of orders (at any price), cost calculations, capacity plans and investments. The borderline between government and corporate responsibility became blurred.'[6] The company eventually collapsed in 1983. More than one billion dollars had been spent on it alone. A parliamentary inquiry into the débâcle brought to light the degree of government interference in what had always remained a private company.

Largely as a result of the RSV fiasco, the amount of government money spent on firms in difficulty has declined sharply. In 1982 the government subsidized private companies (housing and public transport excepted) with a total of 8.8 billion guilders, or 2.7 per cent of the national income. Five years later, this had declined to 5.6 billion guilders, or 1.4 per cent of the national income. Since then it has been reduced to much less than one per cent of the national income because subsidies for investments have been abolished, and the decree authorizing assistance to ailing industries has been withdrawn. The government still provides subsidies to private companies in some cases, but it refuses the publish the criteria for such subsidies as these might possibly 'give rise to the impression that large-scale subsidization is possible'. The Department of Economic Affairs claims that such subsidies are only necessary to 'match' similar subsidies given by other EC countries.

Because of the peculiar structure of the Dutch public sector, this 'demand-side privatizatiton',[7] or desubsidization, has performed the same function as (supply-side) privatization in other countries: the state has retreated from the Dutch economy to a considerable extent. There appears to be no change in government policy with regard to desubsidization. Subsidies for housing (fiscal facilities for house-owners, rent subsidies), public transport (100 per cent of investment in infrastructure, 50 – 80 per cent exploitation), and culture (theatre companies, museums) are likely to decline in coming years. We now return to 'supply-side' privatization to see whether the same prospects exist there.

## Prospects for privatization

At the start of the official privatization programme in 1982, the budgetary motive was probably the strongest of the three motives for privatization (budget, market, and administrative efficiency). The Treasury has been the driving force behind this 'major operation', and not the Department of Economic Affairs ('guardian' of the free market) or the Department of Internal Affairs (responsible for administrative efficiency). Both the budgetary motive, and the free market motive, now seem to be replaced by administrative efficiency. In a letter to parliament in 1990, the Minister of Finance failed to mention the market motive for privatization altogether, only mentioning administrative motives, with budget savings as a likely side-effect.

There could be more than a mere change in emphasis. After enthusiastic endorsement of privatization in the coalition agreements between Christian Democrats and Conservative-Liberals in the first and second Lubbers Cabinets (1982–6; 1986–9), the 1989 coalition agreement between Christian Democrats and Social Democrats (PvdA) completely ignores the privatization programme. Asked in parliament whether there was a change of course, the Minister of Finance (and Social-Democratic Deputy Prime Minister) 'confirmed that a certain change of policy has taken place with regard to privatization and granting greater autonomy to government agencies. I am not as burning for privatization as the previous Cabinet'. Although the current Cabinet does not exclude privatization as an instrument to achieve greater administrative efficiency altogether, it appears to be giving much greater priority to territorial decentralization and also to functional decentralization (to independent regulatory agencies and 'Next-Step'-type agencies). In a letter to parliament dated 21 January 1992, the Ministers of Finance and Internal Affairs announced the discontinuance of the interdepartmental committee on privatization, and the creation of a new committee on functional decentralization.

It should be recalled, however, that divestment of shares is not defined as privatization in the Netherlands. There appears to be a continuation of the gradual shedding of stock holdings whenever it is financially attractive. The 1991 and 1992 budgets included modest sums for income from sell-offs Dfl 325 and Dfl 675 respectively) (Van de Ven, 1992). International mergers may soon result in the sale of state shares in KLM. In internal memoranda, civil servants have warned that after '1992' compliance with expected European regulations on monopolies may force further denationalizations. The management of both Dutch Rail and PTT are actively preparing their companies for the stockmarket.

THE NETHERLANDS                                              **211**

## Appendix 10.1: The Dutch government's shareholdings 1992

*100% holdings*

1. Koninklijke PTT (Post, Telecom)
2. Energie Beheer Nederland (Energy Company)
3. De Nederlandsche Bank (The Dutch Central Bank)
4. Vuilafvoer Maatschappij VAM (Waste Removal and Composting)
5. Verenigd Streekvervoer Nederland (Regional Public Transport)
6. Nederlandse Spoorwegen (Dutch Rail)
7. SDU (former Government Printing Office)
8. Nederlands Meet Instituut (Institute of Weights and Measures)
9. Noordelijke Ontwikkelingsmaatschappij (Northern Development Company)
10. Nederlandse Ondememing voor Energie en Milieu (Energy and Environment Company)
11. Nederlands Inkoop Centrum (Government Procurement Centre)
12. Rijkscomputercentrum (Computer Centre)
13. CF-kantoor voor Staatsobligaties NV (Bureau of Government Bonds)


*At least 50% holdings*

14. Bank voor Nederlandsche Gemeenten (Municipal Authorities' Bank) (50%)
15. Nationale Investeringsbank (National Investment Bank) (50.3%)
16. Luchtvaartterrein Texel (Texel Airfield) (65.3%)
17. Luchthaven Schiphol (Schiphol Airport) (75,8)
18. Ultra Centrifuge Nederland (Nuclear Recycling Industry) (98.9%)
19. Nederlandse Omroepzenderrnaatschappij (Broadcasting Transmitters) (59%)
20. Kon. Nederlandse Springstoffenfabriek (Explosives Industry) (50%)
21. Brabantse Ontwikkelingsmaatschappij (Brabant Development Company) (64.5%)
22. Gelderse Ontwikkelingsmaatschappij (Gelderland Development Company) (68.2%)
23. Nederlandse Financieringsmaatschappij voor Ontwikkelingslanden (Financing Company for Developing Countries) (51%)
24. Industriebank LIOF (Limburg Development Company) (94.3%)
26. Luchthaven Eelde (Groningen Airfield) (80%)
27. Nederlands Congresgebouw (Conference Centre) (50%)
28. Nederlandse Pijpleidingmaatschappij (Pipeline Company) (50%)

29. Domaniale Mijnmaatschappij (State Mines) (99%)
30. OV-Studentenkaart (Student Travelcard) (53.3%)
31. Overijsselse Ontwikkelingsmaatschappij (Overijssel Development Company) (65.2%)


*Minority shareholdings*

31. Internationale Nederlanden (Banking and Insurance Group (including Postbank) (6.6%)
32. Nederlandse Gasunie (Natural Gas Distribution) (10%)
33. Haven van Vlissingen (Flushing Port Authority) (35.5%)
34. Nederlandse Waterschapsbank (Water Authorities' Bank) (18.2%)
35. Eurometaal (33.3%)
36. DSM (Chemical Company) (31.4%)
37. Hollandse Signaalapparaten (Military Electronics) (1%)
38. Hoogovens (Steelworks) (12.3%)
39. AVR Chemie (Chemical Company) (10%)
40. Hoogovens administratiekantoor voor aandelen (Trust Office for Shares in Hoogovens Steel) (2%)
41. Centrale Organisatie voor Radio-actief Afval (Radio-active Waste Disposal) (10%)
42. KLM (Airline) (38.2%)
43. Luchthaven Maastricht (Maastricht Airport) (34.8%)
44. Alpinvest Holding (31.6%)

## Acknowledgements

The author wishes to thank Edith Hafkamp for her invaluable assistance in the preparation of this chapter, and Adrian van de Ven, of the Dutch Ministry of Finance, for his comments on a previous draft.

## Notes

1. De Ru H.J. and Van De Ven A.T.L.M. (1993), *Country Study: Privatization in the Netherlands*, compiled for the Working Group on Privatisation of the International Association of Schools and Institutes of Administration in co-operation with the International Institute of Administrative Sciences, May: 30.
2. A concern which still characterizes Dutch politics. See R.B. Andeweg and G.A. Irwin (1993), *Dutch Government and Politics*, London, Macmillan.
3. Even the state-owned Central Bank enjoys an independence from the government rivalled only by its German counterpart.
4 Calculations by the Secretary of the Interdepartmental Committee on Privatization, Adrian Van de Ven, in a letter to the author.
5. *Verslag van de Enquetecommissie Rijn-Schelde-Verolme (RSV)*, Proceedings of the Second Chamber of Parliament 1984–5, 17817, n.16: 509. The quote is from the well written and entertaining English summary that is included in the report.
6. *Verslag van de Enquetecommissie Rijn-Schelde-Verolme* (RSV), 1984–5, 17817, n.16: 504.
7. For the distinction between 'supply-side' and 'demand-side' privatization, see also De Ru, H.J. and Van De Ven, A.T.L.M. (1993), *Country Study: Privatisation in The Netherlands*, compiled for the Working Group on Privatization of the International Association of Schools and Institutes of Administration in co-operation with the International Institute of Administrative Sciences, May: 4.

## References

Kent, C.A. (ed.) (1987), *Entrepreneurship and the Privatizing of Government*, New York, Quorum p: 171.
Parris, H. Pestieau, P. and Saynor, P. (1987), *Public Enterprise in Western Europe*, London, Croom Helm: p. 186.
Snellen I.Th.M. (ed.) (1985), *Limits of Government; Dutch experiences*, Amsterdam, Kobra: 16.
Van Schendelen M.P.C.M. (1987), 'The Netherlands: from low to high politicisation', in M.P.C.M. van Schendelen and R.J. Jackson (eds), *The Politicisation of Business in Western Europe*, London, Croom Helm: 65.
Van de Ven, Adrian (1992), 'The Netherlands: mix of corporatisation and

privatisation', in Rodney Lord (ed.), *Privatization Yearbook 1992*, London, Privatisation International: 107.

Vickers J. and Wright V. (1989), 'The politics of industrial privatization in Western Europe: an overview' in J. Vickers and V. Wright (eds), *The Politics of Privatization in Western Europe*, London, Cass: 22.

# CHAPTER 11

## PRIVATIZATION IN PORTUGAL

### David Corkill

The wave of nationalizations that followed the revolution in Portugal in April 1974 concentrated ownership in the hands of the state. Scarce resources were poured into inefficient public enterprises that swallowed large subsidies and continued to turn in large operating losses. State funding fuelled a mounting public debt and the criteria used in making investment decisions were more often political and social rather than commercial. While a large public sector preserved the revolution's social achievements it was clearly detrimental to modernization and economic growth. By the mid-1980s substantial restructuring had become essential in order to confront the challenges posed by EC membership (Portugal joined the Community in 1986) and the advent of the single European market after 1992. However, the modernization of the Portuguese economy was delayed by a combination of constitutional constraints and political obstacles. As a result the full privatization of state enterprises only became possible after April 1990.

Comparative studies of European privatization programmes distinguish between the radical model adopted in Great Britain, the 'piecemeal and limited' (Vickers and Wright, 1988) approach taken elsewhere in Western Europe and the rapid disposals undertaken in Eastern Europe. On the whole, in Southern Europe, where traditions of authoritarian rule and state dirigism are more recent and deeply embedded, privatization has not been embraced with the same enthusiasm as elsewhere in the EC. However, a case can be made that Portugal is an exception to this rule as the Lisbon government has pursued an ambitious, occasionally faltering, long-term programme of sales that challenges many entrenched commercial and business shibboleths.

This chapter identifies the main features of the Portuguese privatization project and examines the difficulties encountered in its implementation. An assessment will be made of the following: the ideological, economic, political and financial objectives; the nature and size of the public enterprise sector; the institutional and political context in which the programme is operating; and the economic and financial structures through which the transfer of ownership is carried out.

## The context of privatization

Privatization should not be viewed in isolation from a broad range of policies that can be labelled neo-liberal. Reducing the weight of the public sector is usually but a single component in a multi-faceted policy package. In the case of the Cavaco Silva administrations (1985–7; 1987–91; 1991– ) the declared macroeconomic policy aims encompassed the liberalization of the financial system, the introduction of more flexible labour laws, tax reforms, reductions in public spending by cutting the public administration payroll as well as the disposal of state enterprises.

A consensus existed by the mid-1980s that fundamental structural reforms were long overdue and had become an urgent priority if the Portuguese economy was to respond positively to the challenges presented by closer European integration. Portugal shared the common disenchantment felt throughout Europe with state intervention and public ownership. However, as in other Southern European countries, powerful political interests were opposed to state shrinkage. The provision of jobs in state-controlled firms has long been an effective form of political patronage that governments and political parties have proved reluctant to abandon. In addition, strong pressure existed to maintain the political consensus that strategic industries should remain under state control. However, the massive increase in public debt – debt to GDP ratio stood at 74 per cent in 1988 (OECD 1993) – fuelled by state sector borrowing could not be allowed to continue. State subsidies to inefficient, overstaffed and uncompetitive industries had to be cut in order to tackle inflation and improve long-term industrial competitiveness.

A number of factors specific to Portugal imposed limits on the pace and extent of the privatisation programme:

1. Prior to the April 1974 revolution the structure of the economy, in which a small number of favoured conglomerates enjoyed state protection and monopoly status in key sectors, ensured that ownership was concentrated in state hands when the old regime was overthrown and sweeping nationalization was carried out. This meant that

old, inefficient practices were reinforced and, in some cases, compounded after the revolution as priorities in the state sector emphasized employment generation and protection. Indeed, the survival of the state sector became synonymous with the safeguarding of 'the achievements of the revolution'. This was enshrined in the 1976 constitution which contained references to state enterprises as 'the inalienable property of the Portuguese people' and made redundancies in the workforce almost impossible. However, two developments during the 1980s eased the way for limited denationalization to start. First, the left-dominated Council of the Revolution, which had the power to veto any proposed constitutional changes, was abolished in 1982. Second, the left-of-centre political majority disappeared as the country edged perceptibly in a more conservative direction. Revising a constitution that protected state ownership became a possibility. This required a two-thirds majority in the National Assembly which in practice meant an agreement between the Social Democrats (PSD) and the Socialists (PS). Until such an agreement was reached only a minority holding (49 per cent) in state enterprises could be sold off.

2. Developments in the international economy focused attention on the need to restructure the loss-making state enterprise sector. The most important influence has been the internationalization of both product and financial markets. Protectionism and state intervention had been nationalistic responses to Portugal's subordinate role as a semi-peripheral and dependent component in the world economic system. The disappearance of the guaranteed markets of Portugal's African empire had failed to act as a spur to the modernization and rationalization of the industrial sector. Nor did the external shocks of 1978 and 1983, when stabilization packages were applied under IMF tutelage, encourage a concerted attempt to tackle the financial weaknesses of the state sector. By the 1980s the pressures for internationalization had become intense. Indeed, the challenges posed by Portugal's accession to the European Community were only temporarily cushioned by an extended transition period (seven years) for the elimination of all barriers to the free movement of trade, capital and people and by the transfer of resources in the form of aid to modernize industry and agriculture. The urgency of the task was reinforced by EC competition policy directives that have attempted to limit state aid to industry and signal that inefficient industries could no longer rely on state subsidies for their survival.

3. Until the mid-1980s the political climate precluded any attempt to retrace the public-private sector boundary. However, that particular

constraint was removed by the two successive victories achieved by the Social Democrats under the leadership of Aníbal Cavaco Silva. In the decade following the 1974 revolution Portugal seemed to be condemned to perpetual political instability as shifting coalitions undermined governments and necessitated almost constant electioneering. The political uncertainty was removed in two stages: following the October 1985 General Election, the PSD formed a minority government that was eventually brought down with two and a half years of its term to run. In the July 1987 elections the PSD became the first party to win an outright majority of the vote (50.2 per cent), thereby ensuring an extended period of political stability which was further underlined when the Social Democrats obtained a second overall majority in October 1991.

4. As a relative latecomer to privatization Portugal could learn from the experience of pioneers in the process. Firms like Baring Brothers and Price Waterhouse with experience of flotations in Great Britain were engaged in preparing state companies for privatization. Nevertheless the process has been characterized by numerous delays and setbacks. This can be explained partly by the constitutional constraints, by the lack of experienced administrators to steer the sales through, the negative impact of the 1987 stock market crash and the uncertainty as to future growth prospects generated by the Gulf War. In addition the collapse of Communism in Eastern Europe and the commitment to rapid privatization as the cornerstone of economic reform programmes throughout the region came at an inopportune time. Portugal's privatizations were bound to suffer as investors looked to the alternative opportunities on offer in Eastern Europe.

**The shape of the state enterprise sector**

During the tumultuous revolutionary period (1974–6) a large number of companies came either directly or indirectly under state control. A broad range of industrial and service companies, along with three newspapers, Portucel, the paper and pulp company, and the Pousada hotel chain came under the aegis of Investimentos e Participações do Estado (IPE), a state holding company. The influence and coverage of the public enterprise can be gauged from the following list of industrial companies: Petrogal (oil refining); Setenave (shipbuilding); Siderugia Nacional (steel); Cimpor (cement); Unicer and Centralcer (brewing); Portucel (paper and pulp); Tabaqueira (tobacco); Quimigal and CNP (petrochemicals). In addition EDP and EPAL shared a monopoly of electricity and water provision respectively. The state dominated non-financial services through control of transport companies like: Caminhos de Ferro Portugueses (railways); Rodoviário Nacional (coaches), CCFL (buses and trams in the capital); TAP (national airline) and other services such as: Correios e Telecommunicações (postal services and communications); Enatur (tourism and hotels), as well as the nine largest public banks, two savings banks, an investment bank and eight insurance companies. Baklanoff (1986) noted a resemblance to the public sector in pre-Salinas Mexico: 'Because the private banks in both countries held common stock in their clients, the nationalization of these banks resulted in indirect ownership of hundreds of small and medium sized enterprises'.

The contribution made by the state-owned manufacturing sector to total output actually declined during the 1980s due to financial cutbacks, the expansion of the private sector and the fall in demand during the 1983–5 recession. It made tackling the problem of loss-making state-owned industries an urgent priority. In 1985 total net losses amounted to US$317 million. The chief lossmaker was CNP (US$194 million), followed by Quimigal (US$70 million) and Setenave (US$65 million). Accumulated losses in the public sector stood at between US$7–8 billion (between one quarter and one third of GDP). Restructuring became necessary, if only to ease the public debt burden and rationalize investment allocation. The share of public enterprises in the foreign debt had expanded from 37 per cent in 1978 to 57 per cent by 1982 (Baklanoff, 1986).

## Privatization strategy and objectives

The Social Democrats were pledged to tackle the problem of loss-making enterprises. The privatization programme launched under the slogan '*menos estado, melhor estado*' became the programmatic flagship of the Cavaco Silva administration. When announcing the programme Cavaco declared his determination to 'put an end to the resignation and impotence imposed by our giant state machine' (Pirie, 1988). He made clear that the state sector subdivided into three categories. The first group, public services such as the railways, the national airline, and the postal services would remain in the public domain. The second group, problem companies such as EDAP, Quimigal and Siderugia would require restructuring before any sale. The third, corporations in healthy condition, would be early candidates for a return to the private sector. However, until 1989 full privatization of companies in the nationalized sector was prohibited by the constitution. It was not until June 1989, following lengthy negotiations between the PSD and the Socialists, that amendments to the constitution received the necessary two-thirds majority, thereby removing the political barriers blocking plans to reverse the post-revolution nationalizations. The second set of constitutional changes contained a number of socio-economic provisions. The emphasis was placed on a mixed, rather than a planned economic model. The creation of an 'economic, social and cultural democracy' replaced references to 'the transition to socialism' and collectivist aims.

The Cavaco government embraced privatization for a variety of motives. First, the sell-offs were seen as a means of raising much needed cash which could be channelled directly into reducing the level of public debt, thereby meeting one of the Maastricht convergence criteria, and restructuring state industries to prepare them for the private sector. The declared intention was to use 80 per cent of the funds raised from privatization to reduce the debt which was regarded as a serious structural flaw in the economy. An impediment to optimizing any returns from the sales derived from the poor condition in which public enterprise accounts languished. This made an accurate valuation difficult if not impossible. Preparing state enterprises for a stockmarket flotation was necessarily a lengthy and complicated process. However, there was a marked reluctance to disinvest completely in some key state enterprises and the government has insisted on keeping a substantial stake ranging from 10–30 per cent in 'strategic' companies.

Second, the privatization programme was regarded as a catalyst that would improve efficiency and competitiveness throughout the Portuguese economy. The expectation was that efficient private-sector management would replace an overstaffed, bureaucratically organized and inefficient state sector. In addition, the involvement of foreign capital was expected to bring in its wake higher levels of investment, transfer technology and improve productivity.

Third, the government hoped to promote *capitalismo popular à la portuguesa* (Portuguese popular capitalism), which would create a new shareholder class and give the workforce a share in the success of their company. The disposal of large amounts of capital was also expected to provide the basis for the expansion of Portugal's small stockmarkets. For many years the Lisbon and Oporto stock exchanges merited their description as 'sleepy places that played little part in their domestic economies' (*The Economist*, 1988). The markets were shut down in 1974 and despite reopening two years later remained in a comatose state. As late as 1986 only thirty shares were quoted on the exchanges. By 1987, on the back of the economic upturn and consumer boom, the market quoted 46 listed and 44 unlisted companies. The modest upsurge in activity is explained by companies seeking alternatives to expensive bank loans for investment projects and a growing overseas interest in the Portuguese stockmarkets. Recovery from the October 1987 crash was slow and underlined the dangers faced by such a small, marginal stockmarket. As foreign investors account for more than half the turnover on the Lisbon exchange changes in international market conditions have a disproportionate impact on the financial periphery. When the world markets are weak Portugal is one of the first to suffer.

### The pattern of privatization

Although Cavaco's declared intention was to privatize either fully or partly many of the state enterprises, a gradualist and pragmatic approach was adopted in implementing a programme which it was admitted would take eight years to complete. In fact there was no alternative but to opt for a phased programme. The reasons were both political and practical: a headlong rush to privatize would have provoked stern opposition and thwarted plans to remove the constitutional constraints imposed by the 49 per cent ceiling on any sell-off. Nor could Portugal's small stockmarkets absorb large volumes of shares, particularly when the equity market had still not fully recovered from the October 1987 crash.

The programme began cautiously in 1989 under the shadow of the stockmarket crash and the knowledge that only a partial sale would be possible. The first phase (April–December 1989) involved the part disposal of Unicer, the brewing company, and the Banco Totta e Açores (BTA), the country's fifth-largest bank. Unicer was chosen to kick off the programme because, with more than half the home market, it represented one of the most successful and attractive companies in the state portfolio. The issue was tailor-made for both national and overseas investors as future growth prospects were good (beer sales grew by an annual average 9.7 per cent between 1980 and 1986. The Unicer brands, which include Superbock, Cristal, Tuborg and Lowenbrau, were ideal to take advantage of future market expansion. Unicer's solid financial base and successful management team easily overcame any doubts generated by the partial nature of the privatization.

Portugal's first privatization took place on the Oporto stock exchange. The sale raised Esc9.4 billion for the Treasury and created 11,866 new shareholders. Twenty per cent of the shares were reserved for employees and small savers and ten per cent allocated to foreign investors. No single Portuguese entity was allowed to obtain more than ten per cent in the primary sale. The, second privatization followed in July 1989 when the government offered 49 per cent of the shares in BTA, a bank with a ten per cent market share and 6,000 employees. It initiated the government's programme to dispose of the state banking sector interests with only one exception: the Caixa Geral do Depósitos, the country's largest bank.

Interest in the BTA flotation, which was heavily oversubscribed, centred on the battle between two groups: the first, led by Belmiro de Azevedo and his Sonae group which gained a reported 11 per cent share and the second, headed by José Roquette, linked to the Spanish bank, Banco Español de Crédito (Banesto). Foreign investors resorted to a number of ploys to avoid restrictions by purchasing shares through local subsidiaries and going into partnership with local firms. A Spanish bank's involvement in the contest for control led to fears that BTA would lose its independence and be reduced to a mere affiliate of a larger Spanish bank. Such fears were exacerbated when Banesto later purchased Roquette's share in BTA. Similarly, when shares in Aliança Seguradora, the sixth ranked national insurer with an 8.8 per cent market share, were offered for sale in September 1989 there were claims that the rules were being broken. It marked the first sale in a two-stage offer that would see another of Portugal's largest insurers, Tranquil-idade, fourth ranked with 9.9 per cent of the market, sold to the private sector. In the event the offer was nearly eight times oversubscribed but claims were made that the Paris-based UAP had circumvented the 10 per cent rule and, in fact, controlled 30 per cent of the stock.

## Privatization issues

The issue of foreign control figured prominently in the debate over the new privatization bill that took place during autumn 1989. Two schools of thought emerged. The first was that privatization would *desportu-galizar* (deportugalize) vital sectors of the economy and surrender the country's independence and national autonomy. The government stood accused by some sectors of the press of 'putting the country up for sale' or being prepared to sell the family silver for a quick killing. It ran the risk, according to some critics, of replacing excessive state control by too much foreign control, with the result that decisions affecting the Portuguese economy would be taken abroad and senior jobs awarded to foreigners. The government was clearly sensitive to such criticisms and began to consider limits to the influence that could be exerted by foreign capital. One proposal suggested a prequalifying round in which the Finance Ministry would select a hard core of Portuguese share-holders allowed to make privileged bids in order to ensure that key companies remained under domestic control.

The sensitive issue of foreign, especially Spanish, control has continued to be a focus for debate with each new sell-off. Penetration is greatest in the banking sector, where foreigners exercise effective control at the Banco Comercial Português (BCP), the Banco de Comércio e Indústria (BCI) as well as BTA. Clearly attempts to restrict foreign ownership have been a failure and may, in any case, infringe EC legal rules. Limits on foreign participation do contradict the government's desire to maximize the revenues accruing from the sell-offs. Yet, if comparisons are made with other European economies, the level of foreign ownership in Portugal is not particularly high.

The second perspective on the privatization issue focused less on the origins of capital investment and more on the potential growth and productivity that might result. It was accepted as inevitable that Portuguese capital would have problems competing with foreign capital in an increasingly European and international economic system because of their limited financial resources and their restricted access to credit. The effective response to such developments, it was argued, was to improve the competitiveness of national enterprises so they were fit to compete within the European market and to phase the privatization process to allow for structural adjustments to take effect. The government did encourage the formation of strong Portuguese groups to assume control of the privatized companies, but came under fire for failing to favour national investors. Others asked where these consortia were to come from, given the volume of proposed privatizations. One possible source is former owners of nationalized companies, already involved in legal action over the compensation paid to them. Indeed, one interesting feature of the Tranquilidade sell-off was the attempt by the Espírito Santo group to retake control of the company. The same group, along with Jorge do Mello and others, formed a consortium to acquire a major stake in Portugal's largest company, Petrogal, in which the state decided to retain a 'golden share' equivalent to twenty per cent of the social capital. The re-emergence of the Mello, Champalimaud and other pre-revolutionary business families was confirmed in March 1990 when, in partnership with a Scandinavian consortium, they acquired control of Lisnave, the shipbuilding company, from IPE.

**Privatization policy**

The Lei-Quadro de Reprivatizações became law on 5 April, 1990. It allowed the government to sell more than the previous 49 per cent maximum. The new law tightened the rules on foreign ownership, allowing the state to retain a 'golden share' with a veto in order to protect the national interest, and provided for a case-by-case approach. Each sale required a decree outlining the conditions for the sale. In addition, the privatizations were obliged to set aside a percentage of the shares for previously identified groups: employees of the companies, pensioners, Portuguese emigrants and small investors.

The second stage in the privatization programme differed in a number of ways from the first. A larger number and broader span of companies were to be disposed of. The increased tempo of privatization sales (60 public companies were said to be on the list) generated new difficulties. Inevitably the early privatizations involved companies in reasonable financial shape and with a positive public image. However, the direct sell-off method was considered unviable in the case of loss-making industrial enterprises, such as CNP and Setenave, where management was put out to contract and private capital injected. It was no surprise then, when the debate began on the new privatization law, that greater flexibility was emphasized. While the government regarded privatization as the most appropriate and efficient way to modernize and restructure the economy, it was determined not to be limited to a single model. Apart from the stockmarket flotation (*oferta pública*) other options in the government's armoury included an open or limited public bidding (*concurso público*), as well as direct negotiations with selected national and/or foreign interests. The latter option was regarded as appropriate in the case of companies identified as strategic to the national economy like Petrogal and Cimpor. Foreign participation was to be restricted to ten per cent in full privatizations, but the government reserved the right to increase the percentage in the case of public enterprises with a 'very unfavourable' economic profile.

Concern that the 'national interest' might be in jeopardy shaped opposition and trade union proposals. Torres Couto, the UGT General Secretary, expressed no objection to privatization in principle, but voiced widely held fears that Portugal would be transformed into a mere production platform for foreign operators. He stressed the need to equip Portuguese entrepreneurs with the financial resources to restructure in the face of international competition and argued for worker participation in the ownership of enterprises. The Socialists placed their own proposals before the National Assembly, which would have limited to

20 per cent the share any individual or collective could own and suggested a ten per cent ceiling for foreign purchasers. In the Socialists' plan future privatizations would be overseen by a Reprivatization Commission, which would guarantee a wider dissemination of transferred capital and better safeguards against the concentration of ownership.

Although ostensibly committed to a full programme of privatizations the government was accused, on the one hand, of having no clear policy on which companies should be candidates for sale and, on the other, of lacking the political will to restructure the industrial framework in order to respond to the process of European integration. The government justified the slow progress on the grounds that national groups needed time and assistance in order to compete with foreign investors. However, it is clear that a cluster of factors dictated the erratic pace of the programme. The government's indecisive and overly bureaucratic approach can be blamed for some of the postponements and delays although unfavourable international developments such as the Gulf War and the recession in the international economy in the early 1990s compounded the problems. A combination of scarce domestic capital and the limits on foreign ownership generated uncertainties and posed questions about the success of each venture (EIU, 1993).

The first major 100 per cent privatization was completed in June 1990 when the remaining 51 per cent in Unicer was sold. Effective control went to a Portuguese company, Sogrape, after fending off a determined challenge from the Santo Domingo group. The Colombians had tried to circumvent rules that prevented any foreign-owned company securing more than a 20 per cent holding by transferring all their equity to Cervunião, a company created specifically for the purpose.

During 1990 there were nine privatizations, which included the first newspaper sell-off, the *Jornal de Notícias*. The remaining 51 per cent of the insurers Tranquilidade and Aliança Seguradora were sold, but the cautious approach was confirmed when the second stage of the BTA disposal was limited to a further 31 per cent and a 33 per cent tranche of Portugal's largest commercial bank, Banco Português do Atlántico. However, the flotation of 100 per cent of the brewer, Centralcer, flopped when the underwriters were left with unsold shares on their hands.

By the end of 1990 it was clear that the authorities had underestimated the complexities involved in a major denationalization programme, particularly when political as much as economic criteria played such an important part in the calculations. The political balancing act – safeguarding the national interest, giving priority to employees, small shareholders and emigrant workers – was often incompatible with encouraging foreign investment and technology transfer. The government was open to the accusation that, having accepted the need for the internationalization of the Portuguese economy and EC membership, it was wrong to hamstring foreign investors. However, it was also clear that domestic investment capacity was overstretched and the sales provision that prevented small shareholders from trading their shares for two years prevented any profits being ploughed back into new privatization issues.

## Conclusion

The privatization programme continues to generate controversy within Portugal. Although major companies have been returned to the private sector, a significant number have still to be disposed of. It was argued that Portugal had missed the boat and the optimum time for disposing of the more problematic companies had passed. By 1993 fourteen European governments were involved in extensive privatization programmes, and foreign investors could choose from a selection of attractive sell-offs. It began to be asked whether investors would be interested in the remaining Portuguese privatization candidates, such as Siderurgia Nacional, Portucel and Petrogal, when they carried such large liabilities (totalling 542 million contos) and were currently turning in annual losses. Tensions within the government surfaced between the Industry Minister, Mira Amaral, and the Finance Minister, Braga de Macedo, over the timing of future disposals. Braga wanted the sales to go ahead as quickly as possible in order to help the public finances while Mira Amaral argued for delay on the grounds that, until restructuring was complete, they would excite little interest among national investors.

The internal debate within the Cabinet highlighted a feature of the privatization process. The government has been reluctant to become involved in restructuring companies prior to returning them to the private sector. In so doing, Cavaco has avoided the stigma associated with significant job losses that accompany rationalization, but inevitably private investors have baulked when faced with the costs and uncertainties involved in such a process. There were signs during 1993 that the government was responding to criticism from business quarters. In July the law was changed to allow privatization proceeds to be used to cancel some of the debts accumulated by state enterprises still in the state sector, rather than insisting that 80 per cent must go to repay the public debt (EIU, 1993). It was also an indication that the public debt problem had been reduced to more manageable proportions – the debt–GDP ratio stood at 60 per cent in 1992.

Arguments inside Cavaco's Cabinet do point to a central problem of the privatization programme. Revenue generation has consistently been placed above secondary aims such as wider share ownership and the stimulation of entrepreneurial activity. However, it is undeniable that substantial revenues have been raised by the sales. By the end of 1992 Esc390 billion had been generated for the Treasury In 1993 the aim was to raise a further 225 million contos, but indications are that such an ambitious target is well out of reach as only 59.8 million had been raised by mid-year. By late 1993 the privatization programme faced a new threat. The growing unpopularity of the Social Democrats, as revealed in local election results, could presage a return to political instability and renewed uncertainty about one of the major planks of the Cavaco government's economic policy.

## References

Baklanoff, E.N. (1986), 'The state and economy in Portugal: perspectives on corporatism, revolution and incipient privatization', in W.P. Glade, *State Shrinking. A Comparative Inquiry into Privatization*, Austin, Texas, Institute of Latin American Studies: 257–81.
*The Economist* (1988), 27 August.
Economist Intelligence Unit (EIU) (1993), *Portugal: Country Report*, 2nd and 3rd quarter London, EIV.
OECD Economic Surveys (1993), *Portugal*, Paris, OECD.
Pirie, M. (1988), *Privatization in Theory and Practice*, Aldershot, Wildwood.
Vickers, J. and Wright, V. (1988), 'The politics of industrial privatization in Western Europe: an overview', *West European Politics*, **11**(4), October: 1–30.